M000314989

PAUL GORMAN

INTO TROUBLE

First published by Rain City Cinema LLC 2021

Copyright © 2021 by Paul Gorman

All rights reserved. No part of this publication may be reproduced, stored or transmitted in any form or by any means, electronic, mechanical, photocopying, recording, scanning, or otherwise without written permission from the publisher. It is illegal to copy this book, post it to a website, or distribute it by any other means without permission.

Paul Gorman asserts the moral right to be identified as the author of this work.

Paul Gorman has no responsibility for the persistence or accuracy of URLs for external or third-party Internet Websites referred to in this publication and does not guarantee that any content on such Websites is, or will remain, accurate or appropriate.

Designations used by companies to distinguish their products are often claimed as trademarks. All brand names and product names used in this book and on its cover are trade names, service marks, trademarks and registered trademarks of their respective owners. The publishers and the book are not associated with any product or vendor mentioned in this book. None of the companies referenced within the book have endorsed the book.

This is a true story. The events and people in this book are real. Some characters' names have been changed. Any resemblance to real people, living or dead, is purely coincidental.

First edition

ISBN: 978-0-578-94847-8

Editing by Barbara Noe Kennedy
Cover art by Paul Gorman

This book was professionally typeset on Reedsy.
Find out more at reedsy.com

This book is dedicated to my sons Kelly and Patrick. Thanks for being easy to raise. I would also like to thank my father for his intellect and the toughness he instilled in me.

Youth is quick in feeling but weak in judgement.

Homer

Contents

Acknowledgement   iii

Prologue   iv

  1 Interrogated   1

  2 Badlands   7

  3 Arrival   27

  4 Trier   31

  5 Rejected   35

  6 Liberated   42

  7 Darkness   51

  8 Flames   65

  9 Freighter   70

10 Paradise   78

11 Danny   84

12 Terry   94

13 Airport   100

14 Friendship   113

15 Rich   119

16 Smuggle   129

17 Settlement   144

18 Apprehended   150

19 Guilt   156

20 Confession   161

21 Prison   172

22 Letter   183

23	Martin	187
24	Vulnerable	196
25	Communists	200
26	Escape	207
27	Arrangements	211
28	Ambassador	216
29	Blood	223
30	Brits	231
31	Depression	235
32	Freedom	240
33	Goodbye	244
34	Reflections	248
35	Paranoid	252
36	Hitchhiking	257
37	Favor	264
38	Home	271
Epilogue		277
About the Author		284
Also by Paul Gorman		285

Acknowledgement

I would like to thank my wife Susan for her unwavering love, friendship and support, not only with this book but with life in general.

Prologue

The last time I saw Las Palmas was 1969. I was a shy nineteen-year-old teenager leaving home, seeking adventure, dodging the draft, and yearning for the love I didn't receive from my abusive father. I ended up in the Canary Islands thanks to Andy, a guy I met at a youth hostel in Barcelona who was on his way there aboard a 15-passenger freighter. The weather was colder in mainland Spain than I expected, so, craving sunshine, warmth, and beautiful bikini-clad Swedish girls, I joined him.

Little did I know the trouble that loomed in my future. I barely subsisted on sardines and baguettes; I did not impress any Swedish girls; and—probably the most jarring—I wound up in a prison in Franco's fascist Spain, requiring the assistance of the U.S. Department of State to rescue me.

The experiences are locked forever in my memory. It feels like they happened yesterday, they are that fresh. And yet, they are experiences so unlike the person I am now, I find it hard to believe I actually did the things I did—and survived to tell about it.

That's why, thirty-five years later, I had to return to the Canary Islands. I needed to put the things I experienced into a context that fit the person I had become. But what I found all these years later disappointed me. The vibe was so different. In 1969 Las Palmas was still very much part of Franco's

Spain, though his iron grip was lessening as his health failed. Northern European sun worshipers had recently discovered the subtropical city, especially Swedes who were only a six-hour flight away. The sparkling new hotels combined with friendly locals, low prices, and Spanish/Canarian culture, added to its ambience and sense of excitement.

But now, I was disheartened to find that Las Palmas was like all other tourist traps filled with pushy tourists. At the all-inclusive hotel where I stayed, fellow lodgers stampeded the buffet trough, and arguments threatening a resumption of World War II erupted over lounge chairs at the swimming pool.

Wanting to see more of the island and assess how it had changed, I took a bus to Maspalomas in the southeastern end of the island. I was the second person, behind and elderly local woman, at the transit stop. By the time the bus arrived, a crowd had assembled. *No worries,* I thought. *I'm second in line.* Wrong! When the bus doors sprung open, it was a free-for-all. Tourists, along with a smattering of locals rushed the entrances like they were storming Normandy Beach. Grunts, groans, shrieks, and swearing filled the air. Elbows swung. Needless to say, I missed the transit and so did the elderly woman and several other stunned locals, but I fought like hell to board the next one, even holding off pushy old ladies trying to squeeze past me. It was never like this back in 1969; tourists were polite and orderly then.

Apparently the locals were fed up with rude tourists too. Once I got on, the bus ride wasn't any better. A young Canarian man, came aboard a stop or two later, harassing me persistently with anti-tourist slogans echoing the "*No Turistas*" and "*Turistas* go home" graffiti spray-painted on buildings and walls we passed.

I couldn't say I blamed the locals for the anti-tourist graffiti and the young Canarian man who badgered me on the bus. If I was treated so rudely by fellow tourists, then I can only imagine how the locals were being treated. Having experienced enough, it was time to leave. I felt unsettled and disappointed.

More recently, in 2019, I arrived in Barcelona on the last leg of a Mediterranean cruise, another chance to revisit my past. I hoped this mysterious, gritty, safe city hadn't changed like Las Palmas had. Ostracized from the rest of Europe because of Franco's dictatorship, back then it was a throwback to old Europe, frozen in time. I remembered a city of undiluted Spanish culture and, to a lesser degree, Catalonian. Men huddled around black-and-white TVs in bars eating tapas, smoking, drinking cerveza and port as they watched soccer matches and bullfights. Cafés with rotisserie chickens in the windows roosted on many streets. The Central Market had more flies than the city had tourists as they feasted on unrefrigerated chicken and seafood. In the mornings, a symphony of church bells awakened me, ringing in a new day.

Franco's fascism underlay all of this, which strangely added to the place's allure. I didn't analyze it in these terms at the time, but I was challenging "polite society" by searching for adventure outside the mainstream. I wasn't interested in Paris's cafés or Florence's art museums. The Soviet Union was too far beyond the political spectrum; they were the enemy in those Cold War years. But the fact that Spain was also considered taboo for its politics, though in a more benign way, along with cheap prices, made it irresistible—with the biggest sinner of all being Barcelona.

When I disembarked from the cruise ship into this city so

deeply entrenched in my memory, I immediately felt something was wrong. Hop-on-hop-off tour buses jammed the streets. Street mimes, hawkers, and tourists choked La Rambla. Barcelona was an enormous block party that would make Manhattan blush. A search for local cuisine proved elusive as I ate in a tapas bar staffed by Chinese cooks and waiters serving dim-sum-like foods to mostly Chinese customers. La Sagrada Familia's Passion façade's cubist addition was a mockery of Gaudì's original Croquembouche-like masterpiece. Litter and gang graffiti marred the neighborhood where I stayed, and it was unsafe, making me feel like I was in one of the *Back to the Future* movies set in a dystopian world.

After two days of fighting through throngs, trying to find culture resembling the Barcelona of fifty years before, I was ready to go home. I knew then if I wanted to recreate my experiences in Spain and the rest of Europe, and more importantly, reconcile my past with the present, then I would have to write about it. Those memories were still there. Hidden away in the recesses of my mind they seemed like someone else's. For fifty years I was too ashamed to talk about the bad things I had done, but now I was ready because I came to the conclusion that those experiences had changed my life for the better.

I hope my account will provide a glimpse of Europe and my experiences as I remember them. This is where my story begins. Get ready for a wild ride.

Paul Gorman
Tacoma, Washington
September 12, 2021

1

Interrogated

May 2, 1969 — Las Palmas, de Gran Canaria, Spain

T hree armed policemen led me into an office where Capitán González sat at a heavy wooden desk beneath a framed picture of Generalissimo Francisco Franco. A graying Indian man named Mr. Bhatt entered last, standing slightly behind and off to the side. Open-faced fluorescent bulbs, several hanging light fixtures, and a barred window dimly illuminated the room. Several army-green file cabinets lined the wall to the left of the window.

I was in Las Palmas Municipal Jail. I knew the officer's name was González, by the black engraved name tag pinned to the breast pocket flap of his short-sleeve khaki shirt, exposing his hairy arms.

"Sit down," he ordered in English with a heavy Spanish accent.

An officer wearing glasses motioned for me to sit in one of

two wooden chairs in front of the desk. Seated now, one of the other guards settled beside me.

"What is your name?" González asked, lighting a Ducados cigarette before exhaling a blue, foul-smelling plume that sinuously wrapped its entrails around the overhead lampshade.

Man, I hate the smell of Spanish cigarettes, I grumbled silently. *They smell like burning garbage.* Waving away the smoke, I told González my name was Scott Charles.

"Age?" González queried, writing his report.

"Nineteen."

González blew out another blast of pollution into the air, stinging my eyes. "Nationality?" He scribbled away without looking up.

"American, I'm an American, you know, and I have my rights, you know. I demand to know what this is all about, you know."

González set down his pen, then hammered a meaty fist on the desktop. "This is not America!" he shouted. "In U.S.A., people who think they big shots do this." Lifting his legs, he thrust his black jackboots on his desk and reclined in his chair, puffing a vast cloud of smoke skyward. "You are in España, not America," he yelled, his eyes raging and jugular bulging.

Taken aback by his ferocity, I tried to remain indignant. I would talk my way out of the situation. Of course my name wasn't Scott Charles. The name on the two American Express checks I'd forged and cashed at Mr. Bhatt's camera shop in the port area was. González plucked the two checks off his desk. Squinting, he examined the signatures. Leaning left, he conferenced in hushed Spanish with a gangly mustached officer. The Capitán opened his desk. With a grunt, he turned to me, holding out a blank sheet of paper. "Sign this," he said, sliding the paper toward me.

Panic-stricken, my gut clenched as I rose from my chair, reaching for the pen González pointed at me. "What am I supposed to sign?" I asked, knowing he wanted to compare my *Scott Charles* signature with the name I penned on the checks.

"Sign your name, Señor Charles."

González turned the checks over so I couldn't see the signatures on the face side of them. Droplets of perspiration formed on my forehead as I tried to visualize the signatures on the checks. Conveniently, when I had signed them, I could look at the original *Scott Charles* signatures on the checks. Never having forged anything before, for some peculiar reason forging his signature was easy. Now it was going to be difficult. I drew in a deep breath to relax, closed my eyes, and signed the name, concentrating on the mechanics—the feel of the signature, not the image.

I set down the pen, opened my eyes, and to my astonishment saw my re-creation. It was perfect, exactly as I remembered. González scooped up the paper, comparing the new forgery with those on the checks. He conferred with the lanky, mustached officer. Relaxing, González turned to me. "Señor Charles, sorry for the confusion, you are free to go."

Relieved, I emptied my lungs as I rose. "*Gracias,* Capitán González."

Mr. Bhatt stepped forward. "Capitán González," he said with a British/Indian accent, "the bank will not accept the checks without his passport number. They claim American Express reported the checks as missing. We need his passport number or our money returned."

González's eyes shifted to me. "Where is your passport, Señor Charles?"

"Uh, it's on the ship."

Actually, the ship I had taken from Barcelona docked two months earlier. My passport was in my rucksack at my friend Terry's flat.

For a moment, González pondered, scratching one of his hairy arms. "There's nothing I can do, Mr. Bhatt," he said, gazing in his direction. "This is a federal matter. If you want his passport, you must see the Guardia Civil."

Mr. Bhatt's eyes caught mine. I cast mine away, avoiding eye contact with him. He then spun to González. "Capitán González, with due respect, we checked with the port and there are no passenger ships here at the moment."

I recoiled, wishing I could vanish as González's eyes bore into me. "Señor Charles, is that correct?"

"Uh, uhm, I don't know," I said, biding time to come up with an explanation. "I did come here on a ship and, uh, lost my passport, you know."

González studied me briefly and then scrutinized the names. Opening a smaller drawer, he pulled out a magnifying glass, comparing the signatures with a fish-like eye. I began sweating again. Setting the magnifying glass down, his eyes tilted up at me. "Where are you staying, Señor Charles?"

"Uh, on the beach, you know," I said, forcing a smile.

"Which beach?"

"Uh, I don't know. The one with the fishing boats. You know, the one by the port."

Stroking the five o'clock shadow on his chin, González mused, and then glanced around the room at the other officers and Mr. Bhatt. Finally, his gaze settled on me. "Why are you sleeping on the beach when you have money? One hundred dollars is much money. You can afford a pension. Sí?"

"Uh, because I like it, you know," I said, scoffing at how stupid my story sounded.

Laughing along with his officers, González directed his attention toward me. "You like sand fleas, rotting fish, and being awakened at dawn by fishermen?"

"Hippie," I smirked.

Again, González and his men laughed. As the laughter subsided, he became deadly serious. "Where are your bags, Señor Charles?"

"Bags?"

"Yes, your bags, Señor Charles," González pressed. "Surely you have bags. Even hippies have bags."

Cornered, with no way out other than being honest—at least momentarily, until I could come up with an innovative way to bluff my way out—I responded honestly. "Uh, they're at a friend's, you know."

"And what is the location of your friend's place?"

"In town, you know, the tourist section. I'll go get them." Rising, I did an about-face to leave, walking no farther than one step before González interrupted me.

"Stop," he commanded. A thin-lipped officer stepped in front of me, blocking my exit. "Señor Charles, my men will escort you and Mr. Bhatt there."

Out of the corner of my eye, I could see a conflicted look on Mr. Bhatt's face. On one hand, he just wanted his money back. On the other, he seemed concerned about my well-being. Despite my act, I was a teenager and believe I came across as a polite and likable—albeit vulnerable—kid. Perhaps I reminded him of one of his seven children I'd met earlier in the day, after his two oldest sons accosted me and brought me to clear up the matter at his shop.

As I turned to leave González's office, I noticed an officer who looked vaguely familiar. With dark hair, bangs, and olive-colored skin, the man resembled my brother, Bob, only older. As we drove to Terry's place to get my "bags," I reflected on the day I left home and how my brother dropped me off at a freeway on-ramp. That was nearly four months ago, a life-time ago, and so much had happened since then. There was no way I could foretell the future that day, and even if I could, I probably wouldn't have stayed home, because I was on a one-way trajectory into trouble. And now, by the looks of it, I had arrived.

2

Badlands

January 11–19, 1969 — North Bend, Washington

A light snow fell when my eighteen-year-old brother, Bob, dropped me off at an on-ramp to Interstate 90 just outside North Bend, Washington. Because it was only January 9, it was already getting dark at three p.m.

"Good luck, Paul," Bob said, holding out his hand, trying to hide the concerned look on his face.

"Don't worry," I responded, shaking his hand. "I'll be okay."

"Yeah, but it's snowing," he frowned, looking even more worried.

"I know, but I've decided I'm going."

I grabbed my green army surplus duffel bag and blue athletic bag from the rear seat of my old VW Beetle, which I'd just sold to my father. Standing there in the cold and snow, I grasped the door handle and paused for several seconds with indecision.

There was no turning back now.

"I'll see you, Bob," I said, my voice cracking slightly.

"Write to me."

"I will. I'll send you a postcard when I get to Europe."

Closing the door, I stuck my thumb out, watching my old 1962 powder-blue Bug dissolve away amid a flurry of swirling snowflakes.

My first ride took me all the way to Sioux Falls, South Dakota. The driver's name was Larry. An Army private stationed at Fort Lewis, he was on his way to visit his fiancée. As a stoic man in his late twenties, sporting a bristling flattop haircut, he talked little. We just drove, which was fine with me because when we spoke, he was so boring, regaling me about how much he loved the Army and missed his girlfriend that I'd fall asleep only to be awakened by Larry saying it was my turn to drive.

Taking turns like this, we made great time, keeping his '65 Chevy Impala at ninety most of the way across Montana, after crossing the Continental Divide.

Around midnight we drove through Sheridan, Wyoming, encountering a rodeo of drunken young cowboys cruising Main Street in their jacked-up pickup trucks and Broncos—Ford, that is.

Larry turned to me and said, "So you haven't told me why you aren't flying to Europe."

"That was my original plan," I said, shifting in my seat. "I bought a charter flight ticket to Amsterdam from some Dutch guy named Dirk, who didn't want to go home yet, but I couldn't get on the flight in Vancouver because my name wasn't on the passenger list."

"That's too bad. Well your loss is my gain, I spose," Larry said, honking at a pickup truck stopped in the middle of the street.

"Yeah, I guess so. I called the guy back and asked him to return my money but he'd already spent it. He felt bad and gave me his dad's address in Amsterdam. Said if I ever need help there, to look him up."

"That's good," Larry said, gunning the engine now that we were around the pickup truck.

"Yeah, I've got his address in my wallet for safe keeping." I patted the side of my butt. "I'm sure I won't need it though."

As the sun rose in the morning, we entered the Badlands, silhouetted by an orange horizon to the east. Larry woke up. He took the wheel. "These are the Badlands," he said. "Outlaws used to hide out here in the Old West days after we drove out the Lakota. My fiancée and I plan to get married here."

"Here?" I blurted. "It seems so, you know ..."

"Inhospitable," Larry said, finishing my sentence.

"Yeah man, it's kind of scary, you know what I mean?"

"Well, my fiancée is one-quarter Lakota, so it's a sacred place for her. Besides, she says it will prepare us for any bad times we might encounter in our marriage."

Rising abruptly, the sharp-toothed peaks grew larger as we neared them. I tensed, almost expecting a gigantic roar and then jaws to snap shut, swallowing us up. Larry glanced at me and chuckled. "Don't worry, they won't hurt us. A bit further and we'll be through them."

When we passed them, I exhaled in relief, glancing in the passenger side mirror just to be certain. Fatigued, I fell asleep shortly thereafter. Approximately three hours passed. Larry shook me awake. "We're here," he said, startling me.

"Help," I yelped, fearing a scary monster with huge teeth was about to devour me.

"No monsters here," Larry chuckled. "You were having a bad dream."

"Where are we?"

"Sioux Falls—end of the line," Larry said. "This is where I turn. I'll let you out here. There's an on-ramp over there for I-90. It'll take you all the way to Chicago. With a little luck, you'll be there in time to spend the night at your uncle's place. Well, I've got to go, promised my fiancée I'd be at her place for the Super Bowl. She's pulling for the Jets, says they're going to win."

"Smart woman," I smiled, shaking Larry's hand. "Thanks for everything."

"No, thank you. If it hadn't been for you, I'd still be in Montana."

I grabbed my belongings, bid Larry farewell, walked across the street to the on-ramp, and stuck my thumb out, watching him gun his Impala and roar away, honking his horn goodbye. As dull as Larry had been, I was going to miss him.

Less than fifteen minutes later, a pickup truck carrying bales of hay pulled over and a farmer in his sixties, wearing cowboy boots and hat, beckoned me to get in. I opened the door, and he spoke with a Minnesota accent. "Where're you going, sonny?"

"Chicago," I replied.

"Chicaga," he grimaced. "Why in lordy's name would you be going to Chicaga? Dontcha know there isn't anything there but sin and unhappy folks."

I explained I was on my way to Europe and was going to rest up at my uncle's place for several days.

"Well, I'm only going as far as Austin, Minniesota, will that do, sonny?" the farmer asked.

"Yes," I said, and for the next three hours, the old guy

rambled on about his dairy farm, the *Lordy*, Jesus Christ, and his Lutheran faith. Oh, how I missed Larry's long stretches of silence. Not trying to be impolite, I did my best to nod or say "uh huh" in agreement.

Somewhere close to four p.m., the old farmer dropped me off at a Shell gas station just off I-90 in Austin and I thanked him. "You betcha. Be careful there in Chicaga, sonny, and always remember to call on the Lordy if you need help."

After the dairy farmer drove off, I stood there at the station corner trying to hitch a ride. It was getting dark, and hardly any cars were on the road. *Maybe they're all at church, or watching the Super Bowl,* I surmised. The temperature was dropping too. Working in the garage, the Shell owner kept glancing over at me. Finally, he came out and said, "There's coffee inside and restrooms. You can wait in there if you'd like."

Thanking him, I went inside, used the restroom, and then poured myself a Styrofoam cup of day-old coffee with its own oil slick. Standing there, I watched the Super Bowl on a portable black-and-white TV. To my surprise and satisfaction, the New York Jets were leading the Baltimore Colts 16–3 in the fourth quarter. *Yes.* This was an upset on the scale of Muhammed Ali beating Sonny Liston for the Heavyweight Championship of the World. It was the dawning of a new age. You could feel it in the air, everywhere. Convinced the Jets would win, I took one last gulp of the bitter brew and went back outside. *Perhaps there will be more cars now that the Jets seem to have the game in the bag,* I hoped.

By six, the owner had put away his tools and was sweeping the garage. Pawing his chin, he observed me with a look of concern. The temperature was dropping fast. It was now below freezing, evidenced by an icy sheen on the streets beneath the street lamps. The proprietor could tell I was cold as I stomped my feet and tried to warm my hands by blowing on them. He came out to me again and said, "I'm closing up soon, but you're welcome to stay inside until I do."

"Much appreciated," I nodded. "If I don't get a ride soon, I'll find a hotel to spend the night in." No sooner was the owner back in the garage than a black, muscled-up '63 Ford Galaxy drove past. The passenger waved at me. Pissed, I flipped him off. *Here I am freezing to death, and all he can do is grin and wave.* The car skidded to a stop and then backed up. A tough looking, greasy-haired driver in his late twenties wearing a white tee-shirt and blue jeans jumped out.

Lordy, I thought, *what have I done?*

"Where're you heading?" he asked.

"Uh, Europe," I replied, hoping it would dissuade them from offering me a ride.

"We're going to Waterloo."

Waterloo. Isn't that where some duke defeated Napoleon in Europe, ending his empire? I recollected.

Becoming impatient, the driver crossed his arms and tapped a foot. "Well, actually I'm going to Chicago, you know," I stammered.

"Waterloo's in Iowa on the way to Chicago. Come on, man, get in. I'm freezing my balls off out here."

I caught a glimpse out of the corner of my eye of the station owner leaning on his push broom, watching like a protective father. I gazed at the driver, who was holding the coupe door open. "Last chance, man," he said. "Stand out here and freeze your nuts off or ride with us."

I picked up my bags, tossed them into the back seat of the car, and got in. *Oh my God, these two thugs are going to rob and kill me, and then dump my body in some Iowa cornfield*, I freaked. *Why did I have to flip them off?*

The driver gunned the engine, and we tore out of the gas station parking lot. I peered out the window at the Shell's owner, who squinted while watching us speed away. Almost immediately, I sensed I was in store for the ride of my life, or death, and hoped he would memorize their license plate number.

Heading south on Highway 218, it wasn't long before we started going uphill. "I'm Roland," the driver said. "And this here is my old cellmate Kellen. Folks call me Rumble, and Kellen, *Killer*. Hope you're not bothered by altitude 'cause we are in the mountains and will be going over a pass."

Snickering inside, I assured Rumble and Killer the hills we were passing through were nothing compared to the Cascades and Rocky Mountains I'd crossed yesterday. The more I boasted, the more they seemed to accept me. Using a neighbor as a model, I made up stories about being a drug dealer. By this time, they treated me like one of their own, and I relaxed.

The road became windy and snow covered. Rumble did not slow down. He accelerated as we continued our ascent. Meanwhile, Creedence Clearwater Revival's "Susie Q" blasted from an eight-track tape deck. Certain we were going to crash, I accepted my fate, *if I'm gonna die; I don't want to know about it. I want to go in my sleep.* Minutes after cresting the pass, I fell asleep.

Several hours later, I awoke and we were on a flat, snow-covered freeway that glistened green from the mercury vapor lights. "Where are we?" I asked, thinking we were on another planet.

"Well, look who just woke up," said Rumble, puffing on a

cigarette dangling from his lips. "We thought you were passed out from a lack of oxygen." The two laughed.

Finding little humor in Rumble's comment, I said, "Are we in Iowa?"

"We're on Highway 20, heading for Illinois," he replied, and then nudged Killer. "Put some Gary Puckett on."

My voice quavered as I tried to hide my growing fear. "I thought you said we were going to Waterloo."

"Plans have changed," said Killer, blowing out a cloud of smoke. "We've got warrants here in Iowa."

"Yeah," chimed in Rumble. "Cops know us real good here. We're on a first-name basis with them."

Rumble and Killer laughed hysterically at their joke, then began singing "Young Girl" along with Gary Puckett at the top of their lungs.

As Rumble and Killer continued singing and pounding on the steering wheel and dashboard, a yellow Dodge Charger pulled alongside. The car's engine revved and tore off down the freeway. The next thing I knew, we were racing down the icy highway at 110 mph, neck and neck with the Charger.

I gritted my teeth and braced for impact, as I'd done when I crashed my father's '62 GMC pickup over a fifteen-foot embankment going 70 mph. The truck rolled several times and flipped end over end—at least that's what my passenger friend said happened. Only seventeen at the time, I bounced around like a ping-pong ball inside, before landing outside the truck, unconscious. I spent the night in the hospital for stitches and observation. When I got home, I dreaded my father would do what the accident had failed to do, but he remained calm and never said a word about it. Having survived my father's wrath and one accident, I wondered if my luck had run out.

Killer and Rumble continued roaring down the sheet of ice at triple-digit speeds. For the next ten minutes or so, we took turns leading. We blasted in front going 120 and then backed off, and the Charger darted in front. The road was runway straight and flat to the edge of the Earth. Now and then, we encountered an overpass and slowed down to 100 mph on the uphill side, then accelerated on the downhill. Meanwhile, Rumble and Killer were too preoccupied with racing and singing to notice a cop alongside who was trying to pull them over.

"Oh shit, Rumble, it's the fuzz," Killer barked over the growl of the engine and blasting music. "He wants us to pull over. How far is state line?"

"Twenty miles."

"Can we outrun him?"

"Shit, yeah," Rumble said, flashing a thumbs-up sign.

Rumble floored it and we took off with the cop in hot pursuit, his red light flashing and siren blaring. As fast as Rumble drove, his car was no match for the state trooper's interceptor.

Rumble angrily slammed the steering wheel and pulled over. The cop came up to the driver's window with his gun drawn. "Do you boys know you were going one twenty-five?"

"Is that all?" Rumble chuckled. "The guy I bought it from said it would do one thirty-five."

Unimpressed with Rumble's joke, the cop ordered us to follow him to the nearest police station where Killer and Rumble were booked and then released contingent on posting a PR bond with the local magistrate. Believing this would be an excellent opportunity for me to go my separate way, I explained to the cops that I was just an innocent hitchhiker and asked them to set me free. They ignored my plea and ordered me to

15

go with them.

Released to post bail, we followed a squad car several blocks to a small yellow clapboard house with a white picket fence and a "Justice of the Peace" sign above the gate. Rumble and Killer got out of the car and entered the house. Once they were inside, the cop drove off. Sitting in the car, listening to the tinging of the engine dissipating heat, I wondered if I should just get out and take off. Not wanting to go to jail, nor anger the two cons, who would probably come looking for me, I stayed put. Big mistake.

In approximately thirty minutes, Rumble and Killer came running out of the house, ripped down the "Justice of the Peace" sign, jumped into the car, and tore off, laughing. "You should've seen us. We tied up his wife, beat him up, and knocked over their china cabinet, breaking everything!" Killer roared as Rumble fishtailed the car and did a U-turn on the icy street. In a matter of seconds, we were back on Highway 20, racing for the state line doing 125 mph. *Oh my God,* I thought. *I'm a fugitive now. I wonder if Mom and Dad will read about me in the newspaper, or see me on the news.*

Within minutes, we crossed the waste-water-gray Mississippi River and were in Illinois. An hour and a half later, Rumble and Killer dropped me off at a freeway entrance in Rockford, Illinois, and wished me well. "Good luck in Europe," said Rumble, shaking my hand. "I hear the French girls don't shave their legs or pits, and they've got hairy pussies!"

Killer and Rumble about fell over laughing. Killer patted me on the back. "Yeah, enjoy that pussy."

A man in his early thirties gave me a ride at the on-ramp in Rockford where my adventure with Rumble and Killer ended. Having been in town watching the Super Bowl at his parents' place, he was heading home to Chicago, where he worked as a stockbroker. Not knowing anything about stocks, I had little in common with him other than sports, so we talked about that. It was close to midnight when the driver dropped me off at the downtown YMCA Hotel on Eighth Street and Wabash Avenue South.

Upon entering the hotel, I noticed how rundown and cavernous the lobby was. Banks of elevators lined the walls. Downtrodden men sat around on dilapidated sofas and chairs, trying to stay awake. After checking in, I waited for an elevator, watching bronze clock-like hands on the walls spinning clockwise and counterclockwise as the elevators went up and down. Finally, an elevator dinged and its doors opened. Getting in, I rode it to the fourteenth floor, got off, and went to my room.

Not much bigger than a walk-in-closet, the room was musty and drab, with a single window. I opened it for fresh air. A blast of arctic air slapped me in the face. I slammed the window shut. Inspecting the bed, I found a lumpy mattress, and the springs creaked. *Oh well, it is better than nothing.* I hadn't slept in an actual bed in almost forty-eight hours, so this would have to do. Since it was so late when I got in, I chose not to call Uncle Jim. I could do that tomorrow, or maybe just keep pushing onward. I was dying to see my German girlfriend Hilke.

Fishing toothpaste and a toothbrush out of my blue Adidas athletic bag, I came out of my room looking for the shower room the hotel clerk had mentioned. As I walked down the hallway, a short, dapper middle-aged man with a loosened tie came up to me. "Hi, I'm from San Francisco," he smiled. "I like you."

Wow, how can he like me; he doesn't even know me, I wondered as I about choked on my Adams' apple. "Uh, you do?"

"Yes, I do," he said, eyeing me up and down and locking his eyes on mine. "I'm looking for a place to spend the night. Do you have a room?"

"Uh," I stammered, trying to think of a way to politely get out of the situation. "I, I'll tell you what, you wait right here while I take a shower and get nice and clean. Okay?"

The man smiled, assuring me he'd still be there when I came out.

"Good," I said. "I'll see you in ten or fifteen minutes." With a closed smile and unblinking eyes, the man nodded.

Rather than going into the shower, I rounded a bend in the hallway and hopped on the elevator. My heart palpitated and my throat felt parched when I got off the elevator in the lobby.

At the front desk, I told the clerk about my encounter upstairs. To my shock, he pulled a handgun out of a drawer and instructed a black coworker and me to come with him.

We emerged from the elevator. As we turned the corner in the hallway, we spied the man who had propositioned me. The night clerk pulled his gun and pointed it at the frightened man whose eyes were huge, like an owl's. "Is this him?" the employee asked without looking at me.

"Yeah," I said, shuffling my feet and avoiding eye contact as they grabbed the shaken man and hauled him off.

I returned to my room, sick to my stomach. Unable to sleep much, I tossed and turned most of the night.

I called my uncle early the next morning. While waiting in a lobby full of lustful men, my memory drifted back to several days before I left home. I was lying in bed reading a letter from Hilke.

My darling. I miss you so much and hope you will come to Germany

and see me. Please come right away. I'm sure you can stay at my
father's place with my sister and me.

  Love,
  Hilke

I'd met Hilke at Redmond High School, where she was an exchange student from Germany. She was a junior and I was a senior. I'd read about her in our school newspaper. She was pretty and blond, two pluses as far as I was concerned, and European—even better. It wasn't long before we started dating. Being my first girlfriend, it was an innocent relationship, never going beyond making out. The following fall, she returned to Germany, and within weeks she sent me this letter, which I'd just finished re-reading for possibly the tenth time. Tucking it under my mattress, I glanced around my bedroom at the upside-down American flag, Jim Morrison, and concert posters thumbtacked to the walls.

I can't wait until February. I'm going now, I said to myself, referring to the 737 airplane delivery flight to Oslo, Norway, that my father had arranged for me through his job at Boeing. I'd always dreamed of going to Europe, and Hilke was the catalyst that finally pushed me to commit. Several days later, I packed my bags and headed out, and now here I was in Chicago.

Uncle Jim arrived within half an hour, greeting me with a handshake and warm smile. Upon meeting Jim, the similarities between him and my father struck me. Other than the fact that my father had hair and Jim didn't, they were about six feet tall and 210 pound, had meaty lips, sloping foreheads, and strong jawlines. They commanded attention with slow, deliberate movements, rigid posture, few facial expressions, and long periods of silence. Immediately I felt at home and nervous as my gut tightened. My father's stoicism, combined with his razor-sharp eyes, always turned me into a blathering fool the occasional times I was alone with him.

Therefore, it was no surprise on the car ride to Uncle Jim's home that I spilled my guts about how I was off to see my girlfriend and Europe, and the wild escapades I had survived the day before. Prior to leaving home, I considered the possibility I might not survive my quest. It was a risk worth taking, though. Life at home and not seeing Hilke was killing me, not to mention at any moment I could be drafted, sent to Vietnam and die there.

While Uncle Jim drove, I rambled on. He took it all in stride. Pulling to a stop in his driveway, he said. "Your mother called, and she and your father are concerned about you. You're welcome to stay here with us as long as you like." After the Rumble and Killer and YMCA incidents, I needed time to collect myself.

Like my father, Uncle Jim had been a World War II pilot. My father did a terrific job at dealing with big events. But little things angered him. With Uncle Jim, I sensed he could handle both.

Over the next several days, I slept in the basement on a sofa and became acquainted with six cousins I'd never met. Janice, the oldest at twenty-one, attended a community college. Thinking that protesting was mostly done on the West Coast, I was surprised she spent Saturdays protesting the Vietnam War and other days boycotting grapes to support Cesar Chavez trying to unionize farm workers.

I spent the days lounging while my aunt cooked, cleaned, and did laundry. The daily highlight was dinner, when the family came together after a day spent at work or school. Uncle

Jim started the meal off by reciting grace, followed by a short speech. It was quite a formal presentation, along with wanting to know how everyone's day went. With so many children, he maintained order by asking questions, reminding others to wait their turn, and telling humorous anecdotes. My father likely would tell you to be quiet or worse if you said something he didn't agree with, didn't show good table manners, or complained about the meal.

One supper, Mark, the youngest of Uncle Jim's kids and the only boy, announced he planned to become a priest. Admittedly, I didn't think it would ever happen and wondered if a little brainwashing had something to do with his ambition. My father had unexpectedly proclaimed one day that I would be attending seminary school. The idea horrified me. I intended to run away from home if he brought it up again. He never did. However, a year later, I left home on this journey.

After four nights at Uncle Jim's, I decided to move on. I informed him, and he said I could stay longer if I liked. But I considered myself a freeloader, lounging about all day while everyone else did productive things. Unable to talk me into staying, he made me promise I wouldn't hitchhike to New York and offered to take me to the airport so I could fly there instead. I had little money, but reluctantly agreed, because I didn't want him to worry about me.

When we got to the airport, he told me to wait while he checked on flights. He came back several minutes later, having paid for my ticket. I tried to reimburse him, but he wouldn't let me. Instead, he handed me back a poem I had written and given him several days earlier while everyone was gone. I asked him what he thought of it and he responded by asking if I'd studied poetry. I had not. The message was apparent; I wasn't a poet.

As I would learn later, I was a young man who still had a lot of growing up and learning to do.

Shaking my hand, he said goodbye and wished me well. I watched him walk away, looking debonair with his tweed flat hat, wool scarf, and black London Fog pea coat.

Half an hour after Uncle Jim said goodbye at Chicago O'Hare International Airport, I boarded a TWA flight to JFK. As I entered the plane, a smattering of passengers already sat onboard. Lugging my duffel and athletic bags down the aisle, I noticed a young man in his early twenties with mid-ear-length wavy brown hair who glanced at me as I passed. I plopped down in a window seat several rows behind him. The plane was only about half full, so the entire row belonged to me.

Shortly after takeoff, he got up and came back to my row. "Mind if I join you?" he asked. After the encounter several days earlier at the YMCA, I warily agreed. After all, it was just a flight. We would talk, then go our separate ways. "Hi, I'm Tom, Tom Wilkens," he said, sitting down in the aisle seat. "So, I noticed your duffel bag when you got on. Where're you heading?"

"Europe," I beamed, sitting erect in my seat.

"Wow, no kidding. I've been there several times."

"So, how about you, where are you going?"

"I'm going home to New York to get married," he boasted. "It's a surprise. My parents don't know and neither does she."

"Uh, she doesn't know?"

"Nope, met her at summer camp two years ago and haven't seen her since," Tom replied with a nod.

"Really, so, what were you doing in Chicago?"

"I was going to college there at DePaul. Just dropped out though at the start of the last semester of my senior year. Folks

22

don't know that either."

"Your parents are going to be shocked," I said, thinking this guy was a certifiable nutcase.

"They're used to it," he smirked. "They'll get over it. All I've got to do is tell them I love them and they'll forgive me."

About then, a stewardess came around with meals and Tom returned to his seat to eat. I was glad he was gone. Screwed up as I was, he was a real mess. I wondered if he'd ever seen *The Graduate* because his story about marrying a girl he hadn't seen in two years somewhat reminded me of Dustin Hoffman's character.

The rest of the flight, I spent enjoying my steak dinner and New York's blanket of lights as we landed at JFK, close to 9:30. I had no idea where I would spend the night, other than another YMCA, or just hanging out at the airport. I dreaded the thought, but it would only be for one night. I already had purchased a ticket on Icelandic Airlines departing the following evening to Luxembourg.

While getting off the airplane, I approached Tom, who had waited for me. "So where are you staying?" he asked.

"Uh, I don't know, man," I shrugged. "I don't want to spend much, so maybe I'll stay at the Y."

"Don't stay there, man," he sneered. "The joint is infested with rats, hookers, and drug dealers. Tell you what; you can stay at my folks' place with me. My dad's an exec at Macy's and they have a place on Long Island. There's an extra bedroom since my sister is away at college. I've got a younger brother who's a pain in the ass, but other than that, you can't beat the price—meals included. What do you say, man?"

I hemmed and hawed momentarily. Not wanting to spend the night at another Y, and in no mood to stay awake all night at

JFK, I agreed. As far as I could tell, Tom might be mentally off, but he was nowhere near as dangerous as Rumble and Killer.

A taxi dropped us off in the driveway of his folks' place on Long Island around eleven p.m. Tom was right; his mom's and dad's place was a charming two story brick Tudor with a well maintained yard. By the looks of it, they were well off. While Tom paid the cabbie, I got my bags out and waited for him.

Rather than sneak quietly into his parents' place, upon entering Tom bellowed: "Hello, I'm home! It's me, Tom! Hey mom, and dad it's me!"

As we stood there in the foyer holding our bags, a light came on at the top of the stairs. A moment passed. A middle-aged woman wearing a bathrobe and slippers came out of a bedroom. She stopped at a wooden railing overlooking us. "Tom, what are you doing home, and who is that with you?"

"Mom, I've dropped out of college, and this is a guy I met on the flight. I invited him to spend the night here."

"You dropped out of DePaul?" his mother shrieked. "It's your senior year!"

"Yeah, I know, but I'm getting married!"

Perking up, his mother smiled. "You are? Who's the girl?"

"You know, that girl I met the summer before last at camp."

"Oh, that one, but you haven't seen her in two years ... Well, this certainly is a surprise."

"Yes, especially since I haven't told her yet."

"She doesn't know? ... Tom, I'm going to make an appointment for you to see a psychiatrist tomorrow ... And I want your friend out of here then."

"I love you, Mom," Tom said, like a sweet altar boy.

"I love you too. Now go to bed and we'll talk in the morning," Tom's mom replied, closing the bedroom door behind her.

Checking my watch almost every hour, I flopped around in bed that night, digesting the circumstances. As Tom and I ate a breakfast of cold cereal, toast, and orange juice, his mother came into the kitchen saying she had arranged an appointment for him with a psychiatrist in the afternoon. "And take your friend with you," she instructed.

I couldn't say I blamed her; she didn't know me. Her son was acting bizarre. For all she knew, I could be a fugitive wanted in Iowa in connection with a Justice of the Peace who was beaten. Cognizant of all this, I tried to keep a low profile and excused myself to take a shower.

That afternoon, Tom and I went to North Babylon's quaint town center. The crisp and sunny weather definitely was an improvement over the weather back home and in the Midwest. While Tom had his appointment with the psychiatrist, I sat outside on a bench, waiting. Broken sunlight filtered through the leafless trees, casting crisscross patterns on the sidewalk. I noticed a used condom approximately five feet away. It seemed incongruous, but everything about this place, and my experience with Tom, seemed off-kilter. It all felt unreal, like I was in an episode of *The Twilight Zone* or a *Hitchcock* movie.

Tom was jovial when he came out of the doctor's office. "Well, the shrink says I'm delusional."

"So, what did you tell him?"

"I told him everything he wanted to hear," Tom bragged. "I took some psychology classes at DePaul. The good news is, I'll probably be 4F now and won't be drafted."

Back at Tom's place, I packed for my flight that evening and wondered whether he had concocted the entire situation by dropping out of college and saying he was going to marry a girl he hadn't seen in two years just to avoid the draft. That was the thing about Tom. During my brief stay with him, I never knew what was true and what was a lie—perhaps he didn't either.

That evening, Tom dropped me off at JFK, gave me his address, and said to write him when I got to Europe. "Maybe we can meet there this spring," he said, just before letting me out of his folks' car. I never wrote.

3

Arrival

January 19–20, 1969 — Luxembourg

My Icelandic Airlines flight touched down in Luxembourg late in the afternoon. It wasn't long before a group of us from the flight found a pub in town. Several beers consumed, we left going our separate ways. The exception was Nicole, a good-looking college coed, who had come to Europe to visit her aunt in Paris. She'd sat across from me on the flight and took a liking to me. "What do you say we get a room together?" she asked.

"Uh, uh, thanks," I stuttered, "I'd love to, but I've got a girlfriend in Hamburg, you know, and want to get going."

"Ah, c'mon," Nicole pleaded. "You can always go there tomorrow. You really don't want to be hitchhiking tonight. It's cold and feels like it's going to snow."

Beautiful and educated, Nicole was confident and scary as hell. As attractive as I found her, I didn't have the nerve to tell her I'd never had sex before. Avoiding eye contact, I exhaled a foggy breath and made up an excuse that I couldn't afford it.

Nicole grinned. "Don't worry about it. It's on me."

My eyes met hers, and they begged with lust. She stroked my cheek gently. "I need you."

"I'm sorry," I said. "I'm ... I need to go. My girlfriend is expecting me, you know."

Nicole stroked my arm. "Okay. At least let me walk you up to the highway."

Walking through Luxembourg City's fairy-tale town shrouded in light fog, Nicole stopped to look at pensions and their rates. "Just looking to see where I'll spend the night," she said. "This place looks cozy," she snuggled, stopping at one. "This place is warm inside," she remarked, coming out of the second one. "The rates here are great," she commented, reading the sign out in front of the third pension.

Continuing our walk to the outskirts of town, we came to a fork in the road with white wooden road signs pointing toward villages and cities. Pausing there, Nicole turned to me. "You sure you don't want to change your mind? There are some nice hotels back in town, and you can be on your way in the morning."

I stood frozen with indecision and fear. On one hand, I wanted to have sex with her, but on the other, I was so horrified about not being able to perform that I couldn't think of anything to say. Before I could respond, a car came along. Nicole waved it down. The driver rolled down the passenger window of his 1965 Renault Dauphine and said something to her in French. Nicole replied in the same language. Looking over at me, she translated, "He's going to a village seventeen kilometers north of here. From there you can catch the A-1 toward Trier, Germany."

"Will it be easy to get rides there at night?" I asked.

Nicole spoke to the driver in French again. He nodded, then said something. Turning back to me she said, "The driver says it's busy there so it should be easy."

"Okay, tell him I'll go with him."

Once again, Nicole spoke to the driver in French. He then got out of his car to help me put my bags in the rear seat. Meanwhile, Nicole put an arm around me, kissing me passionately. "You sure you don't want to stay—last chance," she pleaded, her brown eyes drawing me in like two black holes.

She kissed me again. Her kiss sent shock waves of pleasure and fear coursing through my body. My mouth was so dry my tongue wouldn't move. All I could do was nod *yes.*

"Well goodbye then." Nicole planted another passionate kiss on my lips.

"Goodbye," I gasped, getting into the car.

The car sat there for a moment, and the driver said something to me in French: *"Est-elle ta petite amie?"*

"Je ne *parle pas Français,"* I said, having learned the French saying from my mother, who studied French in college.

"Girlfriend?" the driver asked, finally understanding.

"No girlfriend. Friend."

The driver smiled with satisfaction. "Ah, *maîtresse."* When the car pulled away, I turned and watched as Nicole waved goodbye. Suddenly, I felt aroused and wanted to turn around and go back to her. Immobilized by teenage fear again, it overcame my teenage lust. Frozen with fright, I couldn't bring myself to tell the driver to stop. Before long, we'd driven too far. If he let me out now, when I got back, she would be gone. Resigned to the situation, I dozed as the driver maneuvered the car in the snow toward Germany.

4

Trier

January 20, 1969 — Trier, Germany

Sometime in the evening, the Frenchman dropped me off in the village of Grevenmacher, along the Moselle River on the border with Germany. About twenty minutes later, a portly, middle-aged, ruddy-faced man wearing a fedora gave me a lift. Driving a Mercedes 220 SE, he was an industrial engineer on his way home to Trier after a conference in Luxembourg City.

The man spoke passable English, claiming it was the international language of engineering. Wanting to learn as much about the Space Race as possible—not that I was an expert, because I was the farthest thing from it—he warmed up when I told him I was an American. He was glad to get an American's perspective on it. Somehow or another, I mentioned I liked beer, so he stopped at villages along the way to have me sample the local brews. Several hours later, he dropped me off in

Trier's medieval town center, intoxicated.

Like a skid row drunk, I staggered through falling snow, bundled in my hooded corduroy car coat against the cold. Snot running from my nose froze into mini icicles. I chugged onward into the winter night. Before long, the beer's fuel had worn off. I had run out of gas. I dropped my fifty-pound load. Unable to go farther, I unfurled my sleeping bag in a doorway. From what I could tell, the shop looked unoccupied with its curtains drawn. Dog-tired, I climbed into my bag, boots and all, and within minutes passed out.

Awakened by the sound of snow-crunching footsteps going up and down the sidewalk as people made their way to work, I lay there. Still tired and hungover, I tried to sleep more. I couldn't. An hour or so after having customers step over me and seeing shoes go inches past my face, I got up and made my way through a town dominated by Roman ruins and a beautiful cathedral. Enthralled by the majesty of the buildings and history, I would have enjoyed spending more time in Trier, but I had a rendezvous with romance in Hamburg. The portly engineer had said to stay on the street until I reached the on-ramp for the Autobahn. From there, I should be able to catch a ride toward Bonn.

For the next hour, I stood at a clover-leaf on-ramp with my thumb out. Petite snowflakes germinated the air. The temperature had dropped into the low teens. Many Germans weren't overly friendly. They drove past with impassive looks on their faces or grumpy scowls. Policemen driving a Porsche screamed past me, squawking something in German over their PA system. It didn't matter that I couldn't speak German. I understood their message: Hitchhiking is illegal on the Autobahn. Heeding their threat, I gave up and walked back into town.

I found the train station after asking directions from a police officer—having drawn cold, blank looks from passersby. It appeared as if the war still stunned the German people. It had been twenty-four years since the end of World War II, but for most adults over thirty-five, it remained fresh in their minds. Germany, it would seem, suffered from a collective psychosis.

At the station, I bought a ticket for Hamburg Hauptbahnhof. Scheduled to depart at ten thirty-one, it should arrive at seventeen fourteen. About forty minutes before my train departure, I phoned Hilke.

"Hallo," she answered. A phone operator asked in German if she would accept a collect call from me. "Ja," said Hilke, as the operator disconnected from the conversation with a click. "Where are you?"

"I'm in Germany," I said. "A town called Trier."

"What are you doing there?"

"I'm at the train station, and I just bought a ticket for Hamburg. My train gets in at seventeen fourteen—platform eight."

"Okay, I will talk to my father and see if he can pick you up," she said. "Call back when your train arrives. Sometimes they are delayed."

"Okay," I said, feeling a little unwelcome. "Do you want to see me?"

"Of course, but it's my father; he's not well and knows nothing about you possibly coming here. He is afraid to drive. But I will insist that he pick you up. So call me when you arrive."

Hanging up the phone, I stood there for a moment, wondering if coming to see Hilke was a mistake.

A little shell-shocked, I boarded the train, apprehensive

about the reception I'd get in Hamburg. Hilke sounded aloof on the phone. Her behavior differed from the girlfriend who had pleaded for me to join her in Germany. As the train clattered along, I reflected on the phone conversation, *Geez, maybe she didn't like me calling collect. Yeah, that must be it. But I've only been in Germany for less than a day. I don't understand their currency ... their pay phones are stupid ... and I don't speak the language. How else am I supposed to call her?*

5

Rejected

When my train arrived in Hamburg, I stepped onto a bustling platform. Travelers rushed in all directions, disorienting me. Struggling with my belongings, I followed fellow passengers up a long flight of stairs into the main terminal. Out of breath, I plunked my fifty pounds of luggage on the floor and looked around for Hilke and her father—not that I'd know what he looked like, but he would be with her.

A little more than half an hour later, I spotted a row of wooden phone booths along a wall not far away and called Hilke. An operator put my collect call through and the phone rang. Hilke answered it, speaking with the phone employee in German, and then me, saying, "Hello, we were waiting for you to call first. We will be there in about fifteen minutes."

"Okay, I'm in the main terminal building. See you then," I

said, feeling slightly sick to my stomach.

I returned to my spot in the center of the terminal where they could easily find me. Fifteen minutes passed with no sight of Hilke. Thirty minutes went by. I drew looks from suspicious men pretending to be reading newspapers. Checking my watch, lighting a cigarette, reading my expired train ticket, peering around, I fidgeted self-consciously. *Perhaps I'm in the wrong terminal,* I speculated. I grabbed my bags. Heading back toward the stairs, I wondered whether the main terminal was on the other side of the platform. Glancing back, I noticed a man following me. I picked up my gait, scampering down the stairs as he increased his pace.

Now on the platform again, I fought my way through herds of passengers scurrying to catch trains along with disembarking travelers fighting to get off theirs. Looking back again, I saw the man. Clad entirely in black leathers shinning like a snake's skin, he still tailed me. I tried to run, but with my heavy bags, I moved like a ninety-year-old.

A World War II movie unfolded around me, with confused people rushing every which way on the platforms. Chaos. I panicked. I couldn't move faster than a brisk walk or slow trot. Reaching the steps at the other end of the platform, I fought up the stairs like a spawning salmon. Weakened by fifty pounds of luggage, my duffel bag banged and dragged on the steps. Gasping for air, I reached the top and looked over my shoulder. The man was climbing the treads two at a time. I had a choice to make: Go left with the other passengers or down the stairs on the opposite side.

Anticipating the man would follow the herd, I descended the stairs. The farther down I went, the darker it became. Arriving at the landing, I could barely see. I kept moving, heading out of the station onto the tracks. Back in time. Back to the evil. It still lurked out there. I could feel it. It gave me goosebumps and chilled my soul. Not wanting to go farther, or turn back, I stopped and listened. Close by, I could hear the drip, drip, drip of rainwater coming off the edge of the station's roof, hitting the tiled platform floor. I froze. I looked. I listened. I heard his approaching footsteps. *Clump, clump, clump.* Growing louder, they slowed, drawing closer.

My mind went into a frenzy. *He's stalking me. He's Gestapo. He's a killer. He's a Nazi. He's a psycho nutcase. He's a spy.* All these thoughts swirled in my brain, driving me insane. I whirled around. I could see the moon-like reflection from his alabaster face and the reptilian luster from his leathers. He eyed me, zeroing in, slowly. Like a zombie, he moved trance-like. My heart beat faster than it ever had, faster than my high school cross-country races a year ago. He moved closer. He grinned. I wanted to scream, but nothing came out. A nightmare had me locked in. Surely, I would wake up. Please, please let me awaken.

Drip, drip, drip. More raindrops fell. I could hear his breathing. It grew heavy and steady. Whoosh, whoosh, whoosh. It wouldn't be long before he reached me. I feared for my life. Out of the corner of my eye, I spotted another man. He wore a tweed flat cap and a London Fog trench coat. He could pass for Alec Guinness. A cigarette dangled from his lips. He leaned against a column in a pool of light maybe forty feet away. I rushed up to him.

"Do you speak English?" I puffed a pathetic hiss.

"Being that I am English, I would assume that I do," the smoker replied with a British accent.

"Well, that man over there is following me!" I rasped, my

voice barely more than a whisper.

The Englishman glanced over at my pursuer, who had come out of his spell and now stood there impassively. Turning back to me, the Englishman said, "Don't worry about him. He's a *bizzie*." *What's a* bizzie? I wondered. ("Bizzie," I later learned, is Liverpudlian slang for a cop.)

Grabbing my bags, I dashed past my tracker, up the stairs. At the top, I veered right down a corridor teaming with travelers. I looked behind to see whether the man still followed me. To my relief, he was nowhere in sight. Spotting a different row of wooden pay phones, I entered one and called Hilke. I heard her voice. "Where are you?" I hyperventilated. "You and your father need to pick me up right away!"

"My father's not feeling well. I don't think we can come."

"You need to. A strange man's been following me," I blurted. "I don't know what he is. I've come halfway around the world to see you. It's the least you can do!"

"Okay, let me talk to my father. Call me back."

"No, I'm not hanging up. You need to ask him right now!"

Hilke set the phone down. I could hear distant German voices. A moment later, she got back on the phone. "Alright, my father and I will be there in fifteen minutes. Wait out front of the main terminal."

Fifteen or twenty minutes later, a black 220D Mercedes pulled up and Hilke opened the door. "Hurry, get in the back, my father can't park here."

On the drive to her father's place, her father chattered like a cockatiel, telling me how much he loved the United States, and I was welcome to stay at his place indefinitely. *Wow, does that mean, he wants me to marry his daughter?* I hoped. But Hilke didn't seem like that's what she wanted. She remained quiet during the entire car ride.

I spent the night sleeping in the basement after Hilke and her sister made a bed for me on a sofa. Her younger sister smiled and giggled whenever I said something. Hilke remained withdrawn and soon they went to bed. I stayed up late with her father telling me that as widower and disabled war veteran suffering a postwar nervous disorder, he could not work, and lived off government benefits. Complicating matters, his wife had committed suicide, leaving him to raise Hilke and her younger sister by himself.

That night I lay in bed wondering if Hilke would crawl in alongside me. But something had changed between us. I wasn't sure what, but the next day I found out when Hilke came downstairs. "My father wants to speak with you."

I entered the living room. All the curtains were drawn. A table and pole lamp provided the only illumination. Her father sat in a leather overstuffed chair, wrapped in a blanket over his bathrobe. The pleasant-looking and friendly man, in his late forties or early fifties, had made me feel comfortable the previous evening as we conversed for hours. What he was about to say totally caught me off guard. "Yesterday, Hilke opened a letter addressed to me," Hilke's father said, holding the letter with a sullen look on his face. "Today she presented the letter she had read. It is from her American sponsor, the Barrs. May I read it to you?"

I tensed at the mention of the Barrs' name and nodded *yes.*

Glancing at me apologetically with droopy eyes, he paused, and then put on reading glasses.

"We understand a boy is on his way to visit Hilke. There are reports he smokes marijuana and is friends with a student expelled from

Redmond High School. We do not approve of Paul and would not let Hilke see him any longer. We encourage you to do the same..."

Hilke's father put down the letter. Taking off his glasses, he looked at me. "I'm sorry, but I cannot let you stay here. You seem like a nice boy, but I am a widower and must protect my daughters and my reputation in the community. I hope you understand, if it were not for this letter, I would let you stay with us."

Shocked, my eyes stung. It had been such an ordeal getting to Hamburg. I couldn't speak. Devastated as I was, before I'd left home, I had decided that if things didn't work out with Hilke, I would continue my trip until I ran out of money. I wanted to see Europe. Ever since I'd read *National Geographic* articles about sixteen-year-old Robin Lee Graham sailing solo around the world in his twenty-four-foot sloop *Dove,* I wanted to travel. I wanted adventure. *Here I am in Europe. There's no point in going home; it's an opportunity of a lifetime.* I reassured myself.

That evening I skipped dinner with Hilke's family and wandered around the neighborhood, enjoying the sights. I stopped at a food stand and bought a wiener and sauerkraut. In the morning, Hilke and her father dropped me off at the train station. I caught a train to Wilhelmshaven, Germany. In less than three hours, I would be at Grandma Gronzy's place, on the Baltic.

As the mother of our next-door neighbor, she lived with them several years before returning home to be with her husband. While living in Bellevue, she'd taken a liking to me. It might have something to do with my Irish/Norwegian heritage and blond hair. I looked German.

"You are welcome to stay with my husband and me in Germany if you wish," she had said before she returned to her home. Six months later, I took her up on her offer.

6

Liberated

The welcoming I got in Hamburg from Hilke was cool, but the reception I got from Grandma Gronzy was warm and friendly. She proudly showed me off to her friends, along with young girls working in the town's shops. I suspected she wanted to hitch me up.

Her husband was the opposite. He spent his days reading the newspaper or listening to a shortwave radio, never speaking more than one or two words a day. Grandma Gronzy insisted I say "*Guten Morgen*, Herr Gronzy" to him first thing in the morning, and "*Gute Nacht*, Herr Gronzy" in the evening. The remaining daylight hours, she required that I be quiet lest I disturb him.

Fully rested after four or five days, I was ready to move on. Having already nearly forgotten about Hilke, I craved more excitement in my life than what Grandma Gronzy and

Wilhelmshaven presented. I said goodbye to Grandma Gronzy. It disappointed and worried her to see me go, but it was time to explore Europe. Actually, with Hilke out of my life, an immense weight lifted off me. Liberated, I intended to enjoy every moment of my newfound freedom.

On the flight over from JFK, I'd met two Canadian college students, two or three years older than me, from Vancouver on their way to Dusseldorf, Germany. One of the boy's grandmothers passed away and left him an inheritance. The Canadians were off to Europe to spend it. We arranged to meet at the youth hostel there if things didn't work out with Hilke.

Located along the Rhine River in the industrial Ruhr Valley, the city has a charming old town. Celebrating my arrival, the two Canadians took me to a pub. They kept buying beer, and I kept drinking it. It was brown and sweet and went down like a malted shake. The glasses were small, so they would order them by the platter. Unbeknownst to me, the alcohol content of the beer was 12 percent. After about ten beers, I was so intoxicated the two Canucks carried me back to the hostel.

Deciding they were going to cycle around Europe, about a week later, the Canadians purchased bicycles. They encouraged me to buy one too and travel with them. I bought a red ten-speed Puch Bergmeister bicycle, but declined to travel with them. As friendly, nice, and protective as they were, I wanted to be on my own. It would be easier to meet people that way, I surmised.

The day I left Dusseldorf, I said goodbye to the Canadians and set off southwest for a town called Euskirchen. It lay about fifty miles away and had a youth hostel. About halfway there, it started to snow and stick. It was also getting dark.

Earlier, the weather was partly sunny and chilly. Laughing

43

children playing soccer in the streets ran alongside cheering me on, at least I thought that's what they were doing. *The road is flat. This is easy,* I said to myself.

By mid-afternoon, the temperature had dropped. Ominous, steely gray clouds loomed ahead, as did the first snowflakes. I paid little attention to the dandruff size flakes. *Some snowstorm,* I scoffed, mocking what the Canadians had said. Whenever Seattle's weather forecast called for snow, it didn't happen. And whenever the weatherman said it wouldn't, it did. But this wasn't Seattle. The farther south I rode, the larger the flakes became. Having gone almost thirty miles, I'd passed the point of returning. I had crossed the Rubicon. *There's no turning back now, that's for sure,* I reasoned. Before long, it dumped. The roads were deserted now. No people walking about, no bicyclists on the trail. Every now and then, a motorist drove by.

Darkness fell and snow stung my face. My fingers burned from the cold. The socks I wore on my hands helped, but frigid water had soaked through them. I cursed myself for not bringing gloves when I'd left home. Illuminated by yellow pools of light cast by pole lamps, and my bicycle's headlight, the bike trail meandered between small spruce trees. Grass flanked both sides of the pathway. Not that you would know it by sight, because about four inches of snow now covered the ground. I knew it was grass, though, because I had fallen twice earlier; once on the trail, and the other time on the grass—which was definitely softer than the icy trail.

Off to my left, car headlights from a road about one hundred feet away flickered through the trees and flakes. As I rode up a slight incline, my Austrian-made ten-speed wobbled. Fifty pounds of luggage lashed to a rear bike rack will do that. Now, try doing it in on a thin layer of powdery white stuff deceptively dusting a sheet of ice. Complicating matters was my duffel bag. Like a sausage, it straddled the rack. Over hours, the ropes loosened, and it shifted more to one side than the other. When that happened, it would pull the bike over, and I'd have to stop and re-balance the load.

As I continued to peddle up the rise, the front tire lost traction, and I lost steering. My bicycle became a unicycle. The front tire regained traction when I eased off the pedals, although I lost momentum and downshifted. The torque from the lower gear lifted the front tire off the ground. Within a split second, I smacked the trail and yelped in agony. Stars twinkled in front of me, intermingling with snowflakes. My right hand throbbed and my hip ached.

I flung the bike off and stumbled to my feet. I brushed snow off my face and clothes. Using my teeth, I peeled off my snow-covered socks to examine my right hand. A scrape ran along the heel. My fingers resembled red licorice sticks, and my luggage lay strewn about in the snow. The flat handlebar on my bicycle was askew. I up-righted the Bergmeister, put the front wheel between my legs, and straightened the handlebar by twisting it.

Holding the rear wheel between my legs, I carefully positioned my two bags on the rack. Before I could secure them with rope, the front wheel turned left, rolled, and the bike fell over. "Dammit!" I shouted. "Stupid piece of shit bike!" I kicked it. But it wasn't the bike's fault. I had nobody to blame but myself. The Canadians had warned me it might snow, but I had shrugged them off, and now I was paying the price.

I fastened my bags to the bike rack with the icy rope. My bare fingers stung from the cold like a colony of fire ants biting them.

45

My hip had a painful bruise the diameter of a baseball. I shook the snow off the frozen socks I used as mittens. My fingers wouldn't bend, so I pulled the socks on my hands with my teeth. Satisfied that everything was in order, I mounted the bike and began pedaling again. Despite the freezing temperature, I figured if I kept moving, I would survive. If it worked for Shackleton and his men, it could work for me. I worried about frostbite on my fingers, though.

As I peddled on, random thoughts tumbled around inside my cranium like a washing machine. *Keep moving like Shackleton and his men*, I told myself. *Keep moving, don't stop.*

I didn't have sled dogs to bark at as Shackleton did, so I commanded my legs to keep pumping, to keep mushing along through the cold, dark, snowy night.

"Pedal, pump, pedal, pump," I yelled. "Pedal, pump, pedal, pump!" I shouted over and over again. Keep pumping, dammit! Keep pedaling! Yeah, that's it, keep moving!"

Shackleton ate his sled dogs. He ate seals, slaughtering them on the ice, used oil from their blubber for cooking and heat, I told myself. *I have no baby seals to eat, no sled dogs. Only my frozen toes and fingers. Could I eat them? Would I eat my own flesh, drink my own pee, murder baby seals, cannibalize the bodies of my best friends to endure, as had some great explorers, not that I'm an intrepid explorer, because I am not. I'm a man-child learning about myself, learning about the world, wanting adventure, and freedom. I'll probably never be a scientist. But oh, how I admire those scientific adventurers of yesteryear.*

I screamed again at my dogs, my frozen feet to peddle. "Mush. I don't want to die here!"

My thoughts continued to tumble. *I don't want to die now. I don't want to die, ever. I want to live to see the first man walk on the moon. I want to get married one day. I want to have kids of my own and see my grandkids. I want to live forever! Yeah, that's it, I'll survive. I'll make it, and will live forever. Death is a mirage. I'm nineteen, and I like it!*

Several more spills and bruises on my forearms and hips later, I found that there was more traction cycling in fresh snow than on the ice-packed trail. But it required much more effort and was slower. Having no other choice than to continue onward, I did.

When I finally arrived in Euskirchen, my teeth chattered. Exhausted and shivering, I discovered that the youth hostel was closed for the winter. A quick check of two hotels in town indicated they were full. With no place to stay, I wound up sleeping in a church flowerbed under an eave. Like my first night in Europe, it was so cold I climbed into my sleeping bag fully dressed, boots and all.

I awakened to snow pelting my face, except the pellets weren't cold. I opened my eyes and recognized not snow, but rice. Applause shattered the silence, and I spied a wedding party on the porch above me. I peeked out from inside my sleeping bag at the revelers. They laughed and cheered at the sight of me. Embarrassed, I crawled out of the bag, packed up my things, and waved goodbye. Sitting atop somebody's mantel somewhere is a photograph of this uninvited wedding guest.

Soon afterward, somebody informed me it was snowing all the way to Paris, my intended destination. Not wanting to bike again in the snow, I went to the train station and bought a ticket for Paris. Four and a half hours later, I stepped down onto the platform. Carrying my bags and wheeling my bicycle, an hour later, I checked into the Paris youth hostel.

For various reasons, Paris didn't appeal to me. I noticed, though, that the girls had hairy legs and didn't shave their armpits, just as Rumble and Killer had said. But it didn't bother me. I spent the next several days visiting the Eiffel Tower, Notre Dame, Place Pigalle, the Seine River, and some parks. I didn't speak French, other than the few words my mother had taught me, so I affected a French accent. The shop owners laughed, finding it charming, I think. Regardless, I felt like an outsider. The French weren't particularly friendly, and fellow travelers staying at the youth hostel were snobs. I knew little about art and didn't drink wine. Even the clubs didn't appeal to me. I didn't want jazz. I wanted rock. I wanted to dance. I wanted to move, not sit around smoking cigarettes in a holder trying to act like an intellectual. Mostly, though, the weather bothered me. It was cold, wet, and gray like Seattle in the winter. I wanted warmth and sunshine. It was time to head south.

Originally, when I had bought the bike, my plan was to cycle south to Spain. From there I'd ferry over to Morocco, ride across North Africa, and then up through Italy to Northern Europe. I didn't expect snow and rain. When I left Paris, it was a mixture of both. I didn't ride my bicycle; I hitchhiked with it. From my experience, it was incredibly difficult to hitchhike in France. The French just weren't welcoming, and it was even more difficult to get a ride with a bicycle. Who in their right mind was going to give a hitchhiker with a bicycle and fifty pounds of luggage a ride?

After a couple of frigid hours standing in the cold, a car full of young people pulled over. "Where're you going, mate?" asked a girl with long red hair and an Irish accent.

"Barcelona," I replied.

"There's not enough room for you, but we can take your bicycle," she grinned. "Will that help?"

I returned her smile. "Yes, that would be a big help. It'll probably make it easier for me to get a ride."

They tied my bike on top of their Ford Cortina and promised to deliver it to the youth hostel when they arrived about a week later. Standing there watching the car pull away, I wondered if I'd ever see it again. *Oh well*, I rationalized. *I'm not cut out for cycling, anyway.*

Getting rid of the bike helped with the hitchhiking. Although it was still difficult landing rides—especially once it got dark. Desperate, I began waving money, to no avail. Drivers would flash their yellow fog lamps several times at me as they sped past. A beret-wearing, Gauloises-chain-smoking truck driver clad in a plaid wool shirt finally pulled over and offered a ride. He was on his way to Béziers in southern France. He didn't speak English, and didn't understand my French-accented English, so there was little to talk about. Along the way, he stopped at an espresso bar full of beret-wearing old men for a perk-me-up, and I had my first shot of espresso ever. *Disgusting, how can anybody drink this stuff?* I complained to myself. One sip later, I couldn't drink more, and while he was turned, I left it on the counter, since he'd paid for it.

The truck driver let me out in Béziers, where I spent the night curled up in my sleeping bag inside an abandoned car. After awakening to bright sunlight straining through the dirty, cracked windshield, I walked through town past the fortress-like Cathédrale Saint-Nazaire de Béziers, stopping to buy a banana and orange at an outdoor market for my breakfast.

It wasn't long before a bald-headed Swedish man in his early sixties, driving a new cream-colored Saab 96 V4, picked me up. He was on his way to Costa Brava and later Torremolinos for business. As a real estate developer, he had projects in both areas.

Having spent a chilly night in the abandoned car, I was glad to be inside one with heat. About an hour and a half after clearing customs at the Spanish border, we pulled into the development. It was a resort condominium complex along the Mediterranean Sea, composed of white chunks of blocky concrete structures. Parking his car in front of a building with an "Office" sign, the old Swede turned to me. "Please come inside," he beckoned with a wiggling finger.

Upon entering the building, four Spaniards dressed in suits welcomed us with handshakes. They ushered us to an adjoining room. A table laden with cheeses, breads, meats, olives, fruits, and beverages awaited us. The Swede introduced me in Spanish as his son to the suited businessmen—at least I think that's what he said. Unable to speak Spanish, I wasn't sure. From that point on, I was encouraged to eat and drink whatever I wanted. Famished, I gorged myself discreetly as I could, having not eaten a full meal since departing my youth hostel in Paris a day and a half earlier. Meanwhile, the Swede went over architectural plans and models with his Spanish partners at a table in an adjacent room. Two hours later, we were on our way again to Barcelona.

The old Swede kindly took me to the youth hostel and dropped me off. All along the way, he encouraged me to accompany him to Torremolinos, telling me his son had died in an auto accident when he was about my age. "You resembled him. That is the reason I stopped for you," he said. As sad as his story was, I politely turned down his offer. I just couldn't be his son.

7

Darkness

February 8–28, 1969 — Barcelona, Spain

During my stay in the Barcelona Youth Hostel, I met an American named Pete. He was in his mid-twenties, having just completed a two-year stint with the Peace Corps in Angola after college. He hated the Corps and was glad to be done with them.

He was about my height and weight of six feet and 150 pounds. With layered brown hair, a lean, angular build, and sharp features, he resembled a hawk. It didn't take long for me to tire of his constant complaining about the U.S., and the Peace Corps. Nevertheless, he was the only other American staying in the youth hostel. Being Yanks, we had sought each other's company, sharing our traveling experiences and information on our families and hometowns. Mostly, though, we talked about things we missed about the States. We craved things like hamburgers, French fries, and milkshakes, and especially turkey dinner with all the trimmings.

The backpackers I'd met were living in the moment. We enjoyed talking about our adventures. Negative things were the last things we wanted to hear. Therefore, I was annoyed when Pete kept being negative. His only positive comment was how much he liked my leather pants. Made of buckskin, they were rare in Europe. Blue jeans and corduroys were the fashion among backpackers and what I normally wore. On this day, though, I wore my buckskins. Pete couldn't take his eyes off them as we stood around the room I shared with about seven other travelers.

"I want to get a pair of those," he said, feeling them. "Where did you get them?"

"I bought them mail order from a store in Kansas."

"Really. Do you remember the name of the place?"

"No, I saw an ad in *Rolling Stone* and called them. Try checking there," I said, turning to look out a window.

"Thanks, I will, 'cause they're really cool."

Pete left, and I continued looking out the window at high school students below, practicing soccer and bullfighting on the next-door monastery's soccer field.

Later that day, an Englishman named Arthur and I went to lunch, along with Pete, at a café serving rotisserie chicken in the old Gothic section. Arthur and I didn't have enough money, but Pete did. He had concocted a plan where Arthur and I would dine and dash while he provided cover by pretending to pay for us. As soon as we were outside, Arthur and I loitered briefly, as if we were waiting for Pete to pay our bill, and then took off running down the narrow cobblestone passages.

Arriving back at our hostel, Arthur and I learned from a roommate that the police were there earlier, looking for us.

Apparently, Pete had ratted on us, rather than telling them he didn't know who we were, per the plan. I was pissed.

"What an A-hole," I said to Arthur.

"Yes, he more or less set us up, it would seem."

Arthur and I left the hostel. Not long afterward, we went our separate ways for the day. It wasn't until just before ten p.m., when the hostel locked its door, that I was brave enough to return. I went straight to bed in my top bunk after hanging my clothes, including my leather pants, on the bedpost at the foot of the bed.

When I awoke in the morning, Pete's filthy, worn jeans hung where my leather pants had been. During the night, he'd crept into my dorm room, stolen my pants, and left his. Enraged, I went to the front desk.

"When did Pete leave?" I asked the receptionist.

"About forty-five minutes ago."

"Did he say where he was going?"

"Centro Train Station."

Running the entire way to the station, I got there in about half an hour. Pete was nowhere in sight. He had money, so chances were he took the underground metro or a taxi and caught a train right away. The last thing he was going to do was wait around for me to show up. Discouraged, I gave up and returned to the hostel, dumping Pete's grubby jeans in the trash.

Pete wasn't the only American I met at the hostel. One day, not long after Pete left, Arthur told me about an American from Seattle he'd met somewhere in town. Knowing it was my hometown, he had told him about me. The Seattleite wanted to meet me and would come to the hostel the next day at five. After my experience with Pete, I was looking forward to meeting a different American, especially somebody from the "Jet City," as we affectionately called it.

Nobody, I thought, could be as negative as Pete. Fred was the exception. At twenty-four, he was balding and dreading turning twenty-five so much that he frequently wove those two topics into our conversations. Life was unfair to him. Besides his thinning hair, his folks divorced, and he totaled the Ferrari his mother gave him. We sat at a round table in my dorm room. After an hour or so, I was exhausted, and then the conversation shifted and we began talking about home. It didn't take long to learn that he used to work at Boeing.

"My father works there," I said, finally finding something to talk about that wasn't dreary.

"Oh yeah? What plant is he in?" Fred asked. To my surprise, he worked in the same plant as my father. He took a drag off his Marlboro. "Really? What department does your dad work in?"

"Automatic Flight Controls," I replied, putting my Roth-schild cigarette out in a nearly full ashtray.

"You're kidding me," Fred grinned. "What does he do? Maybe I knew him."

"He's Engineering Supervisor," I sat upright in my chair.

Fred's eyes shot wide open and his eyebrows raised. "Oh my God, is his name Richard Gorman?"

"Yeah, do you know him?"

"Do I know him ... he was my boss! This is too crazy. I worked for him as a draftsman, and my old man has worked years for him as an engineer. You and I are going to have to spend more time together. Maybe we should even travel together."

As astounded as I was by the coincidence of Fred having worked for my father, I couldn't stand the thought of traveling

with him. From then on in, I only got together with him spo-
radically. I'd make up excuses I had other things planned—not
that I really did.

Between the hours of nine a.m. and five p.m., the youth
hostel closed. During these hours I'd wander the city, fighting
the chilly days and waiting for the youth hostel to reopen
for the night. I visited Gaudí's La Sagrada Familia several
times. Engrossed with the melting-candle, wax-like facade, I
wondered how artisans created an architectural structure so
unique and bizarre.

By this time in my European odyssey, I'd seen many in-
credibly beautiful and majestic cathedrals, such as Cologne's
Cathedral, the Notre-Dame and Sainte-Chapelle in Paris,
Cathédrale Saint-Nazaire de Béziers, and the Catedral de
Barcelona. Nothing compared to Gaudí's La Sagrada Familia,
though. It stood alone. I can't say I liked it or found it attractive.
But I found it fascinating and distinctive, like the world's only
albino ape, which was at the Barcelona Zoo.

On a day when admission was free, I went to see the great
white ape. There it stood alone in a cage, looking like a
snowman with not a soul in sight. *Strange,* I thought. *Why is
nobody watching the albino ape?* Nearby, a crowd had gathered
at another cage, giggling and pointing. Wondering what all
the commotion was about, I sauntered over and was startled
to see a male gorilla masturbating. Repressed as they were,
Spaniards found ways to amuse themselves. Embarrassed, I
returned to watch the albino ape, feeling sorry that despite all
its media attention, an aroused, run-of-the-mill ape playing
with himself had upstaged it.

Other than the handful of young backpackers, there weren't
many visitors in town. At night, machine-gun-carrying

Guardia Civil officers patrolled the streets. From what I could tell, most of the crime comprised a black market, where you could buy stolen items such as wristwatches. Besides the black market, there was prostitution in an area filled with bars off La Rambla near the Central Market. The girls would proposition men, wait until the police moved on, and then leave the bar, heading for nearby pensions. Sordid as the business was, the cat-and-mouse game they played with the police made it humorous. The hookers would open barroom doors and poke their heads outside, scanning the area for police. When the coast was clear, they'd motion for the Johns to follow them.

Not long after I arrived in Barcelona, I rode the metro on one of my visits to La Sagrada Familia. Even though the underground metro only cost one peseta (about two cents), it was expensive for me. The subway was old and dilapidated. When I boarded the train, all heads turned toward me. Not only was I the tallest person onboard by at least three inches, I also was the only blond. Immediately, I felt self-conscious as all eyes focused on this freak of nature. I couldn't wait to get off. I never rode it again.

Most days I spent hanging out in Plaça Reial, browsing La Rambla's magazine stands or sitting on the steps at the waterfront in the shadow of Columbus' statue, admiring a replica of his ship *Santa Maria* while whistling Otis Redding's "The Dock of the Bay."

Other days I spent meandering in the city's medieval section, getting lost in the labyrinth of narrow winding alleyways. In the dark corridors, I encountered black-robed nuns scurrying to church, hunched old women dressed in black dresses and shawls, merchants with donkeys carrying loads of goods, and old men without limbs or eyes, injured in the civil war, holding out tin cups, begging for money. A layer of soot from years of diesel cars and burning coal blackened its buildings. It was odd and sad seeing old women dressed in black sweeping the streets in the mornings with brooms made from branches lashed together around a wooden handle.

While driving down Costa Brava, the old Swede gave me a history lesson on Spain since Franco came to power. He said that after the civil war, Franco punished Barcelona for its support of the communist Republicans against his nationalists. The Catalonian language and culture were banned, and the city and province fell under hard times. It wasn't until the "Spanish Miracle" began in the late fifties, with the rebuilding of the economy, that life improved. For more than a decade, their economic growth rate was second only to Japan's.

By 1969, Spain enjoyed the world's ninth largest economy, slightly behind Canada. It was this mixture of mostly old and some new that I experienced in Barcelona. It was a great balance, unless, I suppose, you were Catalonian. As hard as Spain's government tried to stamp out Catalonian culture, they could not eradicate the "Catalonian lisp." Hard as it was for me to understand Spanish in broken English, hearing it with a lisp made it doubly difficult. I heard it everywhere, especially in shops, restaurants, and the Central Market. Usually around lunchtime, I'd go there, just off La Rambla, to buy sardines, bread, olives, and a banana or orange.

On one of my roamings around town, a Ford Cortina pulled alongside me with a bicycle on top. The Irish girl I last saw in Paris rolled down her window and yipped, "Hey, do you want your bike back?!"

Having almost forgotten about it, I was surprised and grateful, as I was just about out of money. Within ten minutes, I had sold it for more than I'd paid for it.

Another week or so passed, and one afternoon after lunch, I stopped at a record shop where you could listen to albums using headphones. If there was one thing I missed during my travels, it was not being able to hear rock music. With no radio, and no way to listen to the handful of record albums I'd brought, the only other place to hear music was in the bars. The major problem with this was you had to buy a drink and put money in the jukebox to stay. Having sold my albums to the record store, they didn't seem to mind me listening to their records. While standing there bobbing my head to a Doors album, a beautiful blond woman, who appeared to be in her mid-twenties and resembled Julie Christie, came up to me. "Do you like the record?" she asked.

"Yes," I said, taking off the headphones. I explained that they were the Doors and were one of my favorite bands.

"Do you mind if I listen?" she smiled.

I handed her the phones. It wasn't long before she was tapping her feet and gyrating to the music. She nodded her head in approval as she peeled off the headset. "Yeah, I agree with you. They are great. But I've never heard them before. Where are they from?"

"America," I answered.

"Is that where you are from?"

I nodded *yes*, and spotted the shop owner in the corner of my eye. He looked our way, scratching his head, probably bewildered why such an attractive young woman was interested in a scruffy teen like me.

Returning my attention to her, I asked where she was from.

"I am from Poland," she replied.

"Well, you speak very good English."

"Thank you," she said, with a shy downcast of her eyes. "I studied at university." Tilting her eyes up at me, she asked where I was from and I told her.

"Really? You are such long way from home. What are you doing in Barcelona?"

"Uh, just traveling around." I fiddled with the album jacket. "I always wanted to see Europe—that sort of thing. So, how about you? What brings you here?"

She handed me the headphones. "Uh, work. Only work."

I hung the headphones on a hook and turned to her. "If you don't mind me asking, what sort of work do you do?"

"I am dancer," she shrugged.

"No kidding," I said, with a little hip swivel. "Like a ballet dancer or something?"

She cast her eyes aside. "No, I dance in gentleman's club."

Flabbergasted, I asked her where the club was located.

"It is downtown, just off La Rambla, near Central Market," she frowned.

I glanced over at the proprietor as he greeted a new customer, then back at her. "Well, I'd like to see you dance sometime. I'm sure you're really good."

"Thank you, you are sweet." She winked while I put the record back in the jacket. "I do not want you to come there. It is not good place for nice young man like you. It is full of bad men. I can tell you are not like that."

Speechless, I stood there, not sure what to say next. Our eyes met.

"So are you going to buy record?" she asked.

"Uh, I can't afford it," I said. "Besides, I don't have a record player."

She took the record jacket from my hand. "Don't worry, I

will buy it. I have record player. You can come to my apartment tonight. I get off work at nine. We can listen together. How does that sound?"

"Uh, that sounds ... uh, great." I mumbled.

"My name is Katrina. Here is my address," she said, writing it on a piece of paper and then handing it to me. "And you are?"

"Paul," I said, shifting my weight self-consciously.

"Oh, such a lovely name ... and name of my favorite Beatle. Come," she said, grabbing my arm. "We go pay for this now."

Outside the record shop, Katrina stopped. "See you, tonight dear," she said, giving me a hug and kiss on the cheek. I felt my cheeks burn. "You are blushing," Katrina chuckled. "That is sweet. There is nothing to be bashful about. You are very nice looking man. See you at nine. Ciao."

Katrina turned and walked away, her white, high-heeled, white-rabbit-fur-ringed booties clicking on the sidewalk, her feathery purple boa flapping in her wake. She drew admiring glances and catcalls from yellow-helmeted construction workers dressed in blue coveralls as she passed.

Stunned and scared, I stood there frozen like a modern-day street mime watching her sashay down the street, pondering what I should do.

Half an hour later, I showed up at Fred's one-bedroom apartment. Located on the second floor of an early nineteenth-century building, at busy Avinguda Diagonal and Carrer de Casanova, it was noisy with traffic sounds outside. As much as I disliked him, I sought his advice.

"She's a hooker, man," Fred said, lighting a joint. "She wants you to pay to ball her."

"She knows I don't have any money.

"You're American. They think all of us have money," replied Fred with a squeaky voice as he held the pot smoke inside his lungs.

"Uh, then why would she buy me the record?" I responded as Fred exhaled a gush of smoke and offered me a toke. I declined with a hand wave.

"She didn't buy it for you, man. She bought it for herself," Fred scoffed. "Man, how naïve are you?"

"She's nice. She's not like that."

Fred took another hit. "All women are like that. They all want two things: money and getting laid." A breeze blew the lace curtains in through the nearby bay window, as he let out his own air, infused with marijuana smoke.

I was sorry I stopped by Fred's apartment. He was such a downer. Negative about life in general, he vowed to climb Mount Rainier on his fiftieth birthday and blow himself up. *Why wait until you're fifty?* I wondered.

I left Fred's, reluctantly agreeing to meet him that evening we would go to Katrina's apartment. He was going to show me how to do it. I was relieved, because as a rookie, I was scared to death and didn't know what to do. Katrina was closer to his age, so I was hoping I could introduce Fred to her and get me out of the situation.

At eight thirty, I met Fred at his place, and we walked to Katrina's address. Stopping outside her apartment building, we waited for her. It was an upscale baroque building with balconies and wrought-iron railings with balustrades. Chain-smoking cigarettes, I suffered through Fred's negativism as he continued complaining about everything. The only bright spot was his Swedish girlfriend, who he planned on meeting in Stockholm. But even that he ruined. "The worse I treat her, the better she likes sex," he crowed. "She loves it when I slap her ass and talk dirty to her. I just sent her a letter telling her I couldn't wait to smack her around and then fuck her brains out day and night."

I felt sorry for his girlfriend and couldn't imagine why she was going to marry Fred and then move to Seattle with him. Then again, maybe it was the delusions of a madman. I couldn't imagine any sane girl loving him, because in my opinion, he was mentally ill. Even he had alluded to it, telling me about his many sessions with a psychiatrist.

Despite my dislike for Fred, it was good having somebody I could talk to about Seattle when I was homesick. And now, I hoped he could get me out of the situation with Katrina—who was just getting out of a cab.

"Hello dear, Paul. I am sorry for being late. I am glad you are here," she said, giving me a hug, followed up with a kiss on the cheek. "Let us go inside and get warm."

Hesitating, I glanced at Fred and then back at Katrina. "Uh, this is my friend, Fred," I nodded in his direction.

"Nice to meet you, Fred," Katrina said, with a quick glance at him.

There was a moment of awkward silence as the sounds of passing cars filled the darkened streets. Katrina glimpsed Fred and then looked into my eyes. "Why is he here?" she said, her eyes searching for answers.

"Uh," I paused, frozen with fear.

At that instant, Fred took the initiative. Pulling out a wad of cash, he said, "You can fuck my friend for fifty pesetas."

Aghast at what she had heard, Katrina stood there with her eyes and mouth wide open. Still in shock, she looked at me, then glanced at Fred holding out money, and then back to me again. "I did not invite you here for sex. I invite you here because you seem like nice young man, and look lonely."

"Bullshit!" Fred roared. "You're a slut. Now you can fuck my friend for 150 pesetas, or forget it. Take it or leave it."

"I leave it. I am not that kind of girl," Katrina said, her eyes watering.

"You are a whore," Fred screamed. "You're just holding out for more, aren't you? Well, fuck you bitch, here's three hundred pesetas. Is that enough?"

"I am not prostitute," Katrina protested, her voice rising.

"Bullshit, you filthy cunt," Fred yelled, pointing at her. "Oh, I get it. You want to fuck both of us. Okay, this is my final offer. You can fuck my friend and me for five hundred pesetas. That's my final offer! What's it going to be, huh?"

By then, tears streamed down Katrina's face. She looked at me as if she'd been betrayed. Ashamed, I hung my head and shuffled my feet. I wanted to tell her I was sorry, but I couldn't speak. Meanwhile, Fred was tugging at me. "Come on man, let's go. This fucking whore is playing games with us."

Fred gave me a yank, and we were on our way. About ten feet farther, he stopped and looked back. "Filthy fucking whore," he bellowed, as spittle sprayed from his mouth. "Fuck you! You fucking bitch!"

I turned one last time, to say goodbye to Katrina, but she was already entering her apartment building. Feeling horrible about the way things turned out, I misled Fred, telling him I was going to stop at a friend's place. Several blocks farther, we split up. I couldn't stand being with him any longer, and felt sorry for Katrina. Perhaps she was a hooker, but Fred's behavior was over the top and cruel; there was no excuse for it.

When I got back to the youth hostel, the door was locked. I

spent the night outside trying to sleep, huddled under a covered walkway of the next door monastery, bothered by the cold and the episode with Katrina.

8

Flames

February 28–March 2, 1969 — Barcelona, Spain

"So, if you were drafted tomorrow, what would you do?" Henry asked. He was a young English photographer who had showed up at the hostel soon after the Katrina incident. Earlier, we were sitting at a circular table in the dormitory room of my youth hostel, looking at his amazing portfolio of images shot in New Zealand, India, South Africa, Ireland, and finally the United States. Claiming to be a photojournalist, he'd been traveling the world taking photos of people, trying to become the next Sir Donald McCullin. It wasn't long before he was showing me his portfolio.

"These were taken in Melbourne," he said, handing me a contact sheet of black-and-white stills protected in an insert. "And these here were shot in the Outback."

"Wow, man, these are great," I said, moving the contact sheet closer for a better look. Henry continued displaying photographs he'd taken in New Zealand. "Those were taken at a Vietnam War protest in Berkeley," he grinned, handing me several more contact sheets. "And these at a protest in Washington, D.C."

Being against the war, I was particularly interested in the photos of the demonstrators and told him about the draft and the Selective Service. Henry stopped handing me examples of his work as I became reflective. "Yeah, man," I said, handing him back his photos. "I could be drafted tomorrow, you know."

Henry's eyebrows drew close together as he looked at me. Being a Brit, and therefore free from the draft, he had no idea of the dilemma I faced and was fascinated. That's when he asked me what I would do if I was drafted tomorrow.

His question caught me off guard. "Uh, I don't know, man, you know. Uhm, I wouldn't go home, that's for sure."

Stowing away his collection in a brown leather satchel, Henry nodded. "So, where would you go then?"

"I'd go to Sweden and claim political asylum."

"And what would you do, to convince them that you're a draft dodger?"

"Man, I'd burn my draft card just to prove it."

"You would?" Henry asked.

"Yeah, sure, I'd burn it," I said, slapping the table with a hand for emphasis.

Henry chuckled. "I see, so that would make you a draft dodger," he stated. "Time to burn your draft card, then, I'd say. Do you mind if I see it? I've never seen one before." Pulling out my wallet, I handed him my draft card, and he examined it carefully.

"It says that your classification is 1-A. What does that mean?"

I anxiously folded and unfolded my wallet several times, and then sighed. "Uh, it means that I could be drafted at any moment, man."

Henry flipped the card over and began reading aloud the backside. "Any person who alters, forges, knowingly destroys, knowingly mutilates or in any manner changes this certificate," he recited then paused, looking at me like a judge issuing a stern warning from the bench, "may be fined not to exceed ten thousand dollars or imprisoned for not more than five years, or both."

Slamming his fist like a gavel on the table, Henry shook his head in disbelief. "Wow, that's heavy shit man," he said.

I buried my face in my hands. "Yeah, I know," I murmured.

Henry stroked his face, mulling over the situation for two or three seconds. He handed me back my draft card. "Tell you what. You burn it and I'll shoot you doing it. That way you'll have proof you're fleeing prosecution if you apply for asylum in Sweden. How does that sound?"

I hesitated. I didn't want to go to jail. More than anything, though, the draft was something I wanted to avoid. I'd heard it was getting increasingly difficult to obtain asylum in Sweden. You now had to prove you were truly a conscientious objector, or were avoiding imprisonment. If I was denied, what would I do? Without a work permit, I couldn't get a visa, and without a visa, I couldn't get work. It was a *Catch-22* situation. With no job and without a work permit, I couldn't stay in Europe forever. I'd have to return home and face the draft or face imprisonment for refusing to go.

An idea struck me. I still had my old student deferment draft card listing my classification as 1-HS. Issued to me while in high school, it was now invalid. If I burned my old card, it would give the illusion I was burning my real draft card. I pretended to hem and haw for a moment. "Okay, man," I finally said. "You've got yourself a deal."

While Henry set up his camera, I surreptitiously switched my valid draft card with my old one.

"Alright, all set," said Henry. "Let's get rolling."

Getting up from his chair, he quickly surveyed the room. "We need a little back light, so I'd like you to stand by that open window over there," Henry pointed.

Now that I was at the window, Henry instructed me on the count of three to hold my draft card up and light it on fire while he moved around taking pictures. "Okay, are you ready?" he asked, looking through the viewfinder and setting the focus on his camera. I nodded that I was.

"One, two, three!" he sang out.

At that instant. I clicked the lighter and set my old draft card aflame, making sure my thumb covered the 1-HS classification. The flames licked their way up the card. The paper curled and twisted, turning black as the fire moved closer to my thumb, finally scorching it.

"Ouch," I complained. When I couldn't tolerate the pain any longer, I pinched a top corner with my free hand and let go with the other, just as the flames obliterated my classification. All the while, Henry's Nikon camera shuttered away.

Within ten seconds, my old draft card turned into a small batch of smoldering ashes on the tile floor and Henry was ecstatic. "That was great, man!" he exclaimed. "I've always wanted to shoot someone burning their draft card."

I didn't have the heart to tell Henry the card was fake, and supposed it really didn't matter. He got what he wanted and so did I. He said he would mail a copy of the photograph to my parents' place. "Yeah, man, that's a great idea," I replied. "If I need it, I will have my brother forward it to me."

A day later, Henry had left, and an American named Andy moved in. A little older than me, and from L.A., it was then that he told me he was on his way to the Canary Islands and convinced me to go with him.

The next day I bought a ticket to Las Palmas, Gran Canaria, and went to tell Fred I was leaving. Over the past week, he'd been badgering me to travel with him to Sweden, where he planned to marry his Swedish fiancée. I was so tired of his pessimism I didn't want to go. I prayed Fred wouldn't want to come along. He didn't, thank God, and I was off the hook.

The following day I was on my way to Las Palmas, Gran Canaria, upon a pre-World War II passenger freighter straight out of a Humphrey Bogart movie.

9

Freighter

Enriched with mahogany, steeped in mystery, the old freighter rumbled, thumped, clanged, and shook in the sea. Several hours after getting underway, I climbed into my top bunk in a stateroom shared with seven other passengers. Situated several levels below the main deck, our portholes, perhaps six feet above the waterline, were only good for providing a modicum of daylight and view of cresting waves. Now and then, I'd see a frigate or porpoise from my perch. Mostly, though, it was just wave after wave. I soon felt claustrophobic in such cramped quarters and nauseous from the smell of diesel fuel. Craving fresh air, I spent most daylight hours outside on the main deck.

Our first stop was Valencia, where I disembarked in need of solid ground. As a teenager, seafaring tales of adventure and survival by the likes of Shackleton, Fletcher Christenson,

Captain Bligh, and Robin Lee Graham enthralled me. If my first night at sea was any indication, though, I was a landlubber at heart. It wasn't that the night had been stormy or even rough; it was the constant swaying and droning of the engines, along with the diesel smell, that kept me awake half the night. Besides Terra firma, I needed caffeine.

Within minutes of disembarking the ship in Puerto de Valencia, I found a café selling espresso, pastries, and tea. Conveniently, it was next door to a magazine kiosk overflowing with tabloids displaying Paul Newman's handsome face on the covers. I suddenly felt proud to be an American. I bought a copy of the *International Herald Tribune.* Sitting outside, enjoying the sunshine, I sipped on tea. It was definitely warmer here than Barcelona—not short-sleeve weather, but suitable for just a sweater. Reading about Jim Morrison's arrest for indecent exposure in Miami, the Apollo 9 mission, and war protests back home, it all seemed far away and incongruous. *Americans are crazy,* I said to myself, flipping the page. In the six weeks since landing in Europe, my perspective had changed.

As I took another sip of tea, chattering grade school children attired in parochial school uniforms caught my attention, and I glanced up as they paraded past. Nearby at a table, beret-wearing old men smoking cigarettes and drinking espresso played checkers and chess. Middle-aged commuters raced their way to work riding Vespa scooters, motorcycles, and driving smelly diesel cars. Pedestrians walked past me, looking unhappy.

If there was anything I noticed about Spaniards then, it was that hardly anybody ever smiled. I wasn't certain if it was a cultural thing or because they were poor. Then again, maybe it was because they were living in constant fear of Franco.

In addition, unlike northern European countries I'd visited, from what I could tell, many Spanish people didn't mix with foreigners and didn't speak English. My only friends were travelers like me. By and large, they were Canadians and Brits, since I hadn't encountered many Americans here. I wondered if it was because of the war; if you were male and of drafting age, you were in college or in the service.

Our ship coursed on, with scheduled ports of call ahead in Alicante, Almería, Málaga, Tenerife, and finally Las Palmas. Along the way, we feasted on delicious food: seafood, rice dishes, bread, and fresh vegetables and fruits. I indulged myself, restoring my depleted reserves. In port, I spent part of my time watching men unload and load our ship. Much of the work was by hand. Men carried gunnysacks on their shoulders, wheeled carts of fruit, and rolled barrels on deck to the hatches. They winched the goods on pallets into the holds. Many of the laborers were olive or brown-skin foreigners wearing turbans and muslin clothing.

The second day at sea, I broke up the monotony in the afternoon by going to the ship's lounge. The interior was gorgeously furnished in dark mahogany, Oriental rugs, and brass. I pulled open the door and stood there inconspicuously. Slinking up to the bar to order a hot chocolate, I tried my best to avoid drawing attention from the alcohol drinkers.

"*Que deseas, amigo?*" the bartender asked what I wanted in Spanish.

Struggling to say hot cocoa in Spanish, I replied, "Uh, *uno chocolate caliente.*"

"*Espumoso?*" he queried.

"Foamy," I answered. The bartender shrugged his shoulders as if he didn't understand, and I pointed at his espresso steamer and hissed like a cat. "Ah, *espumoso,*" the bartender hissed back, twinkled his fingers, and then chuckled.

By then, his teasing caught the attention of the boozers who laughed, hissed, and twinkled their fingers. Feeling my face turn red from embarrassment, I left and drank my cocoa outside on the deck. This interplay would become a daily ritual for the remainder of the cruise.

On the third day, we passed through the Strait of Gibraltar, better known to me as The Rock from Prudential Life Insurance's television commercials. I stood on the main deck, exhilarated by the iconic sight as we passed between two continents. I could feel the rhythmic pulsations of the African landmass to the south, and the hum of industrialized Europe to the north. It was definitely a clash of cultures. Primal energy versus Western Civilization.

Strumming his guitar, Andy, who had encouraged me to go to the Canaries, paused and pointed out Gibraltar's massive water collection system, comprising catchment panels on its eastern slopes and cisterns at the base. "That's how they get their water, man," he said. "It's a British territory and highly contested by Spain. Franco cut off the peninsula."

Andy resumed playing his guitar, strumming "Nights in White Satin." I left, walking to the ship's bow to watch the sunset. Having passed through the Strait, we entered the Atlantic. At that moment, I felt homesick.

As I watched from my perch on a hatch cover, the sea became rougher and inky green, contrasting to the cobalt blue of the Mediterranean. Soon darkness fell, and more stars than I'd ever seen sparkled overhead in the night sky. Wind tousled my hair and buffeted my ears. I inhaled a long, deep breath of thick sea air and closed my eyes. I yawned and rubbed my eyes. After four nights on the freighter, I hadn't slept well. Not only did the fumes repulse me, it was hot and stuffy in the communal stateroom. The bunk was too short for someone my height. The constant clanging and thumping noises coming from the nearby engine room made it difficult to sleep. *Thunk, thunk, boom. Thunk, thunk, clang.*

Still sitting on the hatch cover, I reclined against a bulkhead and dozed. A plaintive, distant wailing roused me. It sounded like a baby's cry, or a female cat in heat. The call continued, growing louder, clearer, finally familiar. It was the whine of my brother Bob crying. Had something happened to him? Was he in trouble? I began to worry. Several minutes passed, and the whimpering faded away. I relaxed. Of course, my mother would write if something drastic had happened. Twice, she'd sent me letters c/o General Delivery and wired me money. Cut off from further funds, I wasn't sure whether I'd send her a postcard when I landed in Las Palmas.

The following day, the sea grew calmer and the weather warmer. Having stripped down to my tee-shirt and jeans to bask in the sun, I sat at the bow of the ship with Andy watching porpoises ride the bow wake, performing joyful acrobatics in the air. Meanwhile, Andy strummed "Nights in White Satin" repeatedly on his guitar. As a beginner, he didn't know any other songs. It's not that I disliked his guitar plucking; it's just that I'd have preferred listening to the excited cackles of the porpoises.

The ocean was now aqua colored, and warm trade winds carrying hints of sweet flowers and spices lured us southward. Tomorrow we would arrive in the Canaries—Tenerife in the morning and then Las Palmas in the afternoon. I was ready for an end to the drone and rumblings of engines, Andy's guitar playing, and the monotony of the sea. I was eager for sunshine, warmth, and sandy beaches laden with horny blond Scandinavian girls in need of a Nordic-looking American guy who hadn't washed his clothes or bathed in several weeks.

A storm hit on our last night, pounding the ship. Whitecaps lashed against the portholes in our berth. The constant boom and shake caused by the waves kept me awake half the night. In the morning, the winds had died down and the sea was calm. Shortly after breakfast, we pulled into Puerto de Santa Cruz de Tenerife. I did a double take, surprised to see pastel-colored houses and buildings, along with drab, mostly barren, moon-gray hillsides. I'd expected something tropical and lush. It reminded me of the basalt coulees and outcroppings in eastern Washington, but that was okay. It was warm and sunny—that was all that mattered. I was tired of the cold up north. If I was going to have to spend daylight hours outside, I wanted it to be warm—and it was.

During our layover in Tenerife, while dockworkers unloaded and loaded cargo, I disembarked the ship eager to explore the waterfront shops and go for a swim. No sooner had I stepped onto the golden beach than a tanned young man with long bleached hair ran full blast and somersaulted into the surf. I already liked this place. This was just what I needed after the cold snowy weather back home and up north. Here I could forget about the war, the draft, and my father. Here, I could lie on the beach, tan my embarrassingly pale skin, and ogle Scandinavian girls. I didn't care if the U.S. Army drafted me. Let them find me first.

I didn't have a bathing suit, so I stripped down to my Fruit of the Loom jockey shorts and waded into the ocean. If anyone was watching, they would probably think my "suit" was like the white speedos the paunchy old men wore standing around showing off their spindly stork-like legs—not a pretty sight.

Wading in, I came to a stop and hesitated. The waves lapped my thighs, just below my briefs. The water was cooler than I'd expected, reminding me of swimming in Lake Sammamish. Definitely a chill. I took a deep breath and dove in. *Yep, definitely has a bite to it*, I grimaced. *More like Lake Washington.*

Monitoring the ship, I swam around for about ten or fifteen minutes and then noticed passengers re-boarding. I leapfrogged out of the water and dressed. With no towel to dry off with, my clothes were dripping wet.

As I boarded the ship, Andy saw me and called out, "What'd you do, fall in?"

The other passengers chuckled as I explained I'd gone for a swim, thinking I could dry off in the sun, and didn't expect the ship to leave so soon.

"There're towels in the shower," Andy teased. "Why didn't you just take one of those?"

"There are?" I shot back, quickly realizing my faux pas and looking guilty since I hadn't showered in the six days we'd been on the ship.

"Yeah, there are," Andy replied, knowing I hadn't showered.

Truth was, I hadn't bathed in weeks because, whenever I did, my hair fell out, so much so it would clog the drain. It horrified me. In an era when so much emphasis was placed on a person's hair, my personal identity was at stake. I'd rather smell bad and have my hair a matted and tangled mess than watch it go down the drain. Unlike Fred, who constantly bemoaned his receding hairline, I was too ashamed to talk about it, so I just let the dirt and grime and tangles lock it in place—and mostly it did. My hair felt stiff, as if sprayed with lacquer.

To cover up any body odor, I used an antiperspirant deodor-ant, Old Spice aftershave, and I did wash my face and brush my teeth. Since the rest of me hadn't seen soap and water in weeks, I went swimming. I'd heard that saltwater was a natural disinfectant and would crystallize and mat hair together until washed with soap and water.

Upon arriving in Puerto de Las Palmas that afternoon, my clothes had dried, and I was ready to get off the ship with Andy.

10

Paradise

March 8–March 27, 1969 — Las Palmas de Gran Canaria, Spain

I f Barcelona was dark and mysterious, Las Palmas was vibrant as it basked in a golden Impressionistic glow. While I hadn't really noticed "The Spanish Miracle" in Barcelona, Las Palmas exemplified it. Everywhere I looked there was a crane, and construction workers erecting high-rise apartment buildings, hotels, office buildings, and shops. The boardwalk along Playa de Las Canteras was being extended to accommodate the sprawling construction at the southern end of the beach. Not only was there sunshine, but there was a buzz of excitement—especially in the northern tip, which comprised the tourist section. Other than occasional Guardia Civil officers, it was difficult to tell I was in Franco's Spain. When Andy and I disembarked the ship in the port, this is the Las Palmas we found.

Walking through the port with Andy, with his curly locks

resembling T-Rex's lead singer Marc Bolan, we were the object of catcalls, whistles, and bananas tossed at us. Stopping to see some friends of his, we got stoned on a chillum full of marijuana blended with hashish. A tingling sensation started in my toes, working its way up my legs, exploding in my brain with a rush of euphoria and paranoia.

Surrealistic murals on the walls supposedly painted by Salvador Dalí came to life. It felt like I was going to have a heart attack or lose my mind. Apparently, the other ten or twelve people sitting on the Persian rug felt the same way, because for what seemed like an eternity, nobody moved or uttered a word. I've never been so high in my life. From then on, I rarely bought the stuff. Likewise, I'd often pass up my turn, or fake taking a hit if offered a joint.

Gradually, people started coming out of their self-induced hash stupors. Some staggered out aimlessly without saying a word, some started talking mindlessly, others just wandered around, dazed and confused, tripping out on the paintings and black-and-white checkerboard floor. I decided this was an excellent opportunity to slip out as I was still too high to talk to anybody and needed fresh air.

Outside, I tried to get my bearings. Las Palmas lies on a peninsula. I was aware of this, based on the map in the travel brochure they gave me at the cruise office in Barcelona when I booked my excursion. Unexpectedly, though, it was a maze of side streets and alleys, so it was difficult to know where I was in relationship to the main body of the island. Was I on the west or east side? Looking skyward, I found the sun to my right. Since it was afternoon, I knew that west was to my right, east to my left, and south was dead ahead.

Before I left Barcelona, I checked my copy of *Europe on $5 a*

Day for youth hostels in Las Palmas, and to my consternation found none. I did find the name and addresses of several inexpensive pensions in the area. I wrote down their addresses and marked them on the map. The first one was close to where I was. Within five or ten minutes, I found it and inquired about a room. Unfortunately, it was full.

The next pension had a room available. They'd raised their rates though, from fifty pesetas a night to a hundred, since it was now *turista* season.

Back on the streets, I continued looking for pension signs advertising vacancies. There weren't any. Rounding a corner, I encountered a balding and bearded man in his late twenties playing guitar and harmonica, singing Bob Dylan's "Tambourine Man." I'd soon learn his name was John. With his neck veins bulging, spittle spewing from his mouth, he sang with conviction and sounded great.

I'd only been in town for two or three hours. Already I loved the quaint Spanish colonial houses, pastel colors, modern hotels, weather, and vibe. It was groovy without being pretentious. Above all, I loved the weather. I'd found paradise—my Shangri-La. Now, all I needed was to find a pension, a place where I could make my bed and call home. I needed little. This was the place, this was the time, and I was open to anything—well, almost anything.

John finished playing. As a street musician, he passed the hat, eventually holding it out toward me. Digging into my jeans, I came up empty-handed and pantomimed I was sorry. He winked at me it was okay. While he was putting his guitar in a case, I came up to him. "That was great, man," I said. "Much better than Dylan's version."

"Thanks," John shrugged, more preoccupied packing up his

gear than with small talk.

"No, I mean it, man, you sounded great!" John hesitated, then turned to me. "It doesn't matter what you think, or anybody else thinks, I didn't write the song."

I contemplated what he'd said. He was right. It didn't matter how good he was. It all came down to who wrote and recorded the song. "Uh, so do you have any original songs?" I asked.

"Yeah, I've got a lot of songs," he said with a dismissive shrug. "But I don't have time to sing them right now."

"Well, man, maybe some other time," I said. "I just got here, and plan to stick around."

"That's good, man," John said, and then after exchanging introductions, he asked me where I was staying. "Uh, nowhere. I'm still looking for a place," I replied.

"Well, you should check out Mama Gallenda's pension on Calle Portugal and El Cid. Cheapest place there is. It's on the other side of town. I used to stay there, so tell her that John sent you. Anyway, gotta go now. See you around. I play here every day at three."

Over the weeks, I occasionally stopped by to hear John play and got to know him. At twenty-eight, he was almost ten years older than me. Built like a fireplug, he was a Vietnam Marine vet. He didn't talk about the war, but you could tell it had affected him by the tattered army coat he frequently wore, and the ferocity of his musicianship and singing. Unfortunately, his songwriting didn't live up to his pathos. But I didn't care; we struck a chord and became friends. Perhaps it was because we were the only two Americans other than Andy in town then, or because I liked his music and felt his turmoil. Clearly, he'd seen and experienced things in Vietnam, and it troubled his soul.

81

Eventually he introduced me to his Grace Slick–looking Australian girlfriend, Kate, who was about his age, along with her adolescent daughter and their gay Cuban roommate Miguel. Miguel was a black man in his early thirties with a flair for the dramatic, who spoke with a heavy Spanish accent and lisp, which made him sound Catalonian. Miguel had somehow escaped Cuba and sought asylum in Spain because of Fidel Castro's persecution of gays. *So Franco treats gays better than Castro does?* I wondered.

He was the first gay man I came to know. I liked him. I could never understand his esoteric ramblings, punctuated by his flamboyant prancing, though. One moment he would sprinkle flower petals, and the next he twisted in anguish. It all reminded me of a Greek tragedy.

Miguel was a prolific dancer, and as the weeks and months went by, when I didn't see him at Kate and John's, I'd run into him in town. Usually, though, I'd encounter him at my favorite hangout, El Cofre discotheque, dancing up a storm all by himself, or with anyone else who ventured onto the dance floor. I frequently made a point of timing my trips to the bar and restroom lest Miguel start dancing with me. He was harmless, though, usually going on about how his young Spanish boyfriend left him, and how it ruined his life forever.

One evening at El Cofre I met a Swedish businessman in his mid-forties. He was married but had a strange relationship with his wife. Every year they would vacation in the Canaries. She would go to an island and he would go to another. They did whatever they wanted with the agreement neither one would tell the other what they had done. It just so happened, Miguel showed up later, and I introduced him to the Scandinavian man. The two hit it off, with the Swede telling me how special

Miguel was while watching him prance around the dance floor like a gazelle.

Days later, John and Kate had a party, and Miguel came with the businessman. When Miguel wasn't putting on a show, the two spent the evening dancing and sitting together. *If only his wife knew what he's up to,* I chuckled to myself. *Then again, I wonder what she's doing. What a weird way to spend your vacation. I thought the point of being married was to share your experiences. Oh well, they're not hurting anybody, other than maybe themselves, so who am I to judge?*

Occasionally I'd run into Andy. Having piqued my interest in the Canary Islands and traveled together there, we would chat briefly about our experiences on the island. Beyond that, we had little in common. Andy liked to spend his days getting high, body-surfing in Maspalomas on the island's southern end, and living in a nearby commune. He tried talking me into checking it out, but I didn't want to lie around smoking hash all day, and certainly didn't want to live in a commune. I just wasn't cut out for the hippie life, I suppose.

11

Danny

March 27–28, 1969 — Las Palmas de Gran Canaria, Spain

My involvement, and I suppose you could call it friendship, with Danny began one evening as I nursed a cup of tea at one of the outdoor cafés in Parque Santa Catalina. I often hung out at this palm-and-fig-tree-shaded square in the evenings. Frequented by tourists looking for souvenirs at one of the shops to take home from Las Palmas, or to eat at one of the outdoor cafés, I'd wait for El Corfe to open at ten and then go to the discotheque for the night—usually until around five in the morning. At that point, I'd walk home to my pension on the outskirts of town, sleep in until around two in the afternoon, and then do it all over again the next day. This was my routine since my arrival in Las Palmas almost three weeks earlier.

As I sat there sipping a pot of tea, I noticed a young man, three or four years older than me, walking along the promenade with a black carry-on bag strapped over his shoulder. He had wavy hair cresting slightly over his ears. He wore blue jeans and a tan corduroy sports coat. Standing approximately six feet tall, he was about my height, and a little heavier than my 155 pounds. He was nondescript except for his snow-white mustache. *How odd*, I thought. *He has auburn hair, but his mustache is white. Maybe he dyes it. Go figure.*

As the white-mustached man walked down the promenade, he glanced in my direction before continuing on his way.

A short while later, a waiter came up to my table. "Would you like another tea?" he asked in accented English.

"Uh, no thanks," I said. "I'm still working on this one." The waiter cast me an arrogant sneer, poured the rest of the pot into my teacup, and retreated to his perch, where he watched over his tables like an owl after field mice. A cup of tea cost two pesetas, and you could sit there all day, provided you were consuming something. I'd been there forty-five minutes and still had half a cup left. It infuriated the waiters, but so what; I wasn't breaking any laws. On the other hand, if I just sat there and bought nothing, they would ask me to leave. If I refused, police might arrest me for loitering.

It was now nine thirty, and in thirty minutes, El Cofre would open. It was going to be difficult to make the tea last, because the less frequently I sipped, the more the waiters pestered me. But I'd had lots of practice biding my time with taking a pretend sip, looking around, lighting a cigarette, and rereading, for the umpteenth time, the copy of the *International Herald Tribune* I bought every day at one of the magazine kiosks in Parque Santa Catalina, or rummaged from a tabletop.

The white-mustached man strolled by once more, in the opposite direction. Again, he looked over at me. I watched him for a moment and then cast my eyes away. *If he comes by again, then he's gay,* I reasoned. Not that I had anything against gays because I didn't. But after having been propositioned several occasions in the months of traveling, I was on high alert. Women turned me on and that was that. Therefore, if a man tried picking me up, it made me feel uneasy. I didn't want to offend them, but didn't want to encourage them either. There was a fine line, and I think some gays were so used to being told flat out to *get the hell out of here* by heterosexual men, that they saw my politeness as a sign of acceptance. Therefore, when mustache man strolled by a third time, stopped to gaze at me, and then came over, I was certain he was gay. Immediately, I felt on guard when he arrived at my table.

"Mind if I sit down?" he asked.

"Uh, I was about to leave, you know, but okay."

"Thank you," the mustache man said in perfect English, seating himself across from me. "I just got in from Tenerife, on the ferry, and need to rest a bit. I've been looking for a place to stay, but there aren't many, and the ones with vacancies are expensive. So where're you from?"

I informed him where I was from before taking another false sip of my nearly empty cup of tea.

"Ah, a Yank," he nodded. "Haven't run into too many these days."

"Yeah, because they're all fighting the stupid Vietnam War," I replied.

"Well, I'm Canadian," the mustache man said. "So I don't have to worry about it."

I grinned. "Ah, a Canuck. I've been to Vancouver twice, you know—great city."

"Actually, I'm from Quebec City," mustache man said,

asking me my name, which I provided. "I'm Danny ... Danny Zorro. Nice meeting you," he said, extending his hand, which I shook.

"Likewise. So what were you doing in Tenerife?"

Danny leaned in toward me. "I was there for a month. I wanted to check it out. You see, I have this idea on how to make money, but I need an investor. I'm down to my last twelve dollars."

"Well, good luck, because all I've got is twenty-nine bucks," I said, preparing to leave. Danny held his palms out, pleading for me to consider his idea. "All I need is twenty dollars. Have you got a moment so I can tell you about my plan?"

At that instant, the waiter came up. "Something for you, sir?" he asked Danny.

Danny pulled a dollar bill out of his shirt pocket. "Sure, I'll have a Pepsi and another tea for my friend, please." He turned to me. "It's on me; it takes money to make money," he said, twirling his mustache. "Not sure I can write it off though," he chuckled, "but I'll keep track of it."

Danny's cobalt blue eyes twinkled mischievously, stirring my curiosity.

"Alright," I said. "So what's your plan?"

"My plan is that you invest twenty dollars and I take a ferry tomorrow to Tenerife, spend the night there, and then catch an Iberia airlines flight back here the following day," Danny said. "Are you following me so far?"

"Yeah, but I don't know you, you know," I smirked. "How do I know you won't just take my twenty and I'll never see you again?"

"It's called trust," Danny said, spinning his mustache again. "Rich people invest their money because they believe in a plan.

87

They believe they will make money on their investment. Some people call it greed, but it's not. It's risk. Greed is when you don't share or help those in need, or horde your money. Risk is when you take chances, knowing you could lose your money, but go ahead anyway because you believe in the plan. Risk-takers deserve to be rewarded, wouldn't you say so?"

Before I could respond, our waiter showed up, bringing Danny his Pepsi, and me another pot of tea. Danny gave him the dollar bill, and the waiter left to get change. "So, shall I continue?" Danny said, pouring his Pepsi into a glass, while I squeezed a little lemon juice into my tea and added two cubes of sugar.

"Alright," I said, picking up my spoon to stir my tea.

Danny took a sip of Pepsi. "Okay, here's the tricky part. But don't worry, I've rehearsed it so I know it will work. Just before my plane arrives, you take a bus to the airport, go to baggage claim, grab my luggage, and catch the bus back here. Meanwhile, I go to lost and found and report my bag missing. At that point, the bus will already have arrived back at Parque Santa Catalina and you can meet me here tomorrow. Are you following me?"

Once again, the waiter interrupted us before I could answer, giving Danny his change. I waited for him to leave and then said, "So how is this going to make money?"

Danny glanced around to make sure nobody was listening. Still being careful, he cupped a hand around the side of his mouth and said, "Insurance. I file a claim for the declared value of the contents. When Iberia can't find it, they settle, paying me for my loss."

"Uh, couldn't that take a while?" I asked, remembering how long it took the insurance company to settle for my father's pickup truck I had totaled two years earlier.

While Danny told me it could take a week for the investigation, I panned my eyes to watch a sexy blond girl strolling down the walkway in front of the tourist shops. I'd seen her around four or five times and on each occasion, her face was more sunburned. Now, her face was smeared mime-like with zinc oxide sunscreen—even at night. I returned my sight to Danny. "In the meantime," he continued, "they would have to provide me with a hotel and per diem expenses because I'll claim that all my money was in my bag."

I poured myself more tea and sat there digesting Danny's plan for a moment. "So, what's my cut?"

Danny opened his travel bag and pulled out a camera and his passport. "Your return would be one-third of their settlement, which could be anywhere from two hundred to three hundred dollars, depending on how much they determine the replacement value of my Nikkormat camera, clothing, American Tourister shoulder bag, and passport I'd claim—and, oh yeah, I'd tell them that four hundred dollars cash was in the bag too."

"So, I get one-third and you get two-thirds, but I'm the one putting all the money up and taking all the risk," I scoffed.

"Yes, you are the investor, but I'm the guy with the plan," Danny said, pouring more Pepsi into his glass. "And I'm the one who has to be believable to Iberia. I need to convince them I really had those contents in my luggage, and that it's missing through no fault of my own. Fraud is a serious offense here in Spain. The usual sentence is four years and one day. So, you see, I'm assuming just as much, if not more risk than you."

I took a sip of tea and mulled it over. The money I had would last a week or two, maybe three. And then what? I

89

couldn't ask my parents for more money; they had cut me off. My friends were broke. And I didn't have the heart to ask my high school teacher again, who'd already sent me a hundred dollars—which was dwindling fast. I scratched my beard, thinking about it. Turning to Danny, I said, "So, until the settlement happens, what will I live on? You will get an allowance. What do I get?"

"Good question," Danny replied, stowing away his camera and passport. "You'll get one-third of my daily per diem. I don't know how much that will be, but I assume they will pay me between five and ten dollars a day for meals and miscellaneous items. Which means I'd pay you anywhere from a dollar seventy to three dollars and thirty cents a day. How does that sound?"

I took a deep breath. "I'd like to think it over for a day or two and let you know."

I didn't know Danny's background. He said he was twenty-four. Perhaps he'd gone to college. Regardless, he was crafty, with a good understanding of business. Above all, he was a salesman. When I was sixteen, I was a paperboy. I learned a lot about sales from selling newspaper subscriptions. The number one rule was to close the deal during the first meeting. Invariably, if someone said "let me think about it," it meant "no."

Danny was perceptive enough to know this, too. "So, what's wrong with the plan?" he asked, leaving a tip for the waiter and pocketing the rest of his change. Danny's question caught me off guard, putting me on the defensive, and caused me to squirm. "Uh, nothing. I just don't like risk."

"Well, if there's nothing wrong with the plan, then there's no risk, right?" Danny said. "That's not it," I said. "The risk is that I don't know you, and after I give you twenty dollars, I might never see you again."

Danny reached down into his bag and pulled out his passport. "I won't need this to go to Tenerife and then back here," he said with a confident grin. "If it makes you feel better, hold on to it for me."

With only twenty-nine dollars remaining, I once again reflected on my financial state. I'd never fussed about money. Somehow or another, it would appear when I needed it, as it was right then. *I don't want to go home. I hate Dad's stupid rules, and I especially don't want to go to Vietnam. I'm having the time of my life.* I opened my wallet and handed him my last twenty dollars. "Okay, okay, we've got a deal. But you hang onto your passport."

That night, Danny and I went to El Cofre and hung out, listening to music. They didn't have a cover charge, but required you buy at least one drink. I always bought a Pepsi because it was the cheapest drink on the menu. I bought Danny one too, as repayment for the cup of tea he'd purchased for me. We stayed there for two or three hours, mostly talking about places we'd been and wanted to go. Prior to his stay in Tenerife, he'd come from Cape Town, South Africa. We shared stories about our families, with me telling him about my mother having graduated from the University of Washington and my father from Purdue in engineering.

Danny told me his father was a vice president at ALCOA, Canada. By the sounds of it, his dad had big expectations for him, wanting him to go into business. Danny resented him for it. His relationship with his father sounded similar to mine.

Nearly broke, Danny didn't want to spend money on a pension. After leaving El Cofre, I invited him to spend the night at my place. "There's a vacant lot close to my pension and I've got a sleeping bag. You can use it to sleep there," I offered. He took me up on my proposal and once Danny had settled, I entered my pension. Opening the door to my room, I crawled into bed. On the other side of the room were another bed and a roommate I'd never met since checking in. I knew he was there because he always snored.

Expecting Danny to be gone in the morning, I went outside and gave a quick whoop of laughter. He sat on the hill overlooking the ocean next to my rolled-up sleeping bag. "Hello," I said, "How did you sleep?"

"Quite well, thank you for asking and for letting me use your sleeping bag," Danny said, looking out over the ocean. "Columbus set sail from here in 1492 for the East Indies and discovered America instead. It took him six weeks to cross the Atlantic. Here we are, descendants from the continent he discovered, able to fly across the same ocean in less than eight hours. Remarkable, isn't it?"

"Yes, it is," I said, thinking of my father, who helped make it possible.

"Today I sail to Tenerife. Are you ready?"

"I think so," I said, forcing a smile. I still had reservations about Danny and whether I'd ever see him and my money again. "Believe in the plan," Danny grinned "Believe in it. Okay?" I nodded reluctantly.

"Alright, let's go." Danny got up and handed me my bag.

We dropped my bedding off at my pension and I said goodbye to Mama Gallenda, after introducing her to Danny. Not long afterward, we were on our way to the port where Danny would catch the daily ferry to Tenerife. Along the way, we rehearsed the plan repeatedly. We went over the time the bus departed for Las Palmas International Airport, his flight number, when his plane landed, the layout of baggage claim, the conveyor number, his American Tourister bag, and when the bus returned to town.

When we arrived at the ferry terminal, I'd memorized everything and hoped to see him the following day. Shaking his hand, I bid him goodbye and good luck.

"Luck has nothing to do with it," said Danny, with a confident smile and upright stance. "As long as we follow the plan, there is nothing to worry about. See you tomorrow morning at the airport."

I watched as Danny, carrying his black carry-on duffel bag, boarded the ferry and disappeared inside. After lighting a cigarette, I headed to my favorite restaurant for breakfast.

12

Terry

March 28–29, 1969 — Las Palmas de Gran Canaria, Spain

The morning Danny left for Tenerife, I ate my standard meal for the day at Cafeteria Tasartico. Located in the tourist area, I usually ate there in the afternoons so this was early for me. After finishing my meal comprising two eggs, grilled potatoes, salad, and milk for seventeen pesetas (about twenty-five cents U.S. then), I then went to see my friend Terry. He buzzed me in, and I rode the elevator up to his flat on the fourth floor. I rang the doorbell, and almost immediately a wiry Englishman in his early thirties, with frizzy red hair, opened the door for me.

"Hello man, come in," Terry said, with a grin spreading under his goatee. "What's going on?"

I followed him into the kitchen, where he was frying sausage and eggs. "That smells good," I breathed in the odors.

"It's linguiça."

"It doesn't look like pasta to me, you know."

Terry chuckled. He prided himself as a gourmet, along with his culinary skills. "Not linguine, linguiça; it's a type of Portuguese sausage," he said, stirring the scrambled eggs. "You hungry?"

"Thanks, but I just ate at Cafeteria Tasartico."

Terry cast me a sideways grimace. "Is that the place you took me to?"

"Yeah," I replied, folding my arms. "And you're still feeling well?" he teased.

I snorted and leaned against the kitchen entrance. Terry was like an uncle. For reasons unknown to me, he'd taken me under his wing. Perhaps it was because I spoke English, and English-speaking people seemed to congregate and stick together here, as in other non-English speaking European countries. There's also the possibility he just felt sorry for me. Then again, maybe he was lonely since his girlfriend Judy was in England. Whatever the case, Terry was generous, inviting me over sometimes for gourmet dinners he fixed.

Terry worked for a London travel agency. During the summer, he was a guide on bus tours throughout Europe, and during winter months, he drummed up business for his company. It was the reason he was in Las Palmas. Having arrived two weeks ago, his job was to go to the port, board cruise ships bound for London, get their passenger lists, and then wire them to his office. They would then put together personalized travel packages, handing them out to passengers when they disembarked in London.

As far as I was concerned, Terry had the *dream job*. He never revealed how he was able to get on board cruise ships. He was articulate and sophisticated, and a licensed travel agent, so he might have talked his way aboard vessels. Then again, there was always the possibility he bribed his way on board. After all, it was Spain, well known for graft.

I'd met Terry at Playa de Las Canteras a day or two after he arrived. He was sitting next to me on a towel, and we struck up a conversation. He wanted to know things to do on the island and places to eat. Afterward, he invited me up to his pad to smoke pot. At first, I was leery of him, but took him up on his offer. From that point on, we became friends, and now I was at his pad inquiring if he wanted to go to the beach in the afternoon.

"I'd love to, but I've got to go to the port today. A cruise ship just came in," Terry said, dishing up his eggs, sausage, and toast. "How about tomorrow?"

"I've got something going on," I said. "How about the day after tomorrow?"

"Sorry, man, but Judy arrives that day," Terry said, sitting down at the kitchen table. "Come over for dinner, then. I've told her about you and she'd like to meet you."

"Okay, sure, man," I said, shifting my weight. "Do you mind if I bring a friend?"

"Not at all. What's her name?"

"Uh, it's Danny," I stammered. "He's Canadian."

"That's cool," Terry said, slicing the linguiça. "Bring him, I'd like to meet him and I'm sure Judy would, too. See you around six." I said goodbye to Terry, who switched his fork into his right hand before taking a bite. *He's got good table manners,* I thought as I left.

I'd need to clear with Danny about going to Terry's, although I was sure he would be okay with it. As nice as Terry was, I always felt slightly uncomfortable around him. He was older and more educated than I was, and now his girlfriend would be there too. I needed someone to act as a go-between, and Danny would be the perfect cushion. He was like a ten-year-younger version of Terry.

I also had an ulterior motive; I needed a place to store Danny's stolen bag, as I wouldn't be comfortable leaving it unattended at Mama Gallenda's pension. Stowing it at Terry's flat would be the perfect place. It was secure, Terry was trustworthy; there was little chance authorities could trace him back to Danny or me, and vice versa.

I spent the afternoon at the beach and then walked back to my pension. Along the way, I stopped at a small grocery market and bought a tin of sardines and a loaf of French bread—my typical dinner. Occasionally, I splurged and ate a square from a Cadbury chocolate bar, or bought a piece of fruit.

Nearby, I stopped and ate overlooking the Atlantic. Looking west, I watched the ocean below smashing into the rocky coastline. Beyond that, I could see the snowy tip of Mount Teide rising 12,188 feet on Tenerife.

I'd read in a travel brochure that there are eight major Canary Islands, located as close as sixty-two miles off the northwest coast of North Africa. Volcanic in origin, and with a subtropical climate, they are split into two provinces of Spain, sharing their capitals evenly between Las Palmas de Gran Canaria, and Santa Cruz de Tenerife.

Prior to arriving in Las Palmas, I had heard of the Canary Islands. In the sixties, NASA established a land-based radar tracking station in Maspalomas, Gran Canaria, used for the Mercury, Gemini, and Apollo space missions. During those flights, TV networks showed an up-to-date flight pattern of a launch and announced when the tracking station in the

Canaries picked it up. It always was reassuring to hear that the astronauts had made it safely across the Atlantic.

As I gazed out on the Atlantic, I suddenly was nostalgic, missing my mother and siblings. I wondered what they were doing. It was late March and warm here. In my last phone call with my mother in February, it was snowing. The snowstorm paralyzed the city for two weeks, shutting down Boeing, schools, and freeways. I was envious because I liked snow. It was a rare occurrence in Seattle. As a kid, I enjoyed playing in it, the way it looked, the silence, the slipperiness of it, catching snowflakes with my tongue, pretending it's the Holy Eucharist.

From the bluff, the waves reminded me of lyrics in the Country Joe and the Fish song, "Bass Strings." Singing the tune, I reminisced about seeing them at Eagles Auditorium in Seattle performing the song. With the reverb on their amps cranked up to the max, they sounded so distant then and now in my mind.

Finished with my sardine dinner and reminiscing about my past, I entered my pension, where Mama Gallenda stopped sweeping the roofless atrium's tile floor. As a robust woman in her forties, she hugged me like one of her three children.

"Ah Señor Pablo, nice to see you," she said in a motherly sort of way. "I not see you this time of day."

"I know, Mama Gallenda, I've been busy. Here's my payment for last week," I said, handing her two hundred pesetas. My rent was thirty-five pesetas a day, or two hundred a week—discounted if you paid it all in advance.

"Gracias," she smiled, showing off sparkling white teeth.

"In a few days I'll pay you for this week, if that's okay?"

"*Sí*, it be okay," Mama Gallenda said, tucking my rent

payment into her brassiere, then resuming her sweeping. "When you go home to America? Your mama miss you."

"My mama has six other kids," I chuckled. "I don't think she misses me."

Mama Gallenda, again stopped sweeping and brushed back her thick, dark hair. "She still miss you. Mamas miss all their children."

"I like it here, so I don't know. I might stay forever."

"Oh no, Pablo, you break your mama's heart then." I rolled my eyes a little in disbelief.

"You are young boy, easy to get in trouble. I worry about you," said Mama Gallenda leaning on her broom.

"Don't worry, Mama Gallenda, I can take care of myself." I flashed her a smile so sparkly that she couldn't help but return it.

I said goodnight to Mama Gallenda and headed back into town to El Cofre. It was too early to go to bed. Besides, I wanted to keep intact my record of never seeing my roommate awake. Something about sharing a room with a total stranger was better if you didn't know the person. For all I knew, he could be a leper or a scar-faced killer. I didn't want to know.

Staying just long enough to make sure my mysterious roommate would be asleep when I got back to my pension, I didn't stay late at El Cofre. Not to mention, I had to get up early the next day so I could get out to the airport and snatch Danny's bag.

13

Airport

March 29, 1969 — Las Palmas de Gran Canaria, Spain

T he morning after Danny left, I got up at nine, awakened by my, softball-size, Westclox wind-up alarm clock. By then, my nameless and faceless roommate had already left. Where he went and what he did during the day, I did not know. The fact I was sharing a room with him for three weeks and I was still alive convinced me he probably wasn't a murderer. My curiosity was killing me, though. Many nights I fell asleep listening to his heavy breathing and snoring, wondering who he was. It wouldn't surprise me if he did the same about me.

I got dressed, opened the door, and entered the pension's open-air atrium. Several children played soccer, and Mama Gallenda stirred a big pot on an old gas cook-top. She spotted me and put her spoon down. "Ah, Señor, Pablo, *buenos días*," she said, welcoming me with a hug.

"*Buenos días*, Mama Gallenda." I stretched and yawned.

"You up early, you go somewhere today?'

"*Sí*, Mama." I hastened my words, not wanting to get into a lengthy conversation with her about how young I was, and how concerned she was about me. "I'm meeting a friend this morning at the airport and need to get going."

"One day soon, you fly home to your mama, she miss you."

"*Sí*, Mama Gallenda." I toyed with my room key as I tried to figure out a way to break off the conversation politely. I needed to be at the airport in about fifty minutes. I had to hurry, because it would take twenty minutes to walk to Parque Santa Catalina, where I could catch a bus five minutes later. It would then be a twenty-minute bus ride to the airport, getting me there ten minutes before Danny's flight arrived. If I missed it, the next one would get me there half an hour late.

There was an earlier bus, but it got there thirty-five minutes before his flight was due to arrive, which meant I'd be loitering around and possibly drawing attention from police who Danny said patrolled the baggage claim area. His plan called for me to arrive just as passengers were entering to retrieve their luggage. I could then blend in with them without drawing an officer's attention. Timing was everything, and now Mama Gallenda was delaying me. Unable to spend more time chatting, I elected to cut her off.

"I'd really like to talk more, but I have to get to the airport. Can we talk later?"

Mama Gallenda turned again from her pot and put her spoon down. "*Sí*, Señor Pablo, I be your mama until you go home." Exhaling with relief, I thanked Mama Gallenda and bid her goodbye.

"Adios," said Mama Gallenda, waving as I walked past her

out the door.

Now that I was outside, I took a deep breath, then took off running. I only had fifteen minutes to catch the bus at Parque Santa Catalina.

Sprinting the entire way, I arrived there just as the yellow-and-blue bus was boarding. I got in line at the end. Digging out a five-peseta coin bearing Franco's bust, I paid the driver upon boarding. He handed me a return ticket, and I settled into a window seat about midway on the right side. From there, I'd be able to see the layout when the bus pulled into Las Palmas International Airport. I could then mingle with passengers entering the airport without the guards noticing me.

Twenty minutes later, the bus pulled to a stop at the airport. My heart raced with fear. Danny's instructions whirled in my head. Peering out the bus's window, I could see the baggage claim area to my right and, through the building's glass windows to the left, the ticketing counter. Passengers disembarking from flights were entering the terminal. They milled about, waiting for their baggage to arrive. Getting up from the seat, I made my way forward down the aisle.

Stepping off the bus, I followed the stream of bus riders entering the building through a glass door to my right with a sign marked "*Intra Solo*" ("Enter Only"). An armed guard, wearing aviator sunglasses, stood just inside the doorway.

The group made their way toward the ticketing counter past baggage claim. Along the way, I veered off, doing my best to blend in with disembarking airline passengers. Despite being nervous, I tried to act blasé by reading a travel brochure I'd picked up on the bus advertising excursions to Spanish Sahara.

As travelers jockeyed about, waiting for their bags to arrive, I glanced around to see if any of the three police officers had noticed me joining the assembly. From what I could tell, none did. They paid no more attention to me than the flights' passengers wandering in and milling about. Sweat formed on my forehead anyway. I wiped it away with a shirtsleeve as I looked up at an overhead monitor for Danny's flight information. There it was: Flight 302 from Tenerife had arrived five minutes earlier. The flight's luggage was on its way to Conveyor D. It was the one closest to the door I had entered, just as Danny said it would be. I was in the correct spot.

Scanning Conveyor D's baggage claim area, I glimpsed a pudgy officer watching me. I averted my eyes, pretending to check my watch. Out of the corner of an eye, I noticed he was still observing me. The conveyor rumbled to life. My attention shifted to the machine. At that instant, the plump guard looked over at several porters taking luggage off the conveyor and sorting them on the floor. Relieved I was no longer drawing his attention, I stepped forward to the luggage.

Danny said he would tie a red bandanna around the strap of his bag to make it easier for me to spot. As the machine continued churning out bags, I wondered whether he had actually caught the flight. I half expected to discover he'd taken my twenty dollars, and I'd never see him again. Just about ready to write him off, I caught sight of a black leather American Tourister duffel bag with a red bandanna tied to its handles. I exhaled with relief that Danny had not conned me. But now the butterflies that had been sitting calmly in my stomach stirred. Once I stole his bag, I'd have to make it out the door past the police without arousing suspicion before boarding the bus. I didn't have a baggage claim ticket, of course. If an officer stopped me, it wouldn't take long to determine the luggage didn't belong to me.

I waited one tier back until a porter added Danny's bag to a row. When he did, I squeezed in a crack between two men and grabbed his bag.

Making my way toward the door marked "*Solo Salida*" ("Exit Only"), I noticed a mustached officer there checking claim stubs. Danny hadn't told me about him. Apparently, security procedures had changed in the month since he'd flown to Tenerife. Frozen with fear, sweat dripped off me. I cast an eye around the room. The overweight policeman helped an elderly woman lift her bags onto a cart, and the officer wearing sunglasses at the entrance directed people to exit using the door by ticketing. I pivoted to see the mustached guard by the exit door. He checked a passenger's stub numbers against those on a suitcase. I needed to think of something fast.

Hoping to buy time, I merged in line with passengers heading to check into their flights at the ticket counter. There was no way the guard at the exit door would let me leave with Danny's bag without a claim stub. It was then that I noticed a man at the ticket counter searching his pockets and carry-on bag for something. Unable to find what he sought, the female agent pointed for him to leave through the exit door. When he arrived there, the mustached officer stopped him and asked to see the man's claim stub. The man explained what had happened, and the guard looked over at the female agent who nodded *yes* to let him leave. *Go ahead*, the guard gestured with a curt head bob, and the man exited outside.

The mustached officer provided the gateway between the terminal and freedom to board the bus. There was only one way in and one way out. I glanced back and the sunglasses-wearing officer at the entrance door still instructed people to exit through the door near me. Over by the carousel, the plump one motioned at those who'd retrieved their bags to leave through the door next to ticketing. It was then that I saw Danny searching for his bag at conveyor D. He acted calm, but perplexed, as he stroked his chin.

Returning my attention to the terminal ticketing counter, I came up with a plan: I would pretend to have forgotten my money. *It's my only chance,* I thought, as I moved forward with the queue.

With one person ahead of me at the check-in counter, I started searching my jeans' pockets, feigning to look for something. The person ahead of me finished and then departed. The attractive ticketing agent motioned me forward with a quick uplift of her head. Still rummaging through my jeans, I stepped up to the counter.

"No, money," I said, pulling out empty hands. The female agent's smile turned upside down as I dropped my shoulders in disappointment.

"Sorry," she said, pointing at the nearby door. "Exit there."

Shouldering Danny's bag, I proceeded toward the door. The mustached police officer there put a hand out to hold me back.

"*No dinero,*" I said, pointing toward the female agent, who then nodded at the guard to let me pass. By now I was wet with sweat and nauseous with fright. He studied me with steely eyes for an hour, it seemed. I held my breath. Apparently satisfied I was perspiring because I'd missed my flight, he gave me a single nod to go outside.

When I got outdoors, I sucked in deep breaths, filling my lungs repeatedly with fresh, heavy ocean air. As great as it felt to breathe again, I still had to board the bus and make it back to Las Palmas. Once there, I could disappear into the hordes of

Nordic tourists should anyone be searching for me.

On board the bus, I grabbed a window seat on the right side and watched Danny still faking to look for his bag. From what I could tell, most people on his flight had already claimed their luggage and departed. Other than a few stragglers, he remained alone. Finally, the rotund guard came up to him, looked at his claim stub, and pointed toward a nearby Iberia airlines office.

As the bus pulled away, Danny spoke with an Iberia airlines agent, and then another joined them.

The ride back to Las Palmas was maybe the longest fifteen minutes of my life. Every time I heard a siren or saw a police car, I panicked. I fully expected somebody would remember me acting strangely. Another possibility was that Danny had become frightened and ratted on me, like Pete had in Barcelona when I skipped out on the meal. To my relief, the bus let me off at Parque Santa Catalina. Free for the moment, I wouldn't know for sure until I rendezvoused with Danny. If all went according to plan, we would meet in the evening at my favorite outdoor café. It was only eleven fifteen, so it gave me almost seven hours to kill, and an opportunity to find a place to hide his bag.

A little before noon, I arrived at Terry's after eating my meal for the day at Cafeteria Tasartico. Terry answered the door wearing a bathrobe and toweling off his wet hair.

"Hey man, what brings you here, so early?" he said, rubbing his fuzzy mane. "Aren't you just a little early for dinner?"

"Uh, I, I've got a favor to ask, you know," I stuttered as I followed Terry into his flat, closing the door behind me.

"I've got to pick up Judy at the airport in an hour, man, so hopefully this is quick," Terry said as he stepped into the bathroom.

"You know that friend I was telling you about?" I stood in the doorway, watching him spread the creamy stuff on his face.

"You mean the one who's coming to dinner tomorrow night?"

"Yeah," I said, leaning closer in. "He needs a place to leave his bag, you know, for a few days, and I was going to see if he could leave it here, man."

Terry glanced at me and then started shaving. "I was wondering what you were doing with that bag," he said, working his razor gingerly around his neatly trimmed goatee. "I thought maybe you were leaving town, or looking for a place to stay."

"No, just looking for a place for my friend Danny's bag—that's if it's okay with you."

"Well, it's fine with me just as long as it's full of hashish," Terry cackled.

If there was one thing Terry liked, it was hash, and he was always more than willing to share what he had with guests, me included—usually I declined.

I thanked Terry and said goodbye, leaving Danny's bag along a living room wall by some windows, as Terry had instructed. I looked forward to meeting Judy and having Terry meet Danny. Terry tended to be prim and proper while Danny was laid-back. Perhaps Danny and I meshed because he had spent several years living in L.A., going to art school there, and I'd grown up on the West Coast. As much as I liked Terry, I liked Danny better.

I spent the rest of the afternoon at the beach. Early in the evening, I bought my usual dinner, eating it on the same rocky outcropping overlooking the Atlantic. Again, I grew homesick, and I imagined the water splashing the shoreline below had at one time lapped the shores of Puget Sound. Somehow it comforted me, making the world seem smaller, my mother and siblings closer, and my homesickness less. Home was liquid. It was just a wave away. In a matter of minutes, my melancholy mood changed, as it always did, and I returned to living out my exciting adventure.

About eight forty-five, I arrived at the same outdoor café to meet Danny and seated myself at a table on an outer edge. Within seconds, a waiter came up to my table to take my order or boot me out. They definitely were like Nazis when it came to loitering. I couldn't say I blamed them, but their aggressiveness was harassment and embarrassing. When it came to older, wealthy customers, the waiters gave them a few moments to settle in before pouncing on them. Having been here many other times, I'd grown used to it, though, and said, "Tea, please," before a waiter could hand me a menu. It always irked them I was onto their game, sending a message I wasn't there to eat. The waiters would sneer, then retreat.

Five minutes passed, and my tea arrived. For the next ten minutes, I sipped it, watching Scandinavian tourists walk past, many of them beautiful girls. I poured myself another cup of tea, added sugar, and squeezed in a few drops of lemon. It wasn't long before I checked my watch. It was nine. Danny should be here any moment now, according to his instructions.

Ten minutes went by, then twenty, and Danny was nowhere in sight. I worried something had gone wrong and police had arrested him. *If that's the case, then they'll be looking for me,* I fretted. *If he's not here in ten minutes, I'm leaving. But where will I go? How will I get off the island, and then out of Spain? I have no money, and I'll be easy to spot with my blond hair and reddish*

beard. Wait, I know: I'll shave my head and beard until things die
down, and then I'll sell Danny's camera to pay my ship and train
fares out of Spain—yeah, that's what I'll do.

I swallowed the last sip of my tea and fished out five pesetas
to pay for it. Out of the corner of an eye, I noticed a tall young
man with a white mustache, wearing an ivory muslin lapelled
shirt with sleeves rolled above the elbows. It was Danny, and
he stood there looking around for me. I waved discreetly, and
he spotted me.

Danny arrived at my table and grinned. "Mind if I join you?"
he said, sliding a chair out from the table. Placing a five-peseta
coin on a payment dish alongside my receipt, I asked him what
had happened.

"The plan worked exactly as designed," Danny said, flashing
a thumbs-up sign. "I would've been here earlier, but their
claims adjuster insisted on taking me to dinner, and then
bought me some new clothes."

"He bought you new clothes?"

"She," Danny grinned. "She paid for this shirt, a pair of
corduroys, and some socks, underwear, and pajamas."

"You're kidding me."

"No," Danny said with a smug smile. "And she was beautiful,
too. Afterward, she dropped me off at my hotel." My eyelids
shot open and my eyes about fell out. "Pension? They're
putting you up in a pension?"

"Pension nothing—Hotel Miami," Danny said as he swaggered in his chair.

"Is that the one at the other end of the park?"

Danny blew on his fist, then rubbed it proudly on his chest.
"That's right. And they're giving me one hundred and fifty
pesetas per diem for meals and essentials. So your cut will be

fifty pesetas a day, paid every week."

"But I thought you said I'd get somewhere between seventy-five and one hundred pesetas a day," I said, tripping on my words. "I can't live on fifty pesetas. My rent is fifteen, and my meal at Cafeteria Tasartico is fifteen—seventeen if I buy milk—that's, uh ... "

"Fifty-two pesetas."

"Yeah, and that doesn't include money for my dinner, cigarettes, and a Pepsi at El Cofre." Danny twirled his mustache, processing my concerns. "How much is your dinner?"

"Ten pesetas," I said. "Seven for a can of sardines and three for a baguette."

"Okay, tell you what," Danny said, stroking a bare arm. "The best I can do is sixty pesetas. That'll cover your meals and pension. You'll have to quit smoking and going to El Cofre, or get a part-time job."

Two attractive Swedish girls sat down at a table next to us and I glanced over at them momentarily.

"Yeah, like what?" I said, returning my attention to Danny. "I don't have a work permit and don't speak the language."

"Do something entrepreneurial," Danny replied, reclining in his chair. "Be creative. Sell cigarettes for two pesetas apiece, shine shoes, teach English, babysit, clean apartments, whatever it takes. All you need is fifteen pesetas a day and you can buy your cigarettes and go to El Cofre."

With a snort, I whined, "It's not fair. I put up most of the money and you get almost twice as much as me—and you get to stay in a fancy hotel for free."

A slow, infectious smile spread across Danny's face. "Investing has its risks and rewards," he chortled. "Return on investment is one of those things that can't be guaranteed. I'd say as an investor, you've done well so far—and when there's a settlement, you stand to get one-third of it. My claim is eight hundred. One-third of it is almost 270—that's a return of roughly 1400 percent."

Danny's command of finance impressed me. The astronomical figures he tossed out excited me to the point of forgetting about my paltry allowance. I'd figure out a way to make up the difference. There was no way I was going to give up my cigarettes and El Cofre. All I had to do was hang in there until the settlement. I'd be rich then. I could leave Spain. I'd have enough money to return home if I wanted.

Danny and I spent the next hour talking about his experience with Iberia and the police. As far as he could tell, there was no reason for them to suspect he'd staged the disappearance of his luggage; they were investigating it as "misdirected" luggage. They would put a trace on it with all Iberia flights that left Tenerife today. "Chances are it was mistakenly sent to Madrid or Barcelona and will turn up in a day or two," they reassured Danny. In the meantime, they would take care of him.

Danny instructed me never to come to his hotel in the event they were watching it. "Any meetings between us will have to be here in Parque Santa Catalina. From here we can go to other places together."

Admittedly, it irritated me I was not welcome to come to his hotel. Feeling like a second-class citizen, I sat there, tapping my fingers, stewing about it.

I said goodbye to Danny, arranging to meet him at four the following afternoon in the same spot, before we went to Terry's for dinner. I'd told him earlier his bag was there and Terry wanted to meet him. Danny didn't like the idea of leaving his bag there without knowing him, so going there for dinner should ease his concern—I felt. "It was either that," I told him, "or leave it at my pension in a room I share with a person I've never met." Danny agreed that wasn't a good idea, but he still felt uncomfortable with leaving it at Terry's place. In particular, he didn't want to lose his passport until he got a replacement.

Since there was no Canadian Consulate in the Canaries, he would have to get a new passport through the British Consulate Service. Because Canada belonged to the Commonwealth, it shouldn't be a problem—at least that's what he surmised would happen. It was all part of his plan. With a British passport, he could use their socialized health care to get cosmetic surgery in England on his nose. It's not that he had a bad nose, because if he hadn't mentioned it, I wouldn't have noticed. Uncomfortable about its width, he wanted one that was slimmer. It made me wonder if in order to draw attention away from his nose, he grew the mustache. Whether or not he dyed it, I never asked, and he never mentioned it.

14

Friendship

March 30–April 5, 1969 — Las Palmas de Gran Canaria, Spain

Before going to Terry's for dinner, Danny and I met in Parque Santa Catalina as agreed. Sipping on a Pepsi, Danny told me about his day at the Iberia airlines office in town while I lit a cigarette.

"They said they checked all outboard flight destinations today from Tenerife and can't locate it. They think now it's somewhere in Tenerife and will turn up there tomorrow. On the other hand, they added, occasionally the claim tags will come off on the conveyors and then those bags end up in lost and found. Since it hasn't shown up in lost and found in Tenerife or Las Palmas, they're saying it's possible it got put on the wrong flight and is in lost and found somewhere else, or in transit back to Tenerife."

"So how long will they keep looking before they settle?" I asked, exhaling a cloud of smoke, from which Danny backed away.

"Would you mind blowing it out the other side next time," Danny said.

"Oh, sorry about that," I answered. "I didn't know it bothered you that much."

"I've got allergies," Danny said, wiping his nose with a handkerchief. "So, to answer your question, they didn't say. The only thing they said was these things resolve themselves in two or three days, but could take up to a week. Since they won't find my bag, I would assume they will call off the search and offer a settlement by the end of the week to avoid running up my hotel bill and per diem expense ... speaking of, here's your weekly cut."

Danny pulled a billfold out of the inside breast pocket of his tan corduroy coat, which accompanied a little blue dress shirt, courtesy of Iberia. "One hundred, two hundred, three hundred, four hundred, and fifty. Do you have thirty pesetas? Your cut is four hundred and twenty per week."

"All I've got is one hundred pesetas," I said, checking my pockets.

"Alright," Danny said, handing me the money, "I'll loan you thirty pesetas." Plucking a ballpoint pen and a pocket-size spiral notebook out of the breast pocket of his coat, he recorded the amount.

Terry's apartment was on the other side of the isthmus. Within fifteen minutes after leaving Parque Santa Catalina, I rang his doorbell. "Just a second," Terry said, from inside his pad.

Terry opened the door wearing a red-checkered apron and holding a glass of wine. "Welcome," he danced a little two-two step in place and then turned to Danny. "You must be Danny."

"And you must be Terry," Danny said, doing a little cha-cha-cha of his own.

"I like this guy, already," Terry said, with a nod. "Come in. I'd like both of you to meet Judy."

We followed Terry into the kitchen where a beautiful woman about Terry's age, with long dishwater-blond hair, wearing lots of gold bracelets, fuchsia-colored satin chiffon pants, and a black spaghetti-strapped tank top, stirred a skillet.

Terry set his wine on the counter. "Judy, I'd like you to meet Paul."

She put the spoon down and gave me a hug. "Nice to meet you. Terry's talked a lot about you."

"And Terry's talked a lot about you, too."

"That's good to know," Judy replied, gazing at Terry.

There was an awkward pause in the conversation before I realized that I should introduce Danny to Judy. "Uh, this is my friend Danny," I nodded toward him. Judy gave him a hug while Terry took over the cooking responsibilities.

"Danny, can I get you a glass of wine or a beer or something else?" Judy asked. "We have white Bordeaux, a Merlot, and a Rioja."

Danny, who had been checking out the small kitchen that doubled as a dining room, sniffed the air. Recognizing the scent with a tilt of his head, he said, "Smells like we're having paella." Terry looked up from his sautéing and put a hand on a hip. "Yes, how did you know?"

"I smell saffron and smoked paprika," Danny replied, as he leaned in for a closer look.

"You're right. I'm making paella, with grilled octopus and abalone," Terry responded, stirring a bubbling rice mixture.

"Then I should probably have the white Bordeaux," Danny

115

replied with a little hand on hip stance of his own.

"Good selection, and good affectation," Terry laughed. Glancing over at Judy, Terry said, "Judy, pour him a glass of the sixty-eight Cheval Blanc Bordeaux. Looks like you know your wines, Danny." Picking up his glass of wine, Terry saluted him.

"Yes, along with being a bartender when I was in South Africa, I was also a wine sommelier." Danny replied.

"Excellent!" Terry boomed, and then, turning to me, said, "How about you? What would you like to drink?"

I shrugged. "Well, since we're having pie layered with grilled octopus and baloney, I'll have a beer."

The kitchen erupted into laughter at my naiveté, which I think they misunderstood as wit.

As the evening progressed, Terry grilled the octopus and abalone over a hibachi on the flat's balcony overlooking Playa de Las Canteras. Afterward, we ate his gourmet dinner, drank wine (I stuck to beer), and then smoked hashish and marijuana.

Judy was sweet, caring, educated, and attractive. I could see why she was Terry's girlfriend, although I wasn't sure if he cared as much about her as she did him. As I'd gotten to know Terry better, he flirted with the young girls at the beach and bragged about coaxing them up to his flat to smoke hashish. I wondered if that's all he did.

As for Judy, she said that they'd met on one of his bus tours last summer. He was the guide, and she was the tourist. She fell in love with him and, before long, she shared his flat in England. Being an elementary school teacher, she stayed behind when he'd come to Las Palmas. But now that it was spring break, she had taken an extended leave and come south to be with him and get some sun.

Danny, Judy, and Terry really hit it off. Besides knowing wines, Danny knew famous restaurants and chefs, gourmet foods, and art. Because he was also a wiz at finance, he could talk business with Terry. Meanwhile, Judy and I talked about my travels and family. She genuinely seemed to take an interest and concern in me. Perhaps it was because she was a teacher, or because I reminded her of her younger brother, who was about my age when he died from a drug overdose. Whatever the case, her warmth comforted me.

By the end of the evening, Danny had told Terry and Judy about his swindle with Iberia airlines and his plan to get an English passport and then go to London for cosmetic surgery on his nose. I feared they would disapprove, but they didn't. Like a leprechaun, Danny had charisma, charm, and humor in a dry-witted way. They fell in love with him. He was like Robin Hood, the little guy outsmarting corporations and governments in the name of nobility. How could you not root for him? Terry was a little like him, bribing or conning his way onboard ships to get their passenger manifests. However, Terry worked within a corrupt system to further corrupt the system. Conversely, the way Danny explained it, he worked outside the system, taking back from the system. He made it sound so romantic.

Hearing all of this, Terry didn't mind Danny leaving his bag at his place, and offered to put him up at his flat in London while he awaited his surgery. Within one evening, a friendship blossomed that would last. We continued having dinner at Terry's two or three times a week. We ate at the rectangular wooden table in the kitchen area. Then we smoked hashish. Afterward, Danny and Terry carried on their discussions about food, wine, art, and history in the pie-shaped living room.

Meantime, Judy and I furthered our conversations in the kitchen area about our lives, families, and feelings. In a way, I was falling in love with her, and she perhaps with me.

15

Rich

April 5–13, 1969 — Las Palmas de Gran Canaria, Spain

Every evening I met Danny in Parque Santa Catalina, where he would tell me about the latest developments with his claim. It'd been a week now since I *stole* his luggage at the airport and they were still looking for his bag. He was nonchalant about it while I was going broke. Several days earlier, I'd run out of money and had to borrow 150 pesetas from him. I just couldn't live on sixty pesetas a day and had even tried panhandling to supplement my income—to little avail. On a good day, I would only make three or four pesetas in an afternoon, and risked being busted by police patrolling the area. I gave up and moved out of my pension, sleeping on the beach near the port side of the peninsula. That saved me thirty-five pesetas a day and enabled me to do all the things I wanted to do. But I still owed Mama Gallenda a week's rent of two hundred pesetas. I felt bad for moving out without paying my bill and planned to reimburse her after the settlement.

Hearing all of this, Danny interceded. "Since you can't seem to manage your money," he said, rolling up the sleeves of his light-blue shirt, "I'll manage it for you."

I took a drag off a cigarette, blowing smoke out the side to avoid getting it in Danny's face. "And how will you do that?" I said, keeping an eye on our waiter, who was scowling at us. Putting his hands on his hips, Danny looked at me like a stern banker.

"Instead of paying you weekly, I'm going to pay you daily," Danny lectured. "I can't keep loaning you money. Didn't you ever have a piggy bank or a savings account as a kid?"

"No," I answered. "I came from a family of seven kids. We were poor. I didn't get an allowance. I wasn't wealthy like you."

With a lofty tilt of his head, Danny pretended to play a violin. He drew repulsed looks from several nearby tables. As he continued, it wasn't long before a group of well-heeled tourists got up and left. Annoyed, our waiter pursed his lips. No doubt, he couldn't wait for us to leave too.

Danny grew up in suburban Quebec City. The oldest of two kids, he'd attended private schools along with his sister. As much as he disdained his parent's lifestyle, his father in particular, and his privileged upbringing, he was obsessed with money.

"Rich people are more interesting than poor people," he told me several days earlier over a bottle of Tropical Cerveza at a nearby *cervecería*. "That's why they're rich. You really need to observe them, the way they dress, the way they carry themselves, the way they talk. If you ever want to be wealthy, you need to act like them."

Danny was a walking-talking contradiction. On one hand, he despised his father and the things he represented; on the other, he envied the rich and aspired to be affluent himself. If he was correct about needing to act like rich people in order to be well off, then Danny had it made because he carried himself with an air of aristocracy. No wonder he could convince Iberia airlines his bag was missing. He played the role perfectly without even trying. Of course he was aware of this, and had a whimsical, self-deprecating sense of humor—otherwise he would have been arrogant and intolerable.

Despite his charm, he acted reserved and kept to himself, mostly. He was a study in restraint and self-discipline. Other than only indulging in hashish when we went to Terry's for dinner, he didn't smoke cigarettes, and hardly drank. Neatly groomed as anyone living with two sets of clothes could be, he took pride in his personal appearance.

While I'd spent my days sleeping off late-nighters under my fishing dory, Danny spent his at the British Consulate's office filling out paperwork and getting photographs for his new passport. Otherwise, he occupied the vast majority of his days admiring the old town's colonial architecture, Museo Nestor, art galleries, and Catedral de Santa Ana.

"Surprisingly, there's a lot to see in this town," Danny said, another day at the *cervecería* over a beer, "if you'd ever get up before two."

As much as I protested, Danny put me on a daily allowance. I knew he was right. I had difficulty managing money. I still liked him, though, and happily played the role of the helpless teenager (which I didn't have to work too hard at), and listening to Danny tease me about it. He wasn't serious, and neither was I.

Days dragged on, and I fell deeper into debt with Danny loaning me money, which he would always record in his pocket-size, wire-wound notebook. To save money, I started going to the port after hearing from Pierre, a French panhandler, that some of the ships would feed you their leftovers if you went there shortly after lunchtime.

My first experience at the port almost cost me a leg. As I sat on a pier, contemplating how to talk my way aboard a cargo ship, I dangled my leg between a freighter and the concrete bulkhead. A sudden swell caused the vessel to pinch my dangling limb against the concrete bulked. The surge ebbed, and the transport rolled the other way long enough for me to get my leg out before it rocked back again. Another inch or two and it would have been crushed. With pain erupting from my pinned leg, I screamed in horror and agony, catching the attention of a few deckhands who came to see what all the commotion was. They helped me aboard the ship, took me inside the crew's mess, laid me on a bench, and looked at my leg. Badly bruised, it did not bleed. As I squirmed in pain, they gave me aspirin, then left.

Not long afterward, they came to see if I needed anything else. I pantomimed I was hungry by rubbing my belly and spooning food into my mouth. They smiled and giggled among themselves. Soon, one of them brought me a bowl of rice and kimchi. I was on a North Korean ship.

While I ate the kimchi, they all stood around laughing. Never having had kimchi before, it caught me off guard by how spicy it was. *It tastes like it's marinated in gasoline,* I groaned to myself. *I hope they're not trying to poison me.* Not wanting to offend them and create an international incident, I ate everything. About halfway through the meal, I grew accustomed to the heat and actually enjoyed it. Being famished, I'd lost all inhibitions, and even their fiery food tasted good.

Upon finishing, I thanked my hosts by smiling, bowing, and shaking their hands—doing everything I could think of not to insult them. I waved and said goodbye. The crew waved back and then escorted me off the ship, waving again. My hunger satiated, I limped back to Parque Santa Catalina, where I met Danny and told him about my experience. I didn't tell him how spicy the food was and talked him into going back to the ship with me the next day for lunch. Danny agreed, just to placate me, I think. He certainly didn't need handouts.

When we arrived at the ship, the crew recognized me and welcomed us aboard.

"You didn't tell me it was North Korean," Danny said, holding me back with a hand.

"So?"

"So, they're communists," Danny said, looking concerned. "Once we step foot on that ship, we are at their mercy and are subject to their laws. They can claim we are CIA and do whatever they want with us. And nobody can do anything about it."

"Hey man, they're people just like us. Their government is bad; these people are fine."

A ship's officer walked past us, causing Danny to do a double-take. When the officer was out of earshot range, he whispered, "There's no such thing as a good communist. Either you are loyal to the party or you are dead. And these people are all party members; otherwise they wouldn't be allowed to set foot out of the country."

"Man, you've watched too many Cold War movies," I replied. "These guys are normal people just like you and me."

I headed up the gangway, leaving Danny at the base. About halfway up, I stopped and turned to him. "Okay, don't come, but I'm eating here." I began climbing the wooden ramp again. I looked back at Danny, who sighed and started up the walkway. Meanwhile, a crew member called out to me in Korean and waved for us to follow him.

On board, he led Danny and me to the galley and seated us at a table. Moments later, the ship's cook brought us two large bowls of kimchi and steaming white rice. Not long afterward, more crew members came into the mess hall and stood around, twittering in anticipation.

Having eaten there the day before, I knew what to expect, but Danny didn't. His first bite caught him off guard, and he nearly exploded. His face turned bright red, and his cheeks puffed out like a blowfish. The crew howled at Danny's expressions as he struggled to swallow his first mouthful.

By the time I had finished mine, Danny was only about half-finished with his. Dripping with perspiration, his face was still bright red. Unlike the crew and cook, who were howling, I contained my laughter, secretly enjoying every minute of watching him suffer. Maybe I was relishing his agony as payback for putting me on a daily allowance and not letting me step foot in his hotel. Then again, I did not know he would react so severely to the spices. As we stepped down the ship's gangway, he moaned and groaned, and complained about stomach pains.

"Oh, my God, it hurts like crazy. I need something for it."

On the way back to town, we stopped at a small shop and Danny bought Tums, eating six tablets at once. By the time we got close to his hotel, he was feeling better.

"Don't ever ask me to eat there again. That was pure hell,"

he said as we crossed a street teeming with taxis and busses.

"I know. You should have seen your face," I snickered. "It was beet red."

"Yeah," Danny huffed. "I felt like I was going to burst into flames."

"And you were dripping with sweat," I chuckled.

Danny laughed so hard his face turned bright red again. As horrible as he'd felt, he was good-natured enough to laugh it off. Being able to find humor in himself was a quality I admired, and it endeared him to others and me.

From that point on, I went to eat at the port by myself. Finding the Korean ship had left, it was slim pickings for several days. Eventually, though, I ate on a Russian ship. It struck me as odd: The communist ships were willing to feed me while the Western ships weren't so generous. As the capitalist he was (even though he wouldn't admit it), Danny was irritated when I told him.

"One of these days, you're going to end up in a gulag in Siberia where you'll never be heard from again," Danny said. "The only good commie is a dead commie."

Still a little resentful of the humiliating meal he'd had on the Korean ship, he was certain they'd tried to poison him. "If it hadn't been for antacid, I could have died of acute gastral inflammation," Danny reminded me. "Never trust a commie and never trust a fascist. They're two heads of the same beast. Both require one-party rule to survive. No wonder their foods are so awful."

From that point on, I stopped talking about eating on ships with Danny. On one occasion, though, I teased him, saying I'd eaten on a French ship. "Yeah, they served me caviar, snails, frog legs, some snooty-sounding blue chicken dish, and fancy red wine." This never happened, of course, but it felt good to pull his leg.

Busy doing a crossword puzzle in the *International Herald Tribune,* Danny kidded me back, "You're going to die of heart disease, liver failure, and gout. Do you know how bad French cuisine is for you?"

"Hey, it tasted great," I fibbed, noticing our waiter and the owner glaring at us for being there two hours.

"Okay, I'll make a point of coming to your funeral," he said, making a sign of the cross, "and will get your cut of the settlement."

As I put out the cigarette I'd been smoking, I said, "Speaking of the settlement, how's it going? It's almost been two weeks now. What's taking so long?"

Deep in concentration, Danny looked up from his crossword puzzle. "Iberia's looking at the possibility the luggage was stolen. They don't think it ever left Tenerife. They've launched an internal investigation of the airline employees and baggage handlers on duty that day, and are looking at the possibility it's still somewhere at the airport. If it doesn't turn up in three days, they'll declare it permanently missing and will turn it over to their settlement adjuster."

Danny resumed playing the crossword puzzle.

"Uh, so how long will that take?" I said, adding two cubes of sugar to my tea.

Engrossed in his game, he didn't bother looking up when he replied. "Iberia didn't say. But I would assume it shouldn't take more than a day—two at the most."

"Good, I can't live like this much longer. I'm broke."

"Again?" Danny shook his head in disbelief. "I just loaned you 150 pesetas three days ago. Where does all your money go?"

"I've got expensive taste."

"You've got a hole in your pocket, that's what you've got."

"Hey, my mom used to always say that too!"

"Well, it's true," Danny chuckled. "I could give you a thousand pesetas and it would evaporate tomorrow. You'd spend it." Unable to refute Danny, I just sat there, wayward child-like, after swallowing a sip of tea. Looking at me with a blank look on his face, before cracking a smile, he pulled out his wallet. "Okay, so how much do you need now?"

"Uh, two hundred would be great," I beamed.

"I can't do that," Danny replied, thumbing through the bills in his wallet. "That would leave me with only 150 pesetas for the next four days. The best I can do is one hundred pesetas. Take it or leave it."

"Uh, okay, I'll take it, but it'll mean that I've got to live on twenty-five pesetas a day."

"Well, I guess you'll just have to stop smoking and going to El Cofre," he needled, handing me the money.

While I tucked the money into my jeans, Danny recorded the amount in his little spiral-bound notebook. "So, Terry and Judy invited me over for dinner tomorrow evening," he said, tucking the notebook into the inside breast pocket of his tan corduroy sport coat. "They said to see if you wanted to join us. Do you want to go?"

"Uh, I don't know, I was kind of thinking of hanging out at the beach."

"We can do that the day after tomorrow. Come on, they really like you and it'll be great food—and it won't cost you anything. Just think of how much money you'll save."

Danny grinned, his eyes sparkling like a blue fish lure.

"Alright," I said reluctantly. The truth was, since I'd introduced Danny to Terry and Judy, they'd become more his friends than mine. The more we got together, the more left out and uncomfortable I felt. Jealousy might have also had something to do with it. Originally, Terry was my friend, and it seemed now he favored Danny. Likewise, Danny gave the impression he favored Terry over me. As hard as I tried to put all of this out of my mind, it bothered me whenever we had dinner at Terry's place.

16

Smuggle

April 13–23, 1969 — Las Palmas de Gran Canaria, Spain

Before we went to Terry's for dinner, I met Danny at our usual hangout in Parque Santa Catalina. I was on my second cup of tea when he finally showed up. Dressed in his light-blue cotton shirt with epaulets, sleeves rolled up to just above his elbows, and tan, wide-whale corduroy pants, he looked like a graduate student or a young high school social studies teacher. Always clean-shaven, he was one of those guys who never needed to comb his hair. It was thick and naturally wavy, always looked good no matter if it was wind tousled or not. When he grinned, his straight cream-colored teeth gleamed behind his white Fu Manchu mustache. With Danny, it was all about image. In order to be rich, you had to look and act wealthy. Good thing he did, because he had to convince Iberia airlines he was telling the truth. The fact it'd taken so long for a settlement didn't seem to faze him.

As for me, I hadn't showered in weeks. With my red beard contrasting with my blond hair, people said I looked like a Viking—probably smelled like one too.

All of this vexed Danny to no end. Every few days, he would get on me about my appearance and lack of what he considered good hygiene. Our conversations would go something like this:

"Why don't you ever shower?" he would inquire. "Didn't your mother ever teach you about soap and water?"

"Hey man, I grew up in a big family; we got to bathe once a week."

"Well, you haven't showered since I met you, and by the looks of it, you haven't had one in at least a month."

"I swim in the ocean."

"That doesn't count. You need soap and shampoo for that greasy bird's nest on top of your head. And while you're at it, wash your clothes; they smell."

"Yes, mother ... anything else?" I'd ask. Then I'd break into my mother's voice. "Yes, shave your beard; it makes you look like an old man."

"Not a bad idea," Danny countered. "Seriously, how do you expect to meet girls looking and smelling the way you do?"

"Hey man, I don't see you meeting any girls," I shot back.

"Girls are expensive and take a lot of effort. They can wait. Right now, I've got other plans."

"Yeah, well, so do I."

"Oh, I get it. The reason you look like a slob is so girls won't be attracted to you," Danny laughed.

"Yeah, that's right." I cracked up. It was impossible to get mad at Danny because he always jested with a twinkle in his eyes.

I was on my third cup of tea and Danny was on his second

Pepsi when he finally got down to telling me the latest from Iberia airlines.

"Iberia is now saying it's possible somebody on the flight picked up my bag accidentally, thinking it was theirs," he said. "They're going to check with everyone who was on the flight and see if anybody has it."

"Uh, but nobody has it because we have it."

"Of course, but they don't know that. They need to do their due diligence before their insurance company will pay it."

"I think they're stalling," I blurted. "I think they know we have it and are hoping you will just go away."

Unconcerned as usual, Danny let it roll off. "They might suspect we have it, but they can't prove it," he analyzed. "It's all part of the process and is pocket change for the insurance company. Once Iberia can show they've properly investigated everything, the insurance company will settle. They would rather do that than face a lawsuit and the bad publicity it would bring them. So, stop worrying about it."

"How am I supposed to stop worrying about it? I paid Mama Gallenda the money I owed her and moved back into my pension. I'm already behind on this week's rent. I owe her for three days now and if I don't pay her by the end of the week, she's saying I'll need to move out again."

Danny took a sip of his Pepsi. "Try panhandling."

"I've tried, but I'm lucky to get two or three pesetas."

"That's because you smile too much," he said, affecting an overly cute smile. "You have to take it seriously. Now Pierre, the French guy, knows how to do it. He makes several hundred pesetas every day."

"Pierre's a bum. He never smiles and is always unhappy."

"That's why he makes money," Danny said, adjusting his

shirt collar. "People feel sorry for him. It's all an act, and he's learned how to do it. As for you, people don't feel sorry for you because you're too nice. Learn how to be sympathetic and make people believe you need the money they've worked hard for more than they do."

Danny always had the answers. He made everything seem plausible as long as you had a plan and believed in it.

Half an hour later, Danny and I arrived at Terry's for dinner. Judy, dressed in black pants, turquoise blouse, and cream-colored macramé shawl, greeted us at the door.

"Come in. Terry's on the balcony grilling lamb shish kabobs and swordfish for dinner," she said, hugging Danny and then turning to me as her gold bracelets jingled.

"Hi Judy," I said, rather sheepishly.

"Oh Paul, it's so nice to see you," she said, hugging me warmly. "Where have you been? Danny said you weren't sure you were coming. I'm so glad you decided to. Terry is looking forward to seeing you ... He's fixing a Moroccan feast."

With a wink, Danny nudged me. "See man, I told you it would be worth it." Glancing at Judy, he smiled. "I didn't have to twist his arm too hard. All I had to say was that the food would be great." Judy and Danny chuckled while I pretended to laugh. Then Danny held out a bottle of wine he'd brought. "I think this should pair well with the lamb and swordfish. It's a sixty-seven Bourgogne Pinot Noir."

That evening, we dined on Terry's delicious Moroccan feast. Throughout the dinner, I drank beer, while everyone else sipped Danny's wine. After several toasts to Terry and his culinary skills, Terry raised his glass of wine and said, "Excellent selection, Danny. Not only does it pair extremely well with the lamb, but does so equally with the swordfish—a rare find.

If ever I'm in the position to afford a sommelier, I will know where to find one." Everyone at the table applauded, except for me.

There was a lull in the conversation, then Terry looked my way and said, "So, Paul, Danny tells me you were sleeping on the beach. If that happens again, man, let me know. You can crash here."

"Better be careful what you wish for," Danny teased Terry at my expense. "With meals like this, he might never leave."

"Well, I'm not sure it competes with my sardine and baguette dinners," I responded. Once again, the room erupted into laughter.

"Yes, but it costs less," quipped Danny.

Everyone laughed again, and so did I. But I felt conspicuous—like I didn't fit.

Afterward, I helped Judy clean the kitchen and wash the dishes. Meanwhile, Danny and Terry smoked hashish in the living room, discussing some plan of Danny's involving hashish and Morocco.

I left Terry's place alone, once again feeling left out.

The following afternoon, Danny and I went to Playa de Las Canteras together. Buttered-up Scandinavian girls baking themselves like a tray of Danish pastries crowded the beach. At the northern end of the crescent beach, colorful fishing dories rested on the golden sand. I never tired of spending my afternoons watching the girls and looking at the ocean. Danny, on the other hand, was impatient. If he didn't have something to do, like playing a crossword puzzle or reading a book about art, he was in the water.

"What do you say we swim out to the reef? I did it the other day and there's lots of sea life to watch," said Danny, sitting up on his Hotel Miami beach towel, wearing a new bathing suit purchased by his beautiful Iberia airlines representative.

"Uh, like what kind of sea life?" I answered, keeping my eyes on an attractive, bikini-clad blond spreading coconut oil on her legs.

Danny sprung to his feet. "Like crab, parrotfish, eel, rockfish, pufferfish, damselfish, and many others that I'm not familiar with."

"And sharks?" I tensed, taking my eyes off the buttered blond. "Well, there's always the possibility," Danny shrugged. "It is a reef after all, and where there're reefs there're fish, and where there're fish, there're sharks."

"Well, where there're sharks, there're no Paul-fish."

"Ah, come on, give it a try," Danny urged. "You've got nothing to worry about when you're on the reef. Besides, the sharks here are small reef sharks, unlike the great whites I saw in South Africa."

"Man, you saw great whites there?"

"Yeah, the sharks here are nothing. So, are you coming with me?" Danny asked, summoning with a hand wave.

"Uh," I shrugged, "I think I'll lie here on the beach and watch all the beautiful Swedish girls walk by, you know."

"Ah, come on, don't be a chicken. The girls will always be here, but it's the lowest tide of the month. Now, are you coming with me or do I get all the fish to myself? Man, there might even be a mermaid."

I hesitated while Danny gestured for me to come along. "Alright," I replied, "but I don't have a bathing suit."

"Just wear your jeans, or strip down to your underpants right before we get in the water."

Following Danny, I stripped down to my briefs at the water's edge and we swam to the reef. Sitting where the ocean lapped against the windward side of the reef, Danny schooled me on the hierarchy of fish.

"Fish are like people," he lectured. "The smart ones survive and the dumb ones get eaten. Just look at them; they're everywhere. If only they had a leader and a plan, they could hold their own against the predators."

For the next half hour or so, I sat on the reef with Danny watching fish, as he told me about his plan to smuggle hashish in bales of cotton from India to the U.S.

"Sounds risky to me," I said, watching several small crabs fight over the carcass of a dead minnow.

"Everything has risks," Danny grinned. "Eating an apple has risks. There's a chance that you might choke on it and die. But you've learned to mitigate the risk by taking small bites and chewing it well."

"Yeah, man, but smuggling hash from India to Houston in bales of cotton is not an apple," I scoffed.

"Exactly. That's why having a good plan is essential. One bite, one chew, and one swallow at a time until you are finished. You will have eaten the apple and not choked, and in this case successfully smuggled a thousand kilos of hashish into the U.S. worth five million dollars. I've been researching it since I was in India and am almost finished with the plan. First, I need funds. That's why I've decided to go to Morocco. I'll buy five kilos of hash and ship it to Terry in London. He's financing the deal, which we'll then split. After that, I'll have enough money to finance the India deal."

I turned to watch the waves crashing into the windward side of the reef. "So, is that what you guys were talking about last night?"

"Yeah, we were talking about Morocco, but I have told nobody about my India plan other than you." I looked back at Danny. He went on to say he would need help and asked me if I wanted to assist him.

"Uh, I'll think about it," I replied.

Truth was, I had an ambivalent relationship with him. As fun and likeable as he was, he could be patronizing. I didn't want to be busted for smuggling large quantities of hashish. Defrauding Iberia airlines for eight hundred dollars was kids' stuff compared to the criminal activity Danny was planning. In the meantime, while Danny was thinking big, I was barely scraping by and doing my best to be entrepreneurial, as Danny had suggested. As luck would have it, I soon met Rolf with an offer that was perfect.

I'm not sure how I met Rolf, but he was part of an influx of sixteen-year-old Swedish tourists who arrived in mid-April. In order to rent a car in Spain, you had to be at least eighteen years old and have an international driver's license. Since I was nineteen, age wasn't an issue, and I had obtained an international driver's license before leaving Seattle, so a double plus. Rolf wanted to rent a car and do some sightseeing. Hearing I was of age, he asked if I'd be willing to rent one for him and his friends and drive them around the island. He offered to pay me ten dollars—a deal made in heaven, or so I believed.

When I rented the car, the company made me fill out a contract stating my age, passport number, and international driver's license number. All of this seemed acceptable to me as I drove off in a 1968 VW Bug convertible. I picked up Rolf and two of his teenage Swedish friends at Parque Santa Catalina, a few blocks down the street. Rolf and his pals wanted to see the island's interior. Volcanic in nature, the barren interior resembled a scorched extraterrestrial landscape, making South Dakota's Badlands look tame. The dirt, potholed road was whipped by wind and eroded in many parts. There were no guardrails to keep a vehicle from going off into an abyss. Other areas, if you were lucky in your fall, might land on a terraced slope.

Farther inland, we passed banana plantations and peasants riding wooden donkey carts full of produce. At the midway point, I'd had enough. It'd been a nerve-racking drive so far, with the sixteen-year-olds smoking marijuana, hooting, and hollering, and badgering me to drive faster. While turning the car around, Rolf suddenly yipped, "Let me drive."

"No, you're not eighteen and don't have an international driver's license," I said.

"Yeah, but I have a Swedish driver's license, and there aren't any police here ... Okay, man?"

The three other teenagers began chanting, "Let him drive, let him drive, let him drive."

I had a headache and, to my regret, acquiesced. Rolf was an absolute madman behind the wheel, as his teenage friends laughed hysterically. I honestly thought we were going to die. At one point, he spun the car in a one-eighty going sixty miles an hour on the narrow dirt road. Arriving back in town, I was exhausted. When Rolf said, "Don't worry man, I'll return the car," I replied, "Okay."

I didn't care. Anything to get away from the shrieking sixteen-year-olds. Worn out, I called it quits early that night at El Cofre and returned to Mama Gallenda's.

The next morning, loud voices and pounding on the door rudely awakened me. Four police officers burst into my room, guns drawn, demanding to know where the rental car was.

"I don't know," I said. "I let somebody borrow it. Didn't he return it?"

"No," gruffed an officer, demanding that I come with them to help find the car. We drove around the city and I finally spotted it parked alongside Parque Santa Catalina.

"There it is," I hollered, pointing.

Covered in dirt and mud, the car was a mess. Getting out of the Land Rover, I looked at the console and, to my relief, the keys were in the ignition. Within minutes, I'd started it and followed the police to the rental company. The owner was glad to get his car returned. To my surprise, I had to pay an extra half-day rental. After making sure I paid for the car, the cops left and I spent the rest of the day looking for Rolf, without luck. A few days went by and I ran into him. He was high on codeine-infused Robitussin. I told him he owed me money, and he offered to pay me in cough syrup. There was no way I was going to use that stuff, so I threatened to beat him up if he didn't pay me. He dug into his jacket and pulled out a wad of bills—the kid's dad was rich and so was he, with his allowance and monthly government stipend. "How much is it?" he asked.

"Four hundred pesetas."

"Maybe we can do it again sometime," Rolf said, handing me money. There was no way I would ever rent a car for him again. The kid was totally spoiled and messed up on drugs. He didn't care about the grief he'd put me through, first with his reckless driving, and then with the police.

Over tea a day later at Parque Santa Catalina, I told Danny about my adventure and run-in with the police.

"You're lucky they didn't throw you in prison and toss

away the key. Fascists are almost as bad as commies," he said, putting down the ballpoint pen he'd been using on his crossword puzzle. "But the main difference is that you can bribe a fascist, not a communist. You could give a commie a million dollars and the person wouldn't know what to do with it, because they can't buy anything. So, the lesson here is, never try to bribe a communist and never rent a car for a sixteen-year-old."

"Hey, I needed the money. Aren't you the person who told me to do something entrepreneurial?"

"Yes. But there are less risky ways to make money than to loan a car to a minor that you're liable for. What you should have done is have him post fifty dollars collateral with the stipulation he'd return the car on time in perfect condition. Why do you think car rental companies won't rent to anyone younger than eighteen?"

"Uh, because they can't be insured?"

"Exactly my point. If they can't cover the damages, they can't rent it. Anyway, I've got two *free* tickets to a soccer match. A cruise ship is coming in and Terry has to work, so he gave me his tickets." He waved two tickets in the air. "Do you want to go?"

"Uh, who's playing?"

"Las Palmas and Real Madrid."

"Real Madrid," I cackled. "Sounds fake to me, man."

"Nothing's fake about it. Real Madrid is the best soccer club in Spain and one of the best in the world. This is a big match. Las Palmas is in second place. A victory would put them in a tie for first with Madrid and give them a shot at the national title."

Hearing a light sprinkle falling, I glanced up at the yellow awning above us. Danny cleared his throat. "Well … "

"Ah, man, I know nothing about soccer," I said.

"Well, this would be a great time to learn. It's a lot like hockey."

"Yeah, well, I know nothing about hockey either."

"No problem, I can explain it to you. I played hockey on my high school prep team and Minnesota offered me a scholarship."

"So, when's the game?"

"Kickoff is this coming Saturday at six p.m., which means you'll still have time for tea and then El Cofre."

"Uh, let me think about it."

"What's there to think about? It's a once-in-a-lifetime chance to see some of the best soccer players in the world in a stadium that only holds twenty-two thousand—that means you'll get to see them up close. So, are you coming with me, or do I give your ticket to Pierre? He's dying to go."

As the sprinkle continued, I glanced around at the waiter, scurrying to keep things dry. While this was happening, Danny flapped the ticket in my face and pantomimed, *Going once. Going twice. Going ...*

"Alright man, I'll go, but if it's boring, then I'm leaving."

Danny and I went to the game, and he explained the concept of soccer to me while the first half dragged on to a zero–zero tie. "Have you ever played chess?" he asked.

"Yeah, my dad taught it to me."

"Well, think of it as a chessboard where you have these different pieces. Each one has a specific purpose and function. Each one moves independently. Some can move in more directions than others. Some are there to protect the queen. And some are there to kill the enemy and capture the enemy's queen. Some are cannon fodder. But some of them can become heroes. So far, the match here has been even. Neither opponent has drawn blood. We've lost a few pieces and so have they. But we still have our queen, as do they."

The second half got underway, seesawing back and forth with neither team scoring. As the game progressed, the fans became more restless and intoxicated. With every missed shot, the spectators moaned. With every penalty against Las Palmas, they jeered at the referees. And then Real Madrid scored a goal. By then, the crowd was inebriated. The audience protested. They shouted and whistled. Fights broke out. Empty bottles rained down on Danny and me. And then the game was over. Las Palmas had lost 0–1. More projectiles flew, and more fights broke out in our section. Men swore and objects bombarded us. The crowd yelled and shoved. We pushed back. It was a riot. It was war. It was Vietnam. And Danny was loving it. Elbowing nobody in particular, he roared, "This is what I miss about hockey!"

"This?" I retorted, shielding myself from flying bottles as I fought my way toward the exit.

"Yes, the fighting," Danny grinned. "How do you think my nose got flattened? Some A-hole broke his hockey stick in half on my face."

Mad at nobody specifically, we jostled our way out of the stadium. For Danny, the match seemed to resurrect hostile memories of his youth and father. But for the Spaniards, it appeared like they had a lot of bottled-up energy and it came out as civil war redux—autonomous zone versus Franco's Nationalists. As for me, it had been a harrowing and educational experience. Thanks to Danny, I could understand soccer on a philosophical level and found the sport interesting, but didn't understand the violence.

On the bus ride back into town, we passed beneath a neon Iberia airlines sign spanning the street. Seeing it, I flashed back to first meeting Danny and stealing his bag at the airport. A lot had happened since then. It seemed like a long time ago. Oddly, I was having the time of my life, and never wanted to return home.

Danny and I split up at Plaça Santa Catalina. I stayed for a cup of tea and then went to El Cofre for the evening.

A day or so passed, and I ran into Rolf again. He was high on Robitussin. I could always tell because it made him stutter. He had a Swedish girl with him. I'd seen her around from time to time, and she would babble euphorically one moment, and then would be sullen the next. I was told she suffered from depression and was suicidal.

"We just did a train on her with eight guys," Rolf whispered in my ear, stuttering. "She's all yours, man." Before I could respond, he walked off with his friends, leaving the girl with me.

The girl was in horrible shape. She needed a place to crash, but there was no way I could put her up in my pension. With no other choice, I took her to Danny's hotel.

Since Danny had ordered me never to come to his place, I didn't know what kind of reception I would get. I didn't care. The girl needed a safe place to sleep. Besides, it was past midnight, so there was little chance the insurance company would spy on him now. Holding the Swedish girl, who was ready to pass out, I entered Danny's hotel, catching the attention of the night clerk.

"We're friends of Danny's. What's his room number?" I said, keeping my distance so he couldn't get a good look at me.

"Room 401," he replied.

Standing outside Danny's room on the fourth floor, I rang the buzzer several times before he opened it. Attired in pajamas and with his hair in disarray, he said, "You woke me up. I thought I told you never to come here."

"Yeah, I know, but this girl needs a place to crash, and she sure can't stay with me."

Danny looked at the half-passed-out girl. "Alright, bring her in and put her on the sofa over there by the window," he said, nodding in that direction.

I said goodnight to Danny and left. He never said anything about it, and I never asked—and I never saw the girl or Rolf again. Apparently, their vacation was over.

17

Settlement

April 23–May 1, 1969 — Las Palmas de Gran Canaria, Spain

The payment from Iberia airlines came unexpectedly. One day they were still investigating, and the next day the settlement came in. Danny tracked me down at Parque Santa Catalina. He always knew where to find me in the evening, having tea at my favorite outdoor café.

Danny pulled up a chair. "Well, it's all over. Iberia made an offer, and I accepted it."

"Yay, eight hundred dollars, that's great, man!"

"No, actually, it's three hundred dollars."

"Three hundred!" I groaned. "Is that all? I thought you said your camera alone was worth that much."

"It is. But they prorated it, my clothes, and my bag because they were used."

"Okay, but how about the four hundred dollars in cash you claimed was in your bag, and your passport?"

"They don't cover cash, don't insure passports, and they deducted the new clothes, hotel, meals, and per diem they paid me."

"Huh, why?"

"Because they said I would have to pay living expenses anyway—irrespective of any settlement."

At that instant, the waiter came up and asked Danny what he wanted. It was so funny, because he always ordered a Pepsi. But his time he ordered a bottle of Heineken beer, telling him to bring me one too. The waiter stood there stunned for a moment before rushing off. Once he was out of earshot range, I resumed our conversation.

"So, let me get this straight. They didn't pay you for your camera and passport, didn't pay you for your clothes, and deducted your hotel bill, meals, and per diem." I shifted in my seat and leaned in toward him. "So what did they pay you for, man?"

"My inconvenience and, as I already stated, the prorated value of the items I mentioned. Oh, and the new clothes they bought me."

"Your inconvenience," I snapped. "How about my inconvenience, you know? I put up the money. Your claim was for eight hundred and we were going to split it fifty-fifty, which means I should get four hundred, and now you tell me I'm only getting one hundred and fifty. Yeah man, that's an inconvenience."

Danny whipped out his little spiral-bound notebook from the breast pocket of his light-blue shirt with epaulettes and flipped it open.

"Actually," Danny said, looking at his figures, "the deal was we were going to split it two-thirds, one-third. So, I only owe you thirty-two dollars and thirty-five cents, after deductions."

At that moment, our waiter arrived with our beers and placed them on the table. Danny opened his wallet and handed him a crisp twenty-dollar bill. The waiter's jaw dropped as he rushed off to get change.

For the next half hour, Danny went over every payment and loan he'd given me, subtracting it from my share of the settlement. He did it in such a manner that I wasn't angry, even though I was pretty sure he was swindling me and had received much more, if not all, of his claim. There was no way I could prove it, though, so I let it go. He was still the best friend I'd made on the trip, and if it weren't for him, my twenty dollars would have vanished long ago. *Danny's smart,* I told myself, *but I don't need him to survive.*

Several days later, Danny received his British passport and booked his ferry excursion to Morocco. The night before he left, Terry, Judy, and I went to dinner with him. I dressed up for the occasion wearing my favorite pull-over sweater that I reserved for special occasions. Resembling one Jim Morrison had worn for one of his record jackets, it had a lapel collar and three buttons. Danny razzed me about it saying, "It looks like a pajama top." But Judy loved it and said I looked sophisticated.

As the evening progressed, Danny talked about art school, how much he loved living in Los Angeles, his Indian hashish smuggling plan, and how, after he made millions on it, he would open a gallery in L.A., presenting the best in cutting-edge modern art, the world's finest wines and cuisine, and would fly all over Europe curating everything. He would call his gallery Zorro's after his last name. The way Danny saw it, communists were taking over the world, and its art treasures needed to be preserved. As far as he was concerned, he was just the person to do it. He would create the Louvre of the West.

Terry and Judy found Danny's knowledge of the arts, fine cuisine, wine, and his ambitions mesmerizing. I remained taciturn, keeping to myself my mixed feelings about him and what I felt were his somewhat duplicitous experiences with me. He was such a captivating person; it was difficult not to like him and fall under his spell.

As the evening wore on, Danny ordered appetizers, wines, and *specials of the day* for the table, and we all dined like there was no tomorrow. For Danny, that was true. His boat sailed in the morning for Agadir, Spanish Sahara. From there, he would take a bus to Marrakesh, Morocco, buy the hashish, and ship it to Terry's flat in London. Having been in Marrakesh before, he knew the hotels and restaurants, and, with Terry's assistance, he arranged his transportation to London.

When we finished dinner, Danny paid for it. *Where is the money coming from?* I asked myself. Actually, his actions further confirmed to me that the *settlement* had been much bigger than what he'd told me.

In the morning, Terry and I went to see Danny off at the port. Shortly before he boarded the ship to Agadir, I wished him well, shaking his hand. Danny took me aside. "If you change your mind about coming," he said, "I'll be sending Terry a postcard so he will know where I'm staying."

"Thanks, man, but I'm going to stay right here," I said, twisting the knife in, reminding him I wasn't entirely pleased about the settlement, and the condescending way he some-times treated me.

"Well, have it your way," he said with a weak grin. "But I think you're making a big mistake. You're missing an opportunity to make a lot of money. In a week, maybe two, you'll be broke ... and then what?"

"I'll think of something."

"That's what I'm afraid of."

"Well, don't be; I can take care of myself."

"Yeah, I know." Danny's eyes watered slightly, and he blinked several times before breaking off eye contact. He turned and boarded the ship. Standing at the pier, I watched him disappear inside the vessel. For the first time, I realized Danny was lonely. He'd been looking for a friend, and I'd been it. It's not that I didn't like him, because I did, but the settlement and the friendship he had with Terry and Judy had soured me on him.

On the way back to town, I was criticizing Danny to Terry. "Danny's not as smart as he thinks he is, you know. He thinks I'm not capable of taking care of myself. Well, if it weren't for me, he'd be broke. He never would've been able to pull off the Iberia airlines deal. He's going to get busted one of these days, you know."

Terry stopped and turned to me. "Danny will be okay; he knows what he's doing. You need to go home and get an education. You're just a kid who needs to grow up."

Terry's words hit me like a Joe Frazier left hook. The rest of our walk into town, neither one of us spoke a word. As we entered Parque Santa Catalina, I stopped. "Well, I think I'll get a cup of tea here," I said, barely audible.

Terry glanced at me, looking sorry for his outburst. "Why don't you come over for dinner tonight? Judy would love to see you, and I'm fixing chicken cordon bleu."

"Thanks, but my friends Kate and John invited me over for supper," I lied.

"Okay, man, well, stop by whenever you want," Terry said, forcing a grin. He turned and started walking off, knowing darn well he'd hurt me and I wouldn't be stopping by anytime soon, if ever again.

As Terry continued through Parque Santa Catalina, I watched him and thought: *I don't need Danny's schemes, and certainly don't need Terry giving me advice. I'm not a kid. I'm nineteen years old and can fend for myself. I'll prove them wrong.*

Less than a week later, I was broke again. Unable to pay rent to Mama Gallenda, I was living on the beach. I stopped by Terry's apartment.

"Come in, man," Terry smiled, as if nothing had happened. "I see you've got your backpack. Are you leaving?"

"No, I'm sleeping on the beach and was wondering if I could store it here for a while."

"Sure," Terry replied. "Judy's leaving next week, so I don't see why not. If you'd like, you can crash on the sofa after she's gone.

"Thanks," I responded, still hurting from the things Terry had said, "but I don't mind the beach, so I think I'll stay there."

Truth was, it was spooky and smelly sleeping under overturned fishing dories, and then being awakened early in the morning by young children playing soccer in the sand. Fortunately, their ball never rolled under the boat.

Before departing Terry's flat, Judy gave me a warm hug, and Terry informed me he'd received a postcard from Danny. "He says hello and everything is going as planned. According to his note, he's staying at Hotel Americano, and would like you to join him."

I was happy to hear he missed me. I left Terry's still feeling bittersweet about the way things had turned out, not intending to see him anytime soon.

18

Apprehended

May 2, 1969 — Las Palmas de Gran Canaria, Spain

Having dropped my backpack off at Terry's, I headed into town, worn out from the amphetamine Pierre had given me the night before, when I ran into him at Parque Santa Catalina. "Don't sleep on the beach, man," he said. "Take these and you will never need sleep again."

Pierre used speed to stay awake all night before becoming a panhandling pro. Now able to afford a pension, he no longer needed the drug and gave them to me. Big mistake. Hours after downing a handful, I began dreaming with my eyes open, and my heart beat like a Ginger Baker drum solo. *I'm going crazy and my heart is going to explode,* I thought. *No wonder he said, "You'll never need to sleep again," because I'll be dead.*

After a night wandering the empty streets, certain I would die, I threw the remaining pills away. Burned out and famished, I went to Cafeteria Tasartico to replenish the countless calories

I'd torched the night before. With just 115 pesetas left, I could only afford one meal a day now.

As I ate my usual order, John, with his guitar slung across his back, came over and stood at my table. Sunlight reflected off his hairless scalp. He'd heard I needed money and had an idea. "See that creepy guy sitting alone over there?" he nodded at a skinny guy eating alone. "His name is Kenneth, and he's a drug dealer. He's got some stolen traveler's checks and is looking for somebody to cash them for him. Says he'll split it fifty-fifty. The guy asked me, but I don't need bread that bad. I know you're hurting and thought you might be interested."

Setting my fork down, I glanced at Kenneth, and then back at John. "How much does he have?"

"He's got three fifties," John whispered.

I scratched a leg, considering it. Actually, there wasn't much to contemplate, but I wanted to give the impression I wasn't desperate. Danny had taught me that, and, just as I'd predicted, I didn't need Danny's help. I could take care of myself just fine. With this deal, I stood to make some real dough, more than I'd made off the Iberia swindle. *Eat your heart out, Danny. Just wait until you hear about what I pulled off,* I gloated.

"Well, are you up for it?" John said, snapping me out of my thoughts.

I took a sip of milk. "Oh, yeah, I'm up for it."

"Great," John said. "All I ask, man, is that you pay me thirty dollars as a finder's fee. If that sounds fair, then I'll introduce you to him. Well, have we got a deal?"

"Deal," I said, shaking John's hand.

"Alright," John winked. "Let's go talk to the creep."

Half an hour later, I left the joint with the traveler's checks, agreeing to meet Kenneth tomorrow afternoon at the taxidermied camel, located just inside Parque Santa Catalina's entrance. The stuffed animal welcomed visitors to the park. Situated close to a kiosk selling magazines, candy bars, cigarettes, and postcards, it was a popular photo attraction with tourists. I found it tacky, and didn't understand the significance of it, other than to advertise camel rides on the sand dunes in Maspolamas at the island's southern end.

Singing the Beatle's song "Money" on my way to the shops in the port area, I bounded like a schoolboy with the day off. I had food in my belly and a potential jackpot in my pocket. I could soon reimburse Mama Gallenda and rent a room.

I visited Mr. Bhatt's shop. Originally from India, he sold cameras, transistor radios, cigarette lighters, batteries, watches and other traveler-oriented paraphernalia. Trying my best to act like a typical tourist, I purchased a cigarette lighter with one fifty-dollar check. An hour passed and I returned, purchasing a pair of sunglasses with another. In between purchases at his store, I cashed a third check at another shop, acquiring a transistor radio.

By the time I finished my escapade, it was too late to rent a room at Mama Gallenda's, so I spent the night sleeping on the beach, too tired to go to El Cofre.

At two p.m., I arrived at the stuffed camel to meet Kenneth. As I waited, I remembered John introducing me to Kenneth yesterday in the restaurant. Sitting across from him at a table, he gave me the creeps. His thick-lensed, wire-rimmed glasses magnified his soulless eyes. Unable to look at him any longer, I flicked my eyes away when he said, "Some guy stole the checks and gave them to me because he owed me money for hash."

I didn't like Kenneth, and certainly didn't believe his story. I suspected he'd probably stolen the checks himself. Nevertheless, we came to an agreement. I'd cash the checks, and we'd split it. But I never paid Kenneth his share. Instead, I conned him when we met at Parque Santa Catalina.

Leaning against the camel there, I told him the police had busted me and confiscated the checks. "They're looking for you, man," I lied. Kenneth bought my story and left town for the hippie colony in Arguineguín. Feeling smug about swindling a drug pusher, I swaggered into Cafeteria Tasartico like Danny had at the outdoor café after the settlement. I paid John his cut and then ate my usual, celebrating with a pastry for dessert.

No sooner had I left the joint than two of Mr. Bhatt's sons came up to me. Recognizing them from their father's store, a pang of fear coursed through me, like a bad meal at the cafeteria.

"Hello, Mr. Charles, my name is Ravi, and this is my brother, Bharat," he said, as the two flanked me. "Last night you were in my father's shop where you cashed two fifty-dollar traveler's checks. The bank will not accept your checks without your passport number."

They're smaller than me, ran through my brain. *I'll bet if I make a break for it, I can outrun them.*

I tucked the idea away for the moment. Machine-gun-toting Guardia Civil officers patrolled the area. After all, this was Franco's Spain, probably the most fascist country in the world since Hitler's Nazi Germany. I elected to play it safe, rather than die by gunshot. "Oh, okay, I understand. No problem. My passport is at my friend's place just down the street, you know."

As we walked down a street fairly crowded with tourists, I kept an eye out for Guardia Civil. Continuing onward, the brothers fell back behind me, either feeling more comfortable with the situation or frightened. When we neared Terry's apartment building, they were at least fifteen feet back. If I was going to make a break for it, now was my chance. I could run down the end of the block, turn left, and head to Playa de Las Canteras, a block away. Guardia Civil was rarely there. It would then be a footrace. Four months of hitchhiking, walking, and bicycling had conditioned me. Moreover, less than a year ago, I was a pole vaulter and runner on my high school track team. Convinced I'd win a footrace, I looked for the right moment.

Just when I was ready to take off, a Guardia Civil officer came around a corner down the street and headed in our direction. *Man, that was close.* I was lucky not to have bolted. As I stopped outside Terry's building, the two brothers came up along either side of me.

"Alright," I said, pointing across the street. "It's that place over there. You two wait here. I'll be right back."

Crossing the street, I left the brothers, unable to believe they were so gullible. I didn't intend to come back. I'd punch in the lockout code at the door, go inside the building, and skip out the back door. And before they knew what happened, disappear.

By the time I made it across the street, the two boys came running after me, yelling for me to wait. Just before I could finish typing in the building's code, they pulled alongside me, panting.

"We need to go with you," Ravi declared, still breathing hard.

"You can't come inside. Strict rules on guests. If the manager sees you in there, my friend will be evicted."

Ravi and Bharat exchanged glances, trying to believe me. I sensed their dilemma. "Look, you two wait here. I'll be down in five minutes with my passport. Then you can write the number down and that will be it. Okay?"

The two boys gazed at each other, and then at me. "No," Ravi said. "Never mind the passport. You must come with us to my father's shop, or we call that police officer over there."

Out of the corner of my eye, I spotted the Guardia Civil officer down the street keeping watch over the area. Guardia Civil was the national police, the elite—Spain's S.S. You didn't dare mess with them. His distinctive hat, upturned in the rear, commanded respect and fear. Their hat, Andy had told me, commemorated executed civil war nationalists. As communists lined them against a wall and shot them in the head, the impact of bullets slammed their skulls, crushing the back of their hats upward. Despite their feared reputation, Guardia Civil could be a blessing, preventing drug dealing, prostitution, and petty crime. But from my perspective, they were a curse, hassling backpackers like me for loitering—lest the tourist area get an unsavory reputation.

"Okay," I reluctantly responded, "let's go."

Bharat hailed a cab. Within ten minutes, we were at Mr. Bhatt's shop.

19

Guilt

May 2, 1969 — Las Palmas de Gran Canaria, Spain

When we entered Mr. Bhatt's store, he locked the door behind us. Flipping the hanging "*abierto*" ("open") sign over to "*cerrado*" ("closed"), he waved for us to follow him to the back of the shop. Passing through a doorway, we reached a room doubling as a storeroom and living quarters. It smelled of curry and incense.

We walked past a utility sink, stacks of clean dishes on shelves, and a portable cook-top on a workbench to our left. We came to a Persian rug populated with bright pillows. Mr. Bhatt stopped and turned to me. "Thank you for coming, Mr. Charles. My name is Mr. Bhatt. This is our sitting area. Please," he said, motioning for me to take a seat.

Partitioned by shelves and boxes, I glanced around at the area's lack of furniture, confused. "Here?"

"Ravi, bring him a chair."

Ravi slid a rattan chair over to me on the Persian rug spread upon the tile floor. Like Rice Krispies, the chair snapped, crackled, and popped as I sat. Once I had settled, Mr. Bhatt began.

"Yesterday you visited my store twice and purchased some items from my sons Ravi and Bharat. They are good boys, but know little about traveler's checks and how they can become missing and then used by someone other than the rightful owner. Banks are aware of this and match the serial numbers on the checks against those reported missing. If they find one, they return it to the shop without payment. This is what happened to the two checks you bought items with at my shop."

Mr. Bhatt turned to the son closest to him. "Bharat, bring me my water."

Taking a sip of water from the bronze goblet his son handed him, Mr. Bhatt peered down at me and then resumed, "When you signed the checks, my sons trusted they belonged to you. They accepted your explanation that your passport was on a ship. Believing this, they cashed the checks. We have no reason to think you are not Mr. Charles and can clear this matter up. Either you provide us with your passport so we can verify to the bank the checks belong to you, or you can return the items and reimburse us the balance. Which will it be, Mr. Charles?"

While Mr. Bhatt spoke, five children crept out from behind a curtain. Some stood and others sat on boxes, suppressing giggles. Their ages appeared to range from five to fourteen.

Anxious about my confrontation with Mr. Bhatt, I plucked at the rattan's webbing. The kids made me even more uncomfortable. "Do we really need a peanut gallery?"

"Peanut gallery," he said, as inquisitive lines formed between his eyebrows. "What is a peanut gallery?"

It surprised me he wasn't familiar with the expression. "Uh, it's American slang, you know, for audience."

Mr. Bhatt still didn't understand. "Audience?" he asked, unaware his children were behind him.

"Your children! Do we really need all your kids here?"

Mr. Bhatt turned and, seeing his children, did a double take. "Children, go to bed, at once," he demanded, waving his hands. His children squirreled through every opening they could find. When the curtain parted, I glimpsed three or four bunk beds as the kids scrambled into them. Mr. Bhatt rotated back to me.

"Please forgive me. I have seven children and my wife is deceased." Hearing this, I shamefully bowed my head for robbing Mr. Bhatt of his livelihood.

"My children are my life now," he smiled proudly, showing off gold fillings.

The muscles in the back of my neck tightened. Trying to massage the tension out of it, I muttered, "I'm sorry about your wife, sir."

Mr. Bhatt hesitated to blink away wet eyes before continuing, "So tell me about your family, Mr. Charles. Are you traveling with them?"

"No, I'm traveling alone."

"I see. Do you have brothers and sisters?"

His words made me miss playing baseball and football with my brothers and the silly outfits my sisters wore. I became silent. Mr. Bhatt asked for water to be brought to me. One of his sons handed me an engraved, heavy, golden chalice filled with water. I sipped, swallowed, and then told Mr. Bhatt that I have two brothers and four sisters.

Mr. Bhatt applauded. "Wonderful, Mr. Charles. Where are

you from?"

"Bellevue ... Uh, it's a suburb of Seattle, Washington."

"Ah, Washington! Where the president lives!"

"Uh no," I answered. "Washington State is on the West Coast." I regarded Seattle as the coolest city in the world. It had the Space Needle, the futuristic monorail, majestic Mount Rainier, and made the best airplanes in the world.

Mr. Bhatt cocked his head and scratched his head with a look of bewilderment, so I elaborated. "You know, San Francisco—that side of the country."

"Ah, San Francisco, yes, I understand now," said Mr. Bhatt, staring off into space, as if he were visualizing a map of the country. "You are a long way from home. Do your parents know you are here?"

"Uh, I don't know. They know I'm somewhere in Europe, you know." I shifted uncomfortably in the chair, causing it to creak. Hearing the sound, Mr. Bhatt noticed my uneasiness and asked if I missed them. "I miss my mom," I uttered, looking down at the floor.

"They must be worried about you. You are a young man and are such a long distance from home. The world is full of dangers. It is not safe for you to travel alone."

"Can we talk about something else?" I'd heard it a hundred times before from my mother and from Grandma Grozny, when I'd stayed with her four months earlier.

Sensing my reticence, Mr. Bhatt moved on. "Ah yes, of course, as I was saying, you can provide us with your passport so we can verify the checks or you can return the items you purchased and the balance. If you cannot do either of these things, I will have no other choice but to call the police."

Since I'd forged Scott Charles' name, providing my passport

was not an option. Returning the items was also out of the question because I'd already spent a portion of the funds on frivolous items, and paid John his fee.

"As I informed your sons, you know, my passport is now at a friend's place. If you'll take me there, I will get it and bring it down to you."

Mr. Bhatt looked at his sons, who both shook their heads *no*, and then at me. "I am afraid I cannot do that. Which leaves the other option of you returning the items and repaying the difference. Would you prefer doing that?"

It seemed like a trap. Even if I could repay Mr. Bhatt, I'd more or less be admitting I'd forged the checks if I said *yes*. As fair-minded as he seemed, I'd be putting myself at his mercy, and resolved to hold my ground.

"I don't see any reason I should have to do that, you know," I said. "Those checks are mine, you know. Look at the signatures. This is a waste of time. I'm supposed to meet somebody for a very important business meeting in fifteen minutes, you know. I've got to go now."

I stood up to leave. Before I could take one step, Ravi dead bolted the storeroom door. I heard Mr. Bhatt on the phone speaking in Spanish to the police. All the commotion awakened the children, and they poked their heads out of every opening they could find. Ten minutes later, the police came to escort me, along with Mr. Bhatt, to the city police station.

Following my interrogation by Capitán González, Mr. Bhatt, along with two officers, and I were on our way to Terry's flat to get my passport.

20

Confession

May 2–5, 1969 — Las Palmas de Gran Canaria, Spain

We arrived at Terry's fourth-floor flat. It was dark, and I rang the buzzer. I hoped he wouldn't be there. The door opened. Surprised to see me accompanied by two police officers and Mr. Bhatt, Terry took a step backward. "What's going on?" he asked. But his wide eyes behind his glasses said it all. He knew I was in trouble. So did Judy, who'd just come out of the kitchen holding a dish towel.

"They want to look in my bag," I said.

"It's over there by the window," Terry said, pointing toward the living room, before retreating to be with Judy.

One officer rifled through the French alpine rucksack I'd bought in Barcelona, looking for my passport, while the other policeman and Mr. Bhatt watched. Meanwhile, I stuffed my trembling hands in my pants pockets, hoping he wouldn't find

161

my passport inside the top flap. To my luck, when the officer unstrapped the top flap, it draped over the back of my rucksack, hiding the zippered pouch on its underside.

Frustrated, the officer stood up, glanced at me, and then around the room. He spotted a black leather American Tourister carry-on bag. "Does that belong to you too?" he asked, looking at me. Before I could respond, Terry interjected. "It belongs to a friend of mine, and he is away at the moment. He left his bag here for me to watch." Afraid that police might search his bag, going through customs, and find the items he reported as missing, Danny's plan was for Terry to bring it to him in London.

Good thing the officer didn't look in Danny's bag, because he would have found the things he reported stolen to Iberia airlines. Instead, the police officer grabbed my rucksack, thanked Terry for letting us in, and told the others and me to come with him to the police station. I waved goodbye to Terry and Judy and could tell by the concerned expressions on their faces they saw fear in my eyes and knew I was in big trouble. Just how big I would soon learn.

When we got back to González's office, he had me sit in the same chair while he conferred off to the side with his officers and Mr. Bhatt. Finished with his sidebar, he returned to his desk, seated himself, and looked me straight in the eye. "So, Señor Charles, my officer informed me he could not find your passport, yet first you told Mr. Bhatt's sons it was on a ship and then at your friend's flat. What has happened to your passport?"

"I don't know."

It wasn't my fault the officer was so inept he hadn't found it. Continuing, I said, "It was in my bag a few days ago, you know, before I dropped it off at my friends, you know."

González's eyes narrowed. "And where was the last place you remember having it?"

"Uh, at the beach, I think," I smirked. "That's where I sleep, you know."

González slammed his palm on his desk. "We are going in circles. Now either you tell me where your passport is or I will arrest you."

"I am telling you—I don't know." I tilted my head, touched my face, and gave my best blank look. "I thought it was in my backpack, you know, that's the last place I remember seeing it, you know. I'm just as concerned about it as you are. Without it, I can't leave Spain."

"Without it, Señor Charles, you are not leaving this jail," said González, motioning to the officer wearing glasses. "Place him in a cell until he remembers where his passport is." The officer grabbed my arm and yanked me to my feet. González held a hand up for the bespectacled officer to wait. "Señor Charles, we can detain you indefinitely without a passport. The choice is yours."

The officer with glasses started escorting me to a cell. I glanced at Mr. Bhatt, whose eyes tracked me before bowing his head. At that instant, I was overcome with shame for what I'd done and realized the hopelessness of the situation. *I'm tired of fighting, and tired of lying,* my conscience told me. *My parents didn't raise me this way. What am I doing?*

Wanting to end the charade, I halted. "Wait," I said. "I can show you where my passport is if he'll just let go of me."

"Release him," González said. "No tricks, Señor Charles."

The officer let me go, and I went to my backpack, bent down, opened the flap, unzipped the inside pouch, and pulled out my passport. Downcast, I shuffled over to González and handed him my identification. He opened it, glanced at me, and then at the photo again. "Señor Paul Gorman," González snorted and then nodded with satisfaction.

Over the next several hours, I gave a full confession, explaining how I'd obtained the traveler's checks and what I'd done with the money. I protected John by giving him a fictitious name. However, it probably didn't matter because other than me, the only other person González was interested in was Kenneth. The police already knew him. By the sounds of it, they would be on the lookout for him in Arguineguín. They would be searching for a burned-out hippie who looked like he was forty, not twenty-five.

After signing my confession, I apologized to Mr. Bhatt as my chest convulsed out sobs, my lips quivered, and tears fell in torrents from my eyes. I wiped them away with a sleeve. I was nineteen years old and in jail in a foreign country nine thousand miles from home. Shaking, my mind exploded into fireworks of a thousand thoughts at once. Too terrified to think clearly, one thought stood out above the others. I grasped onto the memory of my mother coming to my bedroom the times my father struck me. She would stroke my back and sing lullabies until my sobs subsided. I missed her more than ever now and wished she were here.

As two of the officers escorted me to a cell, Mr. Bhatt called my name. Stopping, I turned to him. His shoulders slumped, and he wore a sad expression on his face. "Mr. Gorman, I am sorry for you," he said. "I am sorry for your family. I am sorry for your parents. Please understand ... I did not wish it to end this way."

"Thank you, Mr. Bhatt," I said, fighting the urge to weep

again. "It's not your fault, so don't blame yourself."

The guards led me to a cell. One of them unlocked a metal door and pushed me inside. The other officer tossed in my rucksack. My cell door clanked shut, reverberating through areas of the jail. I spent the night in solitary confinement. I paced the cell, measuring ten shoe lengths long by eight wide. There was no mattress or blanket. I ended up sleeping restlessly on a raised stone platform. Despite their subtropical climate, the Canaries can get cold at night because of its desert climate. The jail had no central heating and the windows no glass—only bars. I used my rucksack as a pillow. Between the cold, hard surface, clanging of cell doors, echoing guard's voices, and the dangling light bulb above me that stayed on all night, I barely slept.

In the morning, a burly guard clanking the bars in the window of my cell door awakened me, asking if I needed to go to the bathroom. I only spoke a little Spanish, but *baño* was one of the few words I understood. Although González and his fellow officers spoke English, the guards who had come around did not. Therefore, when I could, I tried communicating with the few Spanish words I knew. "*Sí, por favor,*" I said.

The same guard unlocked my door and escorted me to the restroom, which reeked of feces and urine. It was the typical squat-style toilet comprising a hole in the floor. You stood on two elevated pads, squatted, and relieved yourself. Afterward, you pulled a chain, releasing a gush of water from a holding tank mounted above on the wall. If all went well, you did your business without stepping in shit or getting sprayed by water splashing from the torrent spewing out of the pipe. You were also lucky to find a scrap of unused newspaper to wipe your ass. To my good fortune, the guard had given me a few squares of toilet paper. With no soap, I rinsed my hands in the sink, and the guard escorted me back to my cell. Before he closed the door, he pantomimed eating and said, "*Comida?*"

"*Sí, por favor,*" I replied, sitting on the stone slab as the man slammed my cell door shut.

My breakfast arrived in less than fifteen minutes with the same jailer handing it to me through a slot in the door. "*Gracias,*" I said, thanking him. The breakfast comprised *café con leche*, a small loaf of French bread, and lukewarm gruel. I couldn't tell what the ingredients were. It lacked flavor, but since I was famished, I ate everything.

A little time elapsed, and the same guard returned. I handed him the tray and dishes, thanking him. He offered me a cigarette, which I gladly accepted, having smoked the last of mine when I couldn't sleep. To my surprise, he gave me a Rothschild and not a Spanish cigarette, which I'd only smoked once or twice because they were so wretched. Savoring the cigarette, I read the graffiti scratched into the faded lime-green plaster walls. Most were in Spanish, but some were in English. Evidenced by the dates, the jail had been there at least since the 1930s.

A little before eleven a.m., I got a message from one of González's English-speaking officers that a visitor was here to see me. *Who could it be?* I wondered. *Maybe they are going to release me!*

The officer escorted me to González's office, where he sat at his desk. I noticed a middle-aged man with combed-over brown hair, attired in a dark business suit, white shirt, and burgundy tie, sitting next to him. González welcomed me. "*Buenos días*, Señor Gorman," González said, getting up. "I have the American consul general who is here to see you."

The consul rose and extended his hand. "Hello, Paul, I'm Wayne Brooks, and I'm the chargé d'affaires with the American Consulate Service here in Las Palmas. Nice to meet you."

Overcome with pride the U.S. government had responded, and guilt for what I had done, my eyes misted as I shook his hand. "Nice to meet you too."

"González informed my office of your arrest, and I have read the report—these are serious charges against you. I have notified the State Department, and they are in contact with your parents."

Swallowing hard, I stood there, barely able to grasp the enormity of what he said.

Brooks directed his attention to González. "Could my client and I have a moment alone, please?" Brooks asked.

González closed his desk drawer. "Sì, Consul." He rose to his feet and straightened his hat. "Let my guards know when you are finished and they will open the door for you."

Brooks shook his hand. "Gracias, Capitán González."

González left the room, and Brooks brought his focus to me. "Sit down, Paul. I think you had better." Brooks showed me where I should sit. I seated myself in a chair facing him. "How're you doing, Paul? Are they treating you well? Is there anything you need?"

I fidgeted in my chair. "It's going okay, but I could use a blanket and pillow. It's freezing at night."

"Okay, is there anything else? Cigarettes, magazines, candy?"

"Cigarettes and toilet paper would be great," I said, forcing a smile.

"Okay, I'll see that you get those, and we'll get some candy bars and magazines for you too, in case you decide you want them," said Brooks, jotting notes in a leather notebook. "It looks like you're going to be here for a few days, awaiting your arraignment, after which you will be interned in Prisión de Barranco Seco awaiting your trial, which could take up to two years. If you are convicted, the sentence for forgery is four years and one day."

Brooks' words stunned me to the core. My entire body numbed, and my mind became dizzy like I was going to pass out.

"I'm sorry," Brooks said. "This is a very serious situation. It'll be a miracle if we can get you out of this. Do you understand, Paul?"

Speechless, all I could muster was a nod.

"Okay," Brooks said. "I've got to go. We'll get those things to you and I will be there for your arraignment. It looks like it's set for the day after tomorrow. I'll see you then."

As Brooks rose to leave, I regained my feet, wishing this whole affair would disappear like a bad dream. He extended his hand, which I shook. "Take care, Paul," he said, pursing his lips. After he left, the thin mustached officer escorted me back to my cell.

When the guard was gone, I cried until dehydrated, cursing myself until I fell asleep. Several hours went by. A new guard awakened me. He opened my cell, handing me a blanket, four packs of American cigarettes, a roll of toilet paper, a *Newsweek* magazine, a copy of the *International Herald Tribune,* and two Snickers candy bars. The gifts boosted my spirits for the moment.

On the day of my arraignment, two machine-gun-carrying army soldiers brought me in a military troop carrier to the municipal courthouse in the governmental section of town.

Directed by a traffic cop wearing a white khaki blazer and pith helmet, we pulled to a stop in front of a colonial building flanked by flags and palm trees. The two soldiers escorted me up the steps and inside, past several Guardia Civil officers. They led me handcuffed down a long, wide, marble-floored corridor to a waiting room outside the actual courtroom. A soldier with salt-and-pepper hair motioned for me to sit on a bench along some windows. Ten or twelve other prisoners sat on benches waiting for their hearings, too. My arraignment would be at ten a.m. It was now nine fifty, five minutes past the time Brooks was supposed to meet me. *He'll be here any second now,* I thought.

Five minutes passed and still no sight of Brooks. I panicked. At ten, they called my name, and the two soldiers accompanied me into the courtroom. A black-robed judge sat behind a large raised dark wooden desk, peering down at me. Speaking in Spanish, the judge's jowls jiggled when he spoke. The salt-and-pepper-haired soldier motioned for me to sit at a table. To my right, a dark-robed man with thinning hair and a wispy mustache reviewed paperwork behind a desk. I assumed he was the prosecutor.

Once I was seated, the judge spoke briefly in Spanish, and then the prosecutor read off the charges against me in Spanish. I glanced around the courtroom to see whether Consul Brooks was there. The prosecutor continued speaking, and occasionally the judge would ask a question. Mostly, though, he just listened, scrutinizing me beneath his spectacles now and then. After about ten minutes, the prosecutor finished, and the judge said something to him. The prosecuting attorney rose and handed the judge my charging papers. The judge studied the papers briefly, signed them, and handed them back to the prosecutor, who then slid them on my desk to me. "*Firmar,*" he said, handing me a pen.

My mind was a jumble of confusion and fear. It was like a bad dream. I had no idea what the prosecutor had said and what the papers stated. "I don't understand," I responded, looking at the prosecutor. "*No hablar Española.*"

"*Debes firmar,*" the prosecutor said again, pointing where I needed to sign my name.

"I can't sign it. I don't know what the charges are," I reiterated. "My consul was supposed to be here. I'm an American. I won't sign anything until my consul reads it!" I was getting hysterical, and the prosecutor's jaw muscles tensed like my father's did before he'd hit me.

"*Debes firmar,*" he snapped, tapping his index finger where he wanted me to sign. "*Debes firmar,*" he yelled, slapping his hand on the papers, causing me to wince. The prosecutor turned to the judge and bellowed something to him. Nodding in agreement, the judge's jowls quivered like Jell-O. He responded to the prosecutor. I sat slack-jawed in bewilderment, wondering what they would do. Would they postpone my arraignment until my consul came? Would they drop the charges? My mind swirled with anticipation. My shackled hands trembled.

Meanwhile, the prosecutor added some notes to my charging papers. Finished, he glared at me and said something in Spanish. I didn't understand, but his tone was unmistakable. It was a threat. I shook my head *no* and said, "*No comprendo ... No hablar Española.*"

At that moment, a neatly dressed young woman stepped forward and spoke something to the judge and prosecutor in Spanish. The judge nodded and said, "*Sí,*" and motioned it was okay for her to talk with me.

The attractive brunette leaned over and, in fluent English, said, "Hello, I'm an attorney. The judge says you must sign or he will add two years to your sentence of four years and one day."

Hearing this, my mind dizzied. Looking blankly at her, I could not comprehend her words. It all felt so surreal, like some elaborate hoax. That's it, it's all a joke. That's why the consul isn't here. He's in on it too. The young female attorney patted my hand, snapping me out of my haze. "Please sign it. It's for your own good."

I slowly picked up the pen, paused for a second, and signed my name. Again, I was on the verge of tears. The young woman patted my shoulder and returned to her chair. Meanwhile, the prosecutor picked up my arraignment papers, and the soldiers led me out of the courtroom arm in arm.

A military troop carrier transported me under armed guard to Prisión de Barranco Seco to await my trial. Sitting on a wooden bench shackled to other prisoners, I stared in glassy-eyed silence.

After spending three nights in the city jail and my arraignment, I regretted I hadn't gone with Danny to Morocco, as the troop carrier arrived at Prisión de Barranco Seco.

21

Prison

May 5, 1969 — Las Palmas de Gran Canaria, Spain

I got my first glimpse of Prisión de Barranco Seco through the small, barred, square window of the troop carrier as we pulled to a stop. From what I could tell, it was a white colonial structure sitting above a ravine. An armed soldier and seven other prisoners sat in the rear of the military-style vehicle with me—four per side, with the guard at the far end of the bed.

On our drive up the windy road to the prison, I talked with a prisoner. He was an African from Dakar, Senegal, facing a sentence of six years and one day for transporting hashish. Speaking broken English, he claimed somebody had paid him to deliver a package without him knowing what was in it. I believed him. Wearing his shoes on the wrong feet, he seemed too naïve and mentally challenged to understand he was actually a paid drug courier. After a two-year wait, his trial, which took only fifteen minutes, had just ended. Altogether, he would spend about eight years in prison. As horrible as his sentence was, my outlook wasn't much better. All told, I could spend up to six years in prison.

Outside the vehicle, a soldier unlocked the rear door and opened it. Still chained together, we clambered out individually, followed by the soldier who had been guarding us. Hopping down from the vehicle, it took a moment for my eyes to adjust to the bright sunlight before I could grasp the scope of the building. A circular guard tower with a red-tiled, British-World War II-helmet–shaped roof brimmed at each corner. It was actually an attractive building—almost hypnotic. If it weren't for several Guardia Civil officers posted outside, it could pass for a charming hotel or old monastery; even the guard towers looked quaint. A scattering of palm trees and banana palms added to the resort-like ambience.

After a quick roll call, we were unchained then led single file into the prison, passing through an ornate, heavy, dark, wooden doorway. Inside, guards marched us in a column down a long marble corridor with windowed conference rooms on the left side and barred windows on the other. As we proceeded, our footsteps echoed eerily. It reminded me of Saint Edward's Seminary, which I'd visited while attending parochial elementary school in Bellevue. The similarities quickly evaporated when we reached an iron-barred doorway at the end of the hallway.

One guard unlocked the door, then escorted us inside. The metal door clanked shut behind us, making me flinch. To the left were offices. To the right was a hallway with barred cell doors. We were at the gates of hell, and my legs were shaking out of fear. I shuddered, wondering if I would be tortured, beaten, forced to do hard labor, or worse. I didn't want my mind to go there so I acted nonchalant, remembering how Killer and Rumble had accepted me when I pretended to be like them. I would do my best to bluff my way through this.

A guard whose name-tag indicated he was Gomez brought us into an office one at a time. When my turn came, Gomez put my belongings, including passport and money, into a storage bin. Since I didn't speak Spanish, he summoned an interpreter. A handsome man attired in a white turtleneck cashmere sweater, blue slacks, and loafers, resembling actor Robert Wagner, introduced himself in English with a Spanish accent. From then on, I referred to him as Mundy in reference to Robert Wagner's sophisticated cat burglar character, Alexander Mundy, in the TV series *It Takes A Thief.*

An inmate himself, Mundy claimed to be a famous singer in Spain, jailed for failing to pay alimony to his ex-wife. Whether he really was a famous singer, I never found out, although he had preferential treatment, never sleeping or eating with the other inmates. Likewise, he always appeared sharply dressed, attired in white, black, light yellow, or baby blue turtleneck sweaters.

An upright engraved nameplate on his desk identified Comandante Herrera, a uniformed, dark-haired, stern-looking man in his fifties. With a propensity for snapping his gold metal watchband, he sat in a solid leather chair, beneath a crucifix and photograph of Franco. The guard pushed me to his desk, where I stood before him. Herrera began reading off the rules while Mundy repeated them in English.

"No, gambling, no drugs, no fighting, no disobeying guards, no homosexual acts ... Roll call is at six a.m., followed by breakfast and then exercise yard. Second roll call is at noon, followed by lunch and then siesta. Third roll call is at three p.m., followed by exercise yard. Fourth roll call is at six p.m., followed by dinner, and afterward will be lockdown. Lights out is at nine p.m. Showers and haircuts are optional every other Saturday in the basement. Movies are shown every other Sunday night after supper. Mass is Sundays at eight a.m."

Mundy asked if I understood the rules, and I nodded I did.

"That is good," he said, "because any violation of the rules could result in disciplinary action or additional time added to your sentence. Now, you must sign this agreement acknowledging that you understand and will comply with the rules."

Despite the agreement being in Spanish, I signed it anyway. Mundy handed it to Comandante Herrera, who set it on top of other documents in a wire mesh basket on his dark mahogany desk. Yawning, he resumed snapping his watch wristband.

Turning to me, Mundy said, "Do you have any questions?"

"Yes, when do I get a prison uniform?"

"Your clothes are your uniform," Mundy chuckled. He then instructed me to follow him into the hallway. The other inmates I arrived with were side by side. "Get in line next to him," he said, pointing at the last guy in line, "for a doctor's examination." I got in line and again my knees began shaking. I took several deep breaths to calm myself.

Soon, a gray-haired man wearing a white lab coat, with a stethoscope dangling from his neck, came out of a room next door to the Comandante's office. Starting at the end farthest from me, the doctor began examining us one by one. It was a thirty-second physical. He listened for a heartbeat, flashed a light into each person's eyes and mouth, and then told them to cough while checking for a hernia. When he got to me, he listened to my heart first thing. In junior high school, I had a heart murmur and wondered if he heard it. If he did, he didn't show any change in his mundane expression. I didn't know if that was a good or bad thing. Within five minutes, he was finished with all of us.

Now that our "thorough" physical examinations were completed, Mundy had us follow him under armed guard downstairs to a room equipped with a barber's chair and benches along either side of seagull-gray walls. At the far end of the room, a barred, glass-less window overlooked a scrubby hillside. Daylight streamed in, supplementing three overhead hanging light fixtures. On the window side of the barber's chair stood a man wearing a white barber's jacket, holding an electric hair clipper.

"Haircut," Mundy said to us in Spanish and then English. "First, take your clothes off, down to your underpants, and put them on the hooks above the benches."

No, not my hair, I freaked. *Anything but my hair.* My hair was my identity. For the first time in my life, I could grow it long. My father had detested anything longer than a crew cut, making me keep it short. "Long hair is for sissies," he'd say. "Get a haircut!" Therefore, I'd get a crew cut to appease him, and would feel like a square at school.

At that moment in my life, I'd recently come out of my wallflower shell and established myself as *cool*. After almost dying from drinking furniture polish when two years old, I had suffered pneumonia, and again in second grade when my tonsils were removed. It set me back. I'd always been shy. I didn't have many friends. I wasn't a good student in elementary school, having been sickly and missing class.

During high school, my grades improved, along with my

confidence. To my benefit, my best friend became senior class president, and by association, I'd become part of the in-crowd that distinguished itself as counterculture, listening to the Doors, smoking pot, protesting the Vietnam War, and having long hair. Other than my average grades, my short hair was the only thing separating me from my newly established friends. Although I was already losing my hair, it was a slow process, so having it instantly shorn off in prison, even if it was a onetime initiation, was a major blow to my psyche.

As clumps of my blond locks fell to the floor, I shivered. Partly because it was chilly, sitting in the damp, dungeon-like basement clad in just my white jockey shorts, but mostly because I was emasculated. In less than three minutes, my head bore a buzz cut and Mundy directed me to stand in line with the other scalped inmates. I was at the end of the line. The barber, if you could call him that, opened a metal cabinet attached to the wall and pulled out a container filled with powder. He then put a gas mask on.

Mundy spoke to us in Spanish and then in English. "Take off your underpants, close your eyes, and don't breathe the delousing powder when it's your turn," he said, before retreating.

Dusted with powder from hairless head to toe, we stood like floured chickens ready for pan-frying. It wasn't bad for me because of my pale skin, but the black guy from Africa looked like a witch doctor doing an exorcism. We dusted ourselves off and then Mundy told us to put our clothes on.

Once we were fully clothed, they paraded us farther down the basement's dingy hallway. Inmates gawked and hurled insults at us as we passed several barred cell doors on the left. We came to a similar door. A guard unlocked it with a large iron key and shoved us inside. The room measured approximately twenty feet square. Occupied by six bunk beds and four other inmates, there were now twelve of us all together.

"Find a bunk that's not already taken," said Mundy bilingually. "It is siesta time. Roll call will be in two hours and ten minutes, followed by exercise yard for three hours."

Mundy and the two prison guards left the room, slamming the door behind them with a heavy clang that reverberated off the stone floors and walls with such intensity that the hanging light bulbs vibrated.

The cell's scruffy denizens scowled as they measured us. We did the same, wondering whether they were friend or foe. Off to a side was a hole-in-the-floor toilet. Despite having a large glassless window with bars, the stuffy, humid room reeked of human excrement. *With the addition of eight more of us, it will probably get worse,* I conjectured.

Following the brief sizing up, one inmate jumped down off the top bunk of a bed in the center of the room.

"Welcome to Hades," he said in Spanish and then broken English. "My name, Carlos. Take bed with no blanket. If lucky, guard bring blankets tonight for you."

Frightened, I did my best to mask my fear by standing erect. Since I was the tallest of the arriving inmates, other than the African, I took a top bunk on the right side of the room—nearest the cell door. I would have preferred a bed in the center row nearest the window if Carlos hadn't already claimed it.

Staking out my bed, I took off my khaki jacket and hung it on one of my bunk's wooden bedposts. I patted the mattress, which comprised a soiled, ripped canvas bag stuffed with straw protruding from the corners.

While the other new arrivals settled in and mingled with the old inmates, I went to the window. The fresh air smelled sweet. The scenery called to me. A palm tree rose above the other side of the prison wall. Small birds landed in it and flitted around from frond to frond, chirping happily before flying off. *Ah, freedom,* I daydreamed. *If only I were a bird, I'd fly out of here.* I found it ironic to be trapped in a cage for people while birds soared free.

An altercation interrupted my fantasizing. One inmate clutched a blanket, and another tried to rip it away. The yelling grew louder as the two wrestled. Finally, Carlos interceded, breaking it up just before several guards arrived and opened the door. We all stood there like saints, as the guards examined us.

"*Qué pasa?*" one guard asked.

"*Nada,*" said Carlos. "*Mantas para nuevos prisioneras, por favor.*"

The guard nodded before leaving the cell along with the other guards, pulling the door shut with a solid iron clunk.

Turning to Carlos, I introduced myself.

"Nice meet you, Pablo," said Carlos, shaking my hand.

"What did you say to the guards?" I asked.

"I tell them it get cold here at night. Inmates fight over blanket. I ask guards to bring blanket for all."

"Thank you."

"You welcome," Carlos said. "My English not very good. I like to learn. Maybe you help me sometimes."

"Well, my English isn't all that great either, you know what I mean."

"You much better than me," Carlos nodded. "I pay you. You help me."

I thought it over. "Okay, Carlos, you've got yourself a deal."

When siesta ended, armed guards ushered my cellmates and me to an enclosed outdoor courtyard where about 150 inmates milled around. The tiled courtyard was about seventy feet square. Surrounded by stone walls, a granite bench wrapped around three of the sides. Within the yard, it was an anthill of activity. Some inmates sat on the bench talking to other prisoners or themselves, some played chess or checkers, and many just paced back and forth up one end of the courtyard to the other—repeatedly. Having spent the past three days in solitary confinement, I did some walking, not only to get a little exercise, but I also felt safer moving. I didn't want to talk to anybody yet, other than Carlos, and he was playing checkers with another inmate.

As time dragged by, I became bored and sat down in a space on the bench. I still had about half a pack of cigarettes the consul had given me. I lit one up. It wasn't long before a swarthy middle-aged man with greasy dark hair and tattoos sat down alongside me.

"*Cigarillo, por favor,*" he said, wiggling an index finger and his middle finger.

I handed him a cigarette.

"*Fuego,*" he said, clicking an imaginary lighter.

I lit his cigarette and then turned my head. The guy gave me the creeps.

"*Gracias,*" he said, his evil smile exposing rotten teeth.

Fed up, I got up and started walking again, smoking my cigarette and glimpsing back to see if he would leave. Eventually he did, and I sat down again in my spot.

Carlos came up to me a little later, and I helped him with his English. One of the side benefits of helping him over the next few days would be that I'd learn some Spanish.

Roll call arrived at six, and everybody lined up in columns ten to fifteen deep. A guard ordered us to stay in rank and not speak. As he called inmate's names, they said, "*Sí.*" Somebody said something, causing some inmates to laugh, and the guard stopped until he determined the guilty party. The man was whisked away. Meanwhile, we stayed in rank and did not talk. With so many prisoners, it took about ten minutes to go through the rest of the names.

Immediately following roll call, guards corralled us into a single line like cattle going through a stockade. Herding us into the cafeteria, I choked down a dinner of watered-down beef stew, fava beans, and French bread. It wasn't very good, mainly because there wasn't much meat in the stew. Starved, though, I ate everything. For dessert, we had flan. I sat next to Carlos and another cellmate who asked to join us. I didn't know him, but realized the importance of forming bonds immediately for protection. Dismissing us after dessert, guards led us to our cells.

That evening I didn't sleep well, because at first it was too hot and stuffy in the room, and then, as the evening wore on, it got cold. I appreciated the blanket. As for the mattress, it reminded me of camping with my father and brothers. On the way to our campsite, my father would stop at a ranch and buy a bale of hay. After we set up the tent, he would spread it on the ground, put a tarp over it, and that would be the mattress beneath our sleeping bags.

Since my father never played ball with me, and only came to one of my little league baseball games, those hunting and fishing trips were my favorite experiences with him. However, he was strict and demanding on those trips. He would make us get out of bed first thing in the freezing cold morning to light the campfire, fetch hand numbing icy spring water from the creek, help with dishes, and scrounge for firewood. In the evening, though, we would sit around the campfire as he told us stories about camping with my grandfather and Uncle Walt, both of whom I adored.

Curled up in my itchy wool prison blanket, I fell asleep and dreamed I was in a tent sleeping with my brothers while my father slept in his homemade camper. Thus ended my first day in prison, a day not too much different from the rest of the days I would spend in Prisión de Barranco Seco.

22

Letter

May 6, 1969 — Las Palmas de Gran Canaria, Spain

My second day of imprisonment began at six a.m. Several guards arrived at our cell, announcing it was time to get up for roll call, much like my father commanded us from his camper to "rise and shine" at the crack of dawn. I jumped out of my top bunk, put on my clothes, then got to the rear of an already formed line. A roll call ensued. Moments later, guards directed us out of our cell, then upstairs to the cafeteria on the main floor. Joining the breakfast queue, I grabbed a tin tray, bowl, and spoon, along with a checkered cotton napkin. As I sidestepped my way down the food line, an inmate emptied a ladle full of *café con leche* into my metal bowl. Farther along, another placed a roll of French bread on the tray.

Served, I looked for Carlos and spotted him. Weaving my way over, I arrived at his table.

"Hey man," I said. "Can I join you?

"*Sí*, Pablo," Carlos said, stuffing a piece of *café-leche*-laden bread into his mouth. "I have favor to ask."

"Sure," I replied, dunking my bread in the coffee mixture. It didn't taste great and was unlike any coffee I'd ever had. *Oh well, at least it's nourishment*, I told myself.

"Can you write letter for me?" Carlos mumbled, swallowing a mouthful of soggy bread. "I pay you one hundred pesetas."

"You don't have to pay me, man. You're already paying me, you know, for English lessons."

"But I want to, Pablo."

"Okay, man, who do you want me to write a letter to?"

"My fiancée," Carlos replied, breaking off a chunk of bread. "She Swedish—read English. I no write English."

I gulped down a wad of *café-leche*-saturated bread.

Carlos resumed, "I meet her in Madrid one year ago. We fall in love and have sex. She go to Sweden. Baby come ... baby boy. I supposed to marry her in Sweden ... Now I can no go."

"Wow, sorry to hear that, man," I said, dunking my bread again. "How long are you in for—I mean, what's your sentence?"

"Fifteen years and one day," Carlos said, slobbering another chunk of dripping bread into his mouth.

"Fifteen years!" I whistled. "What'd you do?"

"Nada!" Carlos bellowed, slamming his fist on the table, causing spoons to stop clinking tin bowls and heads to turn. "I on vacation here with Ingrid. Police arrest me. Say I have *el coche* accident in Madrid three years ago and kill man. I no kill him. He run into me!"

Carlos fell silent for a moment and then tore his bread in half. Setting both pieces on the table, as if they were cars, he

184

showed how the accident had happened. "Light green, I go," said Carlos, moving the imaginary car in his left hand. "He no stop ... hit me like this," he said, as he moved the pretend car in his right hand to the point where it broadsided the fictional car in his other hand. "He die, I no kill him! He hit me!"

Carlos put the bread back on his tray, then bowed his head, resting his chin on his folded hands and sobbed.

"Don't worry, Carlos," I said. "I'll write your letter for you."

I slurped down the last chunks of my bread, then drank the remaining crumb-thickened batter. It was the same breakfast every day. While I finished the slop, Carlos sobbed and sulked until our dismissal.

That afternoon, I helped Carlos compose a letter to Ingrid. He explained the accident, proclaimed his innocence, and told her he loved her. The letter went on to say he'd hired an attorney and in a few days would obtain bail and then come to Sweden and marry her.

When I finished composing Carlos' letter, he said to me, "I marry Ingrid, I become legal Sweden citizen. I claim asylum."

I wondered whether he really loved Ingrid or was conning her to gain legal protection in Sweden. But I liked Carlos, so I gave him the benefit of the doubt.

Earlier in the afternoon, I ate my first lunch of gruel served out of the exercise yard commissary where you could purchase cigarettes and candy bars charged to your prison account. Mine had nearly eighty-five dollars left from the forged traveler's checks. To my surprise, they hadn't confiscated it.

As for the gruel, I wasn't sure what the hot, mushy substance comprised. Based on its gritty texture, though, it had to be some type of grain or blend. Again, it was something that didn't taste great. Figuring it was sustenance and wanting all the nourishment I could get, I ate all of it. Before embarking on my trip, I had purchased a bottle of vitamins, taking one every day to supplement any nutrients I might be missing, and now I needed them more than ever.

While sitting on the bench after eating my gruel, my thoughts drifted back to Danny. I wondered if he was still in Morocco, or if he was in England now. I felt like I'd known him for years, not weeks. I missed him.

23

Martin

May 7–9, 1969 — Las Palmas de Gran Canaria, Spain

My fourth day in prison started out like the others, with roll call followed by the same *café-con-leche* concoction along with a small baguette. Afterward, guards funneled us to the exercise yard, where I spent hours smoking, walking, and helping Carlos learn English. He still tried to arrange bail. My pidgin Spanish improved to where I could order things from the commissary without too much problem.

Other than Mundy, as far as I knew, nobody else spoke English in the prison. That was about to change. While pacing back and forth in the yard, I'd hear snippets of hushed conversation coming from two men in their forties. One of them was tall with straight black hair slicked back with Brylcreem, while the other was short and stocky with short hair. I nicknamed them Curly and Moe to myself. After three or four laps, I stopped them.

"Excuse me, I heard you guys speaking English, you know, and was wondering where you're from."

"Ontario," Moe said, looking a little annoyed, his shiny hair glistening in the morning sun.

I didn't have a clue as to Ontario's location, other than remembering there was a Great Lake called Lake Ontario. "Oh, Lake Ontario, what state is that in?" I asked.

"It's a province in Canada," replied Moe, looking perturbed.

"Oh yeah," I said. "I've been to Vancouver. I bought a charter flight, you know, from a Dutch guy who didn't want to go back to Amsterdam. Only thing was, I couldn't get on the plane, you know because …"

"Vancouver's on the other side of the country," Curly interrupted.

"But my flight was from Vancouver."

"Look, kid," Moe snapped. "We'd like to be left alone, if you don't mind. Our sailboat's been impounded and we need to figure out how to get it back before the authorities sell it."

The two explained they'd sailed to Las Palmas from England and brought along a crew member who'd stolen their money and passports. It was the reason they were in prison. Without passports, they'd entered Spain illegally, and their sailboat was impounded. Moneyless, they were powerless to get their boat back when they got out of jail. Without passports, they couldn't enter another country.

I wondered whether Terry had anything to do with it. He'd come to Las Palmas crewing on a sailboat, and more or less fit their description. And he also looked to buy a sailboat here and sail it back to London with Judy. *Wouldn't it be something if he's the guy who ripped them off?* I humored myself. I put the idea out of my mind and made a point of not telling the Canadians—not that I had a chance, because they pretty much avoided me after that conversation.

It wasn't long before a tall, rawboned, Aryan-looking man with gray-speckled hair and high cheekbones came up to me while I sat on the bench smoking a cigarette. "So, I hear from the two Canadians you are American," the man said with a German accent. "Kurt Mueller is my name." He extended his hand.

Surprised he spoke English, I responded by introducing myself and shaking his vice grip handshake.

"Where do you live?" Kurt asked, pulling an address book and a ballpoint pen out of the inside breast pocket of the gray suit he wore every day.

With a sigh, I told him where I was from.

Kurt must have sensed my reticence, since he gave me a teammate like nudge with his elbow. "I ask because I am American merchant marine captain. There is possibility I might be in Seattle sometime. It would be nice to say hello. May I have your home address?"

I gave him my parents' address and phone number and immediately regretted it. The man acted strange in an evil sort of way. The past few days, I'd watched him play chess with a small, young Spanish inmate. Mueller would show him where to move a piece. The Spaniard would do it, and Mueller would slap him for taking one of his pieces. The game went on like this. He would then accuse the poor fool of cheating and beat the crap out of him. Several hours later, they would make up and it would begin all over again.

Having obtained personal information from me, Mueller abruptly left to play chess with his recovered masochistic opponent who called to him. Following lunch, guards returned us to our cells for siesta. As I was passing the Comandante's office, Mundy came out to me.

"Señor Gorman," he said, "a visitor will be here to see you right after siesta. Guards will escort you here, and then, along with me, accompany you to a meeting room in the hallway near the main entrance doorway."

Oh my God, I murmured to myself, lying on my bunk. *I wonder who it is. Man, I hope it's not Dad.*

There was a good chance it was. Brooks had mentioned something about the State Department notifying my parents, so perhaps both had come—or just my father. That was more likely, because with five kids ranging in age between eighteen and seven still at home, they needed their mother.

The thought of him coming horrified me. Surely, he would be angry, and I'd break down when I saw him. I'd start to say, "Sorry Dad, for putting you and mom through all of this." But before I'd be able to say anything he liked would hit me. Spankings and restrictions were common during my adolescent years. He doled out punishment for the slightest infractions. Finally, it escalated with openhanded wallops to the side of the head he called "clouts." He'd swing and the impact would nearly knock me off my feet. My head exploded with pain like a hand grenade detonated inside it. The throbbing and ringing in my ears lasted for an hour, it seemed. Clouting continued until one day during my senior year in high school, I can't remember what I'd done, but he struck me.

"Don't ever hit me again," I warned.

He swung once more and missed. I decked him with one punch. Jumping on top, I pummeled him. Shrieking, my mother rushed in and pulled me off. My younger sisters were hysterical. Shouting erupted between my father and two younger brothers, spilling out into the front yard. During the commotion, my mother called the police. They arrived shortly thereafter, asking my father if he wanted to press charges against me.

"No," he replied. "We can handle this on our own."

The cops left, and a little later, so did my father for the evening.

As bad as I felt about hitting my father, it had a beneficial effect in that he never struck my younger brothers or me again. By then, though, I had too many painful memories and couldn't wait to leave home.

Siesta ended with a barked roll call. Afterward, the guard named Gomez (who I'd nicknamed Gomer) called my name. Accompanied by a tall guard I referred to as Lurch, because of his high cheekbones and sunken eyes, they escorted me upstairs to the main floor, where Mundy greeted me.

"Señor Gorman, your visitor is here. Follow me."

Flanked by Mundy, Gomer, and Lurch, I passed through the gated doorway and strode down the marble-floored corridor, past conference rooms on my right and barred glass windows on the other side. *For a prison, this section is nice,* I thought.

Mundy stopped us at a dark mahogany door. "Your visitor is in here," he said, holding it open. "When you're finished, knock on the door and a guard will let you out."

I braced to meet my father. Instead, a handsome, athletic man in his early thirties, with short bristly dark hair, sat at a heavy wooden table. Attired in a blue blazer, gray slacks, baby blue shirt unbuttoned at the collar, and penny loafers, he looked as if he'd just come from a country club. Rising, he greeted me when I entered.

"Hello Paul, I'm Martin Alvarez," he said in perfect English, shaking my hand. "I'm the junior consul here. Consul General Brooks has assigned me to your case. Please be seated."

As I sat in a solid, leather-upholstered chair, the heavy wooden door behind me closed with a solid thud. Glancing in that direction, I could see Gomer monitoring me through a window next to the door. I swiveled back to Martin.

"How're you doing, Paul, are they treating you well?

"Yeah, other than that I'm in a tiny cell with eleven other inmates."

"Okay, we'll see what we can do about that," Martin said, scribbling something in a leather notebook. "Even though Consul Brooks couldn't be at your arraignment, don't think we've forgotten about you. We're working on a deal to get you out of here within the next three days—perhaps four. So, here's where we're at: Mr. Bhatt likes you. He feels badly about your incarceration and will drop the charges—provided he's reimbursed the one hundred dollars for the traveler's checks. The State Department has been in contact with your parents, and they've agreed to wire the funds to a bank here in Las Palmas, along with enough money to get you out of Spain ... How does that sound?"

"Wow, that sounds great," I said, wiping my eyes with a shirtsleeve.

"Yes, it is," Martin said. "A few formalities have to happen after the money clears the bank. We will need to petition the court, so it could take a day or two before your case comes before the judge. Second, a hearing will need to happen where Mr. Bhatt will formally request that they drop your charges, and I will enter a plea on your behalf to assume responsibility for you while you remain in Spain. Do you have any questions?"

"Uh, is there any chance the judge won't approve it?" I shifted in my seat.

"Yes, there's a slight risk," Martin said, shuffling papers. "Prosecutor Hernandez will be present and will argue why you should not be released and should serve your sentence. However, don't worry, this isn't more than a formality. The U.S. ambassador to Spain has been following your case and has requested your release through the highest levels of diplomacy. Our relations with Spain are very good right now with the Nixon administration. If needed, he will leverage a military agreement we are negotiating with Spain as we speak."

I couldn't believe how much attention my case had attracted. On one hand, I was proud to be an American. On the other, I was ashamed to have caused such an international incident. I broke down. Martin handed me the white handkerchief from his blazer breast pocket, reached across the table, and patted my shoulder.

"Everything is going to be okay, Paul. We'll have you out of here soon," he said, as I regained my composure. "In the meantime, I'd like you to write a letter to Ambassador Robert Wagner thanking him. Can you do that for me?"

Finding the coincidence of Ambassador Robert Wagner having the same name as the actor who played Alexander Mundy and the nickname I'd given one of the inmates humorous, I shook my head *yes*.

"Good," Martin said. "Here're some cigarettes, a couple of candy bars, and two dollars to tide you over. Is there anything else you need?"

"No, this is plenty," I said. "Thank you for everything you're doing."

"You're welcome. Helping you get out of here makes my job even more meaningful."

Immediately following my meeting with Martin, Mundy and Gomer brought me to the exercise yard where I taught English to Carlos. A short while later, Mundy, accompanied by Lurch and Gomer, summoned Carlos to come with him.

With Carlos no longer there, I started pacing and smoking, reflecting on my meeting with Martin earlier. Thirty minutes or so later, Mundy appeared at the doorway and called my name.

"Señor Paul Gorman, Señor Paul Gorman." Ending my ruminating, I approached Mundy, stopping at the entrance.

"What is it?" I asked, perplexed.

"Come with me to get your belongings," Mundy said. "You're being transferred to another cell."

Accompanied by Gomer and Lurch, I followed Mundy to my old cell in the basement and collected my clothes and rucksack. After I finished packing, they brought me to an enormous empty cell on the third floor. By the looks of it, the room housed about sixty prisoners. I stood there with uncertainty, holding my rucksack, overwhelmed by the size of it.

The room had more light, and the air smelled fresh compared to the basement cell, but it looked like something out of a World War II concentration camp film. What had I gotten myself into? Beds lined the entire length of both walls, along with two rows in the middle. A smaller alcove to the right had two rows of double-decker bunk beds and wooden lockers. At the end nearest the cell door, next to the alcove, was the latrine. Stinking of human waste, the bathroom had two sinks, a trough urinal, and three hole-in-the-floor toilets separated by stalls with half-high wooden doors. Now that the tour was completed, Mundy took me to a bed at the far end of a middle row.

"This will be your bunk," Mundy said, patting it and sending a dust cloud in the air. "Twice a week, everyone has two hours of guard duty at night. Your nights are Tuesdays and Fridays from two to four a.m. You are required to walk around and call the guards if there are any disturbances. Do you understand?"

"Yes," I said, scared at the thought of having so many prisoners under my charge.

"Do you have any questions?" Mundy asked.

"Will my friend Carlos be moved here too?"

"No," Mundy said. "Carlos is being transferred to a prison in Madrid tomorrow for his trial."

Following the tour of my new cell, they returned me to the exercise yard, where Carlos told me that the judge had denied his bail. It made me wonder if perhaps the prison censors had intercepted the letter, read about his plan, causing the court to deny bail. *He never should have sent it through the prison mail.*

That night I slept fitfully, afraid I might be gang raped by my new cellmates or beaten. Neither one happened. I eventually fell sound asleep about two a.m. and woke up at six with an order for roll call.

24

Vulnerable

May 9–12, 1969 — Las Palmas de Gran Canaria, Spain

Now that Carlos was gone, I really didn't have anyone to talk with who spoke English. The two Canadians still wouldn't speak to me, and I avoided Kurt Mueller, the merchant marine captain. Good thing I did, because when Martin visited, he asked if there were any other English-speaking inmates in the prison.

"Yeah," I replied, telling him about Kurt Mueller and the Canadians. Martin informed me that the Canadians were international jewel smugglers. As for Mueller, he wasn't an American merchant marine captain. He was really a World War II Nazi war criminal picked up by Interpol, awaiting extradition back to Germany for war crimes. *Oh my God, he's a mass murderer.* I fretted.

I suddenly agonized about having given him my family's name and address. My imagination went wild, envisioning him

escaping or released, tracking down my family and slaughtering them. Learning these things, I began distrusting everybody
in the prison. What they proclaimed to be wasn't necessarily
who they were and what their actual crimes were. I even
questioned whether Carlos had been honest.

Oh well, I reassured myself, *I'll be out of this hellhole in a few
days, so it really doesn't matter. I liked Carlos, and everyone needs
a friend in prison.*

With Carlos gone, I spent even more hours alone, pacing the
courtyard and smoking. During this period, I wrote a letter to
Ambassador Robert Wagner. I sent another one to my mother
apologizing for my wrongdoings along with any pain I inflicted
on her and Dad.

Prison officials censored letters for anything negative about
the prison or Franco. Because of this, I coded my corre-
spondence to my mother with non sequiturs and statements
followed by erroneous facts, such as, "It's really nice here.
I heard that the Baltimore Colts won the Super Bowl." In
reality, since the New York Jets had just won, almost any
American would know it was untrue. In all likelihood, though,
the censors wouldn't be aware of the fact and would not censor
my letter.

With no friends, inmates started demanding things from
me. Tattoo man insisted on having more cigarettes. Finally, I
yelled at him, "This is the last one. Get the hell out of here!" It
seemed to work because he didn't ask again. But after Mass on
Sunday, when I stood in the queue for the glass of red wine we
were allowed, he came from behind.

"*Vino para mi,*" he growled, goosing me hard, demanding
my wine.

"No," I replied, gritting my teeth. I stood my ground, and

he finally moved on, trying to coerce others. While sipping my wine, I glanced around the vestibule, and sure enough, he'd strong-armed somebody out of his ration of wine. He sneered at me, slashing a finger across his throat. I acted unconcerned by his threat, but fearful he would follow through. From then on, I kept a careful eye on him, distancing myself whenever I could. I needed protection, and without a friend, I was susceptible.

It wasn't long before a band of Africans from Dakar showed up, almost immediately creating friction with some Spanish inmates. The Spaniards called them *negra* and "Cerda" along with other racial slurs and tried to pick fights. On one occasion, a full-fledged fight broke out between a group of Spaniards and several of the Africans. One of them, Abdul, fought back with such ferocity he scared off his attackers, and they left him alone.

I became friends with Abdul, along with his friends, for protection. He spoke English well, albeit with a thick British–Senegalese accent, having studied in neighboring The Gambia's colonial schools. Even though the rest of his compatriots didn't speak English well, all I needed was Abdul's friendship for their acceptance and security.

Abdul and his friends had left Dakar hoping to find work in Europe. After arriving in Las Palmas, they were arrested for loitering, or so they said. I had no reason to doubt them. I'd seen police harassing African migrants around Las Palmas for doing nothing more than sitting on a bench or standing around in a cluster in Parque Santa Catalina.

I won Abdul's friendship by showing an interest in where he was from, along with telling him about the civil rights movement in the U.S. It helped that he wanted to immigrate to the U.S. someday.

25

Communists

F our days had elapsed since Martin visited me with news about my impending release.

Even though he had thrown out three days as an estimate for how long it would take, I knew it could take longer. This was Spain, and bureaucratic things crawled along. In fact, *mañana* was a word heard almost every day.

While in Barcelona I phoned home asking my mother to wire money and she did. It took three or four days for the money to show up at the bank, only to find out later she had sent it on the same day I called. When my high school history teacher wired a hundred dollars because I was broke again, it took a week for the money to arrive at a Las Palmas bank. Every day I'd check to see if the money was there. Inevitably, I got the same response: "*Mañana.*"

In a way, it was infuriating, but once you got used to the pace of life, it was refreshing. What's the big rush? Enjoy life.

There was one exception, though. When I told Martin about my overcrowded cell in the dungeon, he saw to it I was moved to the upstairs dormitory the same day. And, despite my initial misgivings, the dormitory room was vastly superior to my old room. Ocean air blew in and sunshine shone through the glassless barred windows, offering a view of semi-barren hillsides. The density in the dormitory was lower than in my previous cell. Even though there were more than sixty other inmates, we had more space to move around and be *alone*—if that was possible.

One day, a black French citizen named Dominic moved into our dormitory cell. He spoke fluent English with a Creole accent, having grown up on the French side of the Caribbean island of Saint-Martin. The other half of the island, Sint Maarten, was the Dutch English-speaking side. Because of this, he was bilingual. He resembled a young Sidney Poitier, and I was glad to have someone else to converse with.

It was siesta time, and I was heading to my bunk when Dominic came up to me. "Hello, I'm Dominic. People tell me you are American," he said with a backhanded tap on my shoulder.

"People?" I replied, surprised that he spoke English.

"Oui, cellmates. My comrades."

"Comrades?"

"Oui, I'm from America too."

Never having heard an American accent like his before, I said, "Really?"

"Oui, Saint-Martin," Dominic said, formally adjusting his shirt sleeves. "My ancestors were slaves, brought to Saint-Martin by white slave traders to harvest sugar cane. The same people who brought my ancestors there brought them to the U.S. As you can see, that makes me an American. I'm as American as Indians, who had their land stolen by European colonists, and blacks whose ancestors were slaves. We are the true Americans."

Gee, I wonder if Dominic would renounce his "American citizenship" if the U.S. Army drafted him. I snickered to myself.

Fueled with resentment, Dominic took his political fight to the European colonists. He married a French woman, becoming active in leftist organizations and protests.

Dominic claimed to be an innocent bystander in the May 1968 student protests in France. The demonstrations turned into deadly riots, nearly toppling the government, and causing Charles de Gaulle to flee briefly to Germany. Believing he played a role in the insurrection, Interpol picked up Dominic at recent May Day protests in Madrid. Because of overcrowding in the prison there, they sent him here to await extradition.

After Junior Consul Martin's revelations that Kurt Mueller was really a Nazi, and the Canadians were jewel thieves, I wasn't sure whether I believed Dominic. It seemed he must have done something more egregious than just being an innocent bystander to be arrested by Interpol. Furthering my suspicions, he talked mostly about his love of communism and leftist politics. Repeatedly, he denounced Charles de Gaulle, Nixon, and Kissinger as fascists, lumping them right in with Franco. Denouncing Franco was a serious offense in Spain, and could extend your prison sentence or, from what I'd heard, get you the death penalty. I didn't know if this was true and didn't want to find out.

Fashionably clothed in a black leather sports coat, white Nehru collared shirt, flared black slacks, and dark sunglasses,

Dominic confided in me over several days. "The French police are trying to extradite me to France," he said, showing me a letter one day in the dormitory. "They've just charged me with treason, which is a capital offense."

"But you were only a bystander," I said, pretending to believe his story.

"Oui, but a policeman and bystander died, and I was a member of the Socialist Workers Committee. We are a peaceful organization. We merely organized the protests and handed out leaflets to protest the war, the French government, and Charles de Gaulle. Fascist government infiltrators hijacked it, created the unrest, and they blamed us."

"Of course," I said, uncertain about his innocence and ambivalent about his opinions. It wasn't that I opposed the Vietnam War, because I did. Before leaving the States, I'd gone to several antiwar protests in downtown Seattle and at the University of Washington. I believed the war was unnecessary. There was no strategic reason we were there. They weren't attacking us and didn't hold an existential threat to the country. From that standpoint, I morally opposed the war. After seven years of Catholic school, I couldn't imagine killing a human being. However, I drew the line with leftist protests denouncing capitalism, Nixon, Kissinger, and the West in general.

"What do they have to do with the Vietnam War?" I asked Dominic.

"Everything. The U.S. government tells banks what to do. The banks control the International Monetary Fund, and member nations such as France better do what the IMF says or lose funding. Nixon, Kissinger, and Charles de Gaulle are behind it. It's all a right-wing conspiracy."

"Wasn't it Kennedy who got the U.S. involved in Vietnam in the first place? And then Johnson escalated it?"

"They were just following orders from Kissinger and right-wing bankers such as the Rockefellers and ..."

It was useless trying to carry on a conversation about anything other than politics with Dominic. And if it wasn't left leaning, it quickly died a death of redundancy and propaganda. Rather than getting into an argument with him, I usually agreed and politely listened to him pontificate, or avoided him all together. There was one occasion when I talked to him about my case.

"Four years and a day for forging a signature on two traveler's checks?" Dominic whistled. "But they're insured, man!"

"Yeah, I know," I replied, standing next to his double-decker bunk bed.

"So man, when's your trial?" Dominic asked, leaning against the top rack.

"There's not going to be a trial. The consul was here and said they're working a deal to get me out. I should be out of here any day now."

Dominic pirouetted and took a couple of steps over to the row of lockers. Opening the top half of one, he pulled out an addressed and stamped envelope. "Well, since you are a short-timer, would you mind taking a letter out for me when you're released? I don't want to send it through the prison mail."

"Yeah, I can't say I blame you. Who's the letter for?" I asked, leery about my involvement.

"My wife in Paris. She doesn't know where I am. Nobody knows I'm here, other than Interpol, and the French and Spanish police."

While Dominic put the letter away, I agreed to mail it, hoping he'd forget about it. I didn't know what the charge would be, but it would be foolish trying to smuggle a letter out on the day of my release. With my luck, they would throw me back in prison.

Others apparently noticed my association with Dominic, because one day in the exercise yard an inmate who had special privileges like Mundy came up to me and said in broken English, "I know why you here."

"Yeah, forgery," I said, barely looking at him.

"No, no ... you are *comunista.* You here for denouncing Franco."

Suddenly, a spasm of fear sent shock waves through me. "No, I'm not a communist, and I've never denounced Franco," I retorted, looking him in the eye.

At that moment, a commotion sprang up around me with other Spanish prisoners chiming in: "*Comunista, denunciar a Franco, denunciar a Franco, denunciar a Franco!*"

Shaken, I pushed my way through the chanting throng and sat down on the stone bench at the far end of the exercise yard. My hands trembled as I lit a cigarette. I puffed on it nervously until the smoke calmed me enough to walk laps in the yard. By this time, the agitators had dispersed and paid no more attention to me than anybody else. With about 150 men in the yard, there was always a new disturbance going on.

The incident convinced me it was dangerous to associate with Dominic. At the moment, there was a lot of political unrest in Spain. Franco had been in power since the 1930s, and he was getting old. In declining health, he would die before long. For years, he'd suppressed all opposition with an iron fist, and now his adversaries smelled victory and rebelled. There was a new group of young, Spanish, leftist university students in the prison. Arrested in Madrid during May Day riots, they were sent here because of overcrowding in Madrid's prison, and they carried attitudes of wealth, elitism, and moral superiority.

A day or two before the loyalists accused me of denouncing Franco, the young communists surrounded me, wondering if I was pro-Franco. Apparently, they'd heard something about my impending release along with possible back dealings going on between the U.S. ambassador to Spain, Robert Wagner, and military deals with the Franco government. They wanted to know whether I was on their side or Franco's. The communists and loyalists scared me to death, putting me in a quandary. If I denounced Franco, I could be in big trouble. If I stood up for him, no telling what the communists would do. Hemmed in, I began singing the anti-Vietnam War song "Fixin' to Die Rag" by Country Joe and the Fish.

The communists laughed hysterically, and I was able to stop singing. From that moment on, they pretty much let me be. It taught me a lesson. With the tumultuous political situation in Spain, I had to be careful with what I said, and to whom I spoke.

26

Escape

May 16, 1969 — Las Palmas de Gran Canaria, Spain

Every few days, a fight flared in the yard or in my cell, mostly over gambling debts, theft, or insults. Unnerved by these skirmishes and my incidents with the communists and Franco loyalists, I feared for my life. During our first meeting, Martin assured me my release would happen within four days. It was almost ten days later. What was taking so long? I no longer believed him, as I did my fellow prisoners, and wondered if I'd ever be released.

If I had to serve my entire sentence, I'd be twenty-three when I finally got out, provided no one murdered me. If by some miracle I survived long enough to serve my entire sentence, and depending on when my trial occurred, I could be even older, since my sentence wouldn't start until after my trial ended.

The prospect of spending up to six years in prison numbed

my mind. I tried to imagine what the world would be like then. What would I be like when I got out? Twenty-four or twenty-five seemed so old, and far away. By then, my friends would probably have graduated from college and perhaps married with kids of their own. The thought of incarceration for so long seemed unreal. I would lose a huge chunk of my life—almost like having a limb amputated. Would I try to escape if I had to spend that many years in prison? The thought certainly crossed my mind, as probably with any prisoner incarcerated for more than a few days.

Escaping from the upstairs dormitory looked nearly impossible, as it was on the third floor, and the windows had iron bars. In order to escape from there, I'd have to find a way to cut through them and lower myself to ground. Still within the prison compound, I'd need to have a means of climbing the outer wall and lowering myself to the ground outside the prison—without the guards seeing me. Machine-gun-carrying guards kept watch day and night, with searchlights from the guard towers at each corner of the walls. Overall, I pretty much ruled out this method of escape.

My best chance of busting out, I surmised, would be to escape from the long corridor I'd passed through when I first arrived, and where I had met Martin. Although the hallway's windows had bars, they looked like they traveled with the windows when swung open. In addition, there weren't any guards in the area, other than the ones who escorted me in when I first arrived and when Martin came to see me. Once in the corridor, I could possibly open one of the ground-floor windows and escape into the parking lot. I'd still be within the prison walls, but if I could stow away in a vehicle that was leaving, I could then get through the main gate. Once outside the gate, it would only be a matter of getting out of the vehicle unspotted.

Another option would be to steal a car in the parking lot and drive through the gate by pretending to be a prison guard. In order to accomplish this, a uniform would be required, which wasn't impossible, because everyone knew guards could be bribed with cigarettes and candy bars. Some guards were informers, so this would be risky. Rather than arouse suspicion, though, it would be safer to buy items from the inmates. With the large number of fellow prisoners on my floor, somebody likely had a hat, shirt, and jacket resembling what the guards wore. It wouldn't be difficult to fabricate stripes and labels from clothing and sew or glue them on with chewing gum. A belt buckle along with coins could imitate the metal emblem on their hats. I felt this might work and presented my best option.

Attired as a guard, I might be able to gain access to the corridor alone, and from there make my way into the parking lot where I could steal a car. If I couldn't find one with keys in the ignition, I could always hot-wire it. A friend had taught me how to do this in high school when we snuck my parents' car out, and I could do it in less than a minute.

Escaping from the prison solved only half the challenge. Every policeman and Guardia Civil officer would be on the lookout for a blue-eyed teenager with short, blond hair. I'd have no money or passport. They'd check the return ship to Spain and the airport for me. Even if I got to mainland Spain, they would watch for me at border crossings. My best bet, I figured, would be to find a yacht looking for crew members, going anywhere other than mainland Spain.

Satisfied that I had an escape plan gave me hope and a means of dealing with the possibility of receiving a lengthy sentence.

If it came to escaping, I believed I could do it. I would have lots of time to plan and make it happen.

27

Arrangements

May 17, 1969 — Las Palmas de Gran Canaria, Spain

L ooking out a barred window at a hillside and thinking how similar it looked to the semi-desert hills of eastern Washington, I remembered hunting there with my father and brothers. Gomer and Lurch cut short my reminiscing when they unlocked my dormitory cell door during siesta and called my name.

"*Ven,*" Gomer said, as I scurried up to the door. Escorting me down two stories of stone steps, our footsteps echoed throughout the turreted stairwell. *What's going on? Am I being punished for supposedly speaking out against Franco, or am I being released?* As we passed the second-floor dormitory, communist university students jeered me from behind their barred doors. When we got to the main floor, Mundy stood there just outside Herrera's office.

"Señor Gorman, come with me," Mundy said, leading the

way. "The consul is here to see you."

Accompanied by Mundy and Gomer down the corridor, I studied the barricaded windows out of the corner of my eye as a means of escape. Built like French doors, they split in the middle and were locked shut, with a key, evidenced by a large keyhole. *Very good,* I thought. *All I need is a key and I can get into the parking lot.*

We stopped outside the same conference room where I'd met earlier with Junior Consul Martin Alvarez. I could see him conferring with Comandante Herrera through the window next to the closed door.

"We'll have to wait here until they are finished," Mundy said, pulling up the sleeve of his yellow turtleneck sweater to check his wristwatch. "It should be any minute now."

Meanwhile, I used the delay to study the window and its keyhole directly across the corridor. Gomer turned to look down the hallway as the heavy wooden main entrance door creaked open and a guard wheeled in a delivery of bread and sacks of potatoes. While Gomer had turned, the keys on his keyring jingled, catching my attention. It was then I noticed three keys. One was large. I assumed it was for the cellblocks. The middle-size key must be for conference rooms, like the one we were standing outside now, and the smallest key looked like it could be for the windows.

Having an excellent visual memory, I made a mental snapshot of the key intending to draw it when I returned to my cell. Surely, it wouldn't be difficult to make one. Plenty of pilfered cutleries floated around my cell. For a few cigarettes, I could get all the materials I needed, and for a pack of smokes, I could get one of the dormitory's craftsmen to make a key according to my sketch.

The door next to me opened and Comandante Herrera came out. "*Buenos días,* Señor Gorman," he said to me. Herrera then conferred with Mundy.

Mundy looked at me and translated, "Comandante Herrera says not to worry about the inmates the other day that harassed you. They are communist troublemakers and will be dealt with accordingly."

Flabbergasted that he'd heard about it, and not wanting the leftists to seek retribution, I glanced away for a second and then back at Comandante Herrera.

"Uh, thank you, Comandante Herrera," I said, "but it wasn't a big deal, you know. I think they were just joking around."

Mundy translated my response to Herrera, who stiffened, then walked away.

Turning toward me, Wagner said, "He's old guard, and like a lot of officers and guards here, Franco loyalists to the bitter end. They would rather fight another civil war than give in to the communists. Be careful what you say and do here."

All I could muster was a nod. I was frightened of the communists and Franco's loyalists. I wanted nothing of their dispute and potentially looming civil war. All I wanted was to get out of this hellhole. I hoped Martin had positive news for me about my release. As I entered the room, Martin acted cordial and businesslike, but not as upbeat as before.

"Hi Paul, take a seat," he said, rising to shake my hand. "Sorry for the delay, but I've got some good news and bad news. First, for the bad news. The bank still hasn't received the money wire from your folks. Without it, we can't proceed. The State Department has been in contact with them, and they assure us they have wired the money. We've checked with the bank here in Las Palmas and they show no record of having received it. Is there any reason for you to believe your parents haven't wired the money?"

"Uh," I muttered, "I, I don't know."

The truth was, my father could have deliberately withheld the money to make me sweat it out in prison for a while. On the other hand, my mother was kindhearted and stood up for my siblings and me, so I couldn't imagine it. She didn't always stand up for herself, but when it came to her kids, she was like a mama bear with her cubs.

I didn't want to assume the worst, so I just kept shaking my head *no.* In my heart, though, I wondered if my father had abandoned me.

Martin noticed my uncertainty and patted my shoulder. "The State Department advised your parents, if they are thinking of making you sweat it out for a while, this is not the place to do it. I'm sure it's just a foul-up with the wire service. I will check into it again."

My confidence climbed with his reassurance, even though my doubts about my father wiring the money lingered. Martin was a great junior consul. He would make a terrific consul general, coach, or father someday, I thought.

Martin continued. "U.S. Ambassador to Spain Robert Wagner will arrive here the day after tomorrow from Madrid. He's read your letter and would like to meet you. My meeting with Comandante Herrera was to go over the arrangements with him. He is being diplomatic and will host a luncheon along with Consul General Brooks and myself to welcome the ambassador. Afterward, you will be summoned to meet him."

I really didn't know what to expect and really didn't care. Either my father had cast me to the lions or I'd become a pawn in some sort of back-channel deal—not that it really mattered, because it didn't. Freedom counted more than anything. I didn't care how I got out, as long as I got out.

Soon after being returned to my cell, I borrowed a pencil from Dominic and drew a sketch of the key to the barred windows in the main entrance corridor. One way or another, I would get out of this place.

28

Ambassador

May 18—19, 1969 — Las Palmas de Gran Canaria, Spain

Two days later, Mundy, Gomer, and Lurch summoned me to come downstairs for my meeting with the ambassador. I'd never heard of Ambassador Wagner. Unaware of his stature, I really didn't care.

I hadn't showered and shaved. Maybe I'd changed clothes, brushed my teeth, and scrubbed my face, but nothing more. After three days in the city jail, and fifteen days in Prisión de Barranco Seco, I had come to the point where I didn't trust anybody, and didn't value my personal hygiene. I only cared about my self-preservation. Besides, the showers still weren't working, and even if they were, I feared I'd be raped.

Leaving Lurch at the "gates to hell," Mundy and Gomer escorted me down the corridor to meet the ambassador. We passed the meeting room where I'd met twice with Martin. Farther down the hallway toward the main entrance, pools of sunlight shone through the windows on my left. I stole a glance outside at the parking lot. I could see a row of ten to fifteen cars, two Land Rover military jeeps, and the army transport that brought me to the prison. I assumed the cars belonged to the guards and other prison staff. Two of the automobiles were Volkswagen Beetles, which was good because, having owned one, I knew how to drive it. We stopped at the last door before the main entrance.

"This is where you'll meet the ambassador," Mundy said, as Gomer unlocked the door with the key I had suspected would fit.

"Follow me," Mundy said, guiding me inside the room. Ornately decorated with heavy mahogany chairs, marble floors, chandeliers, and a desk on a platform, the chamber resembled a courtroom. The formalness of it overwhelmed and frightened me. Turning, I looked at Mundy for an explanation.

"If you're thinking it looks like a courtroom, that's because it is a courtroom," he said. "You're not here for court, though. This room is for the infirm and those deemed too violent to have their trials in the Municipal Court in Las Palmas. The judge, prosecutor, attorneys, and defendants come here for the trial."

Pulling back the sleeve of his powder-blue turtleneck sweater, Mundy checked his watch. "They'll be here any minute now. Wait here with Gomez."

Crossing an Oriental rug to the other side of the courtroom, Mundy pulled back a curtain, revealing an empty barred prison cell with a table and a wooden chair. He opened the cell door.

"Alright, Señor Gorman, you need to go inside this cell now. You may sit in the chair if you'd like, but if you do, Consul Brooks has instructed me to tell you to rise when the ambassador comes into the courtroom."

Gomer led me into the cell and locked the door behind me. Humiliated, my pulse quickened and vision narrowed. *Why am I in this cell? I'm not a danger to anybody, least of all the ambassador who's supposedly trying to secure my release. This doesn't make sense. What is going on?*

Unclear what would happen, I grew increasingly light-headed and sat down in the chair. My head hanging, I took deep breaths to calm myself. I heard the courtroom door open and voices.

"This way, Ambassador Wagner," said Mundy. "He's in a cell."

Hearing footsteps, I craned to see a group of men standing just outside my cell. From left to right were Martin, Consul Brooks, Ambassador Robert Wagner, I assumed, Comandante Herrera, Mundy, Gomer, and somebody I didn't recognize.

"Hello Paul, on my left here is Ambassador Robert Wagner," said Consul Brooks. "He would like to meet you. Before we do that, we have someone here who is going to set up some lights. Then the ambassador will come inside and meet with you. We'd like to get some photographs of him shaking your hand and talking with you. Do you have any questions?"

"Uh, no," I said, swallowing reflexively and suddenly fighting the urge to pee.

"Okay, go ahead and relax then," Brooks said. "It should only take five or ten minutes before we're ready."

So, I'm the star of the show, but what show? I wondered. *And why?*

My heart thumped in my chest, and my mouth dried. I wormed in the chair, watching the photographer set up lights outside the cell while the bureaucrats mingled together in a group. The photographer turned the lights on and motioned to Consul Brooks that he was ready.

"Okay, Paul," Brooks said, "the guard is going to open the door, and the ambassador is going to come in now to meet you. Remember to rise and shake his hand."

Gomer unlocked the cell door and the ambassador, protected by him, came into the cell. I could hear the *click, click, click* of the photographer's camera as the ambassador entered.

Attired in a light brown suit, white shirt, and brown tie, his slicked-back brown hair glistened as he came up to me. Meanwhile, Gomer hung back about five or six feet.

"Hello, Paul, I'm Ambassador Robert Wagner," he said, extending his hand.

Dizzy with confusion, I shook his hand, but absentmindedly forgot to get up.

"Cut," said Brooks. "Alright let's do it again, but this time get up when you shake his hand, okay, Paul?"

I nodded *yes*, as bubbles of moisture formed on my forehead. The ambassador came into the cell again and up to me as the camera clicked away. Extending his hand, he said, "Hello Paul, I'm Ambassador Robert Wagner. I received your letter and have heard a lot about you from Consul General Brooks."

"Cut," said Consul Brooks. "That was good, Paul, but you forgot to shake his hand."

Embarrassed, my face burned.

"Okay, Paul, let's do it again. Alright, from the top," said Brooks.

Ambassador Wagner interrupted him. "Why don't we just get some shots of him shaking my hand, so we can get done with this deal?"

"Alright, let's do that," said Brooks. "Okay, Paul, on the

count of three, shake his hand. Okay, here we go. One, two, three."

On three, I shook the ambassador's hand. By now, my hand was sweaty.

"Hello Paul, I'm Ambassador Robert Wagner ... and ... oh my, your hand is wet ... Can we just stop now and get some shots of me talking to him?" He glanced at Brooks.

"Makes sense. We already have photos of you coming in, him standing up, and both of you shaking hands," Consul Brooks said. "Okay, Paul, just stand there while the ambassador talks to you and that will do it. Okay, on the count of three, just stand there and look at the ambassador, one, two, three."

Standing there, the ambassador said, "Hi Paul, I am Ambassador Robert Wagner. I received your letter. I have heard a lot about you. We are doing everything we can to get you out of here. Consul Brooks and Junior Consul Martin Alvarez have been in touch with the State Department, and so have I. Unfortunately, the prosecutor is asking the court to rule against our petition to revoke the charges based on Mr. Bhatt's desire to dismiss the charges against you. Have no fear, the U.S. government is very close to signing an extension of military agreements with the Spanish government. We have requested your release as one of the quid pro quo provisions for the agreement. On behalf of the entire State Department, the United States government, and President Nixon, we are doing everything we can to obtain your release. Do you have any questions?"

Unable to talk because of the enormity of the situation, I shook my head *no*, then sat down.

"Okay, Paul, it's been nice meeting you. You'll be out of here any day now," the ambassador said, patting me on the shoulder as the camera clicked away.

The ambassador exited the cell along with Gomer, who then locked me inside. For the next five minutes, the photographer took group photos of the officials outside my cell with me inside. His last shots were some of the ambassador standing outside my cell and me sitting in the background.

"Okay, Paul," Consul Brooks said, "the ambassador has to catch a plane back to Madrid and must go. If you need anything, let Martin know before he leaves."

Back in my barracks-style cell ten minutes later, I tried to make sense of the event. But I couldn't. Word had spread about my meeting somebody important, and Dominic was all over it. Coming up to me while I looked out a window, he said, "What's this I heard about you meeting somebody important today?"

"Who told you?" I asked, still gazing out the window, my mind rehashing my meeting with the ambassador.

"It's all over the place."

"Uh, it is?"

"Yeah, something about an ambassador," Dominic said, moving alongside me. "So who was he?"

"Ambassador Robert Wagner," I said, my voice trailing off. "U.S. Ambassador to Spain."

"*The* Robert Wagner. Former three-time New York City mayor, Robert Wagner. Appointed by President Johnson as ambassador to Spain, *that* Robert Wagner?"

"Uh, I don't know. Is that who the guy is?" I asked, unimpressed, continuing to look outside.

As a political aficionado, Dominic knew exactly who Ambassador Robert Wagner was, and it was killing him why he had come to see me. It wasn't killing me, though. I didn't care. When it came right down to it, I knew little about life and politics. But the broken promises over the past two weeks and today's bizarre events had turned me increasingly into a skeptic. Not that I'd given up hope, because I hadn't, but none of what they'd told me added up.

Despite hating Nixon and the U.S. government, that a man of such stature came to see a lowly proletariat like me impressed Dominic. Continuing his probing, he asked about what my father and mother did for a living. Were they rich? What had I done before coming to Europe? Growing tired of his questions, I turned to Dominic and said, "Maybe he came here to get information on you."

Dominic tensed with paranoia. His eyes darted around the room. "Promise me you won't tell anyone I asked about the ambassador," he whispered. "I am a sought-after man and there are a lot of informers here."

"Don't worry, man," I murmured. "I'm just as baffled about the whole situation as you are." Unconvinced the ambassador hadn't been there today to get information on him, Dominic slinked back to his bunk, jumping up to the upper mattress. Lying on his back, staring at the ceiling, he crossed his arms and emptied his lungs with a loud *whoosh*.

Poor tormented radical, I thought. Confused about life as I was, I was glad I wasn't a druggie, and even more thankful I wasn't a political extremist.

Overall, Ambassador Robert Wagner's visit neither buoyed my spirits, nor diminished them. If anything, his visit left me ambivalent and bewildered. Time would tell if they were telling the truth or if they were lying to me.

29

Blood

May 23–26, 1969 — Las Palmas de Gran Canaria, Spain

Four days passed since the ambassador's visit. I was in the exercise yard when Mundy called my name. I stomped out my cigarette on the tile floor and sprang to my feet. The morning's breakfast churned in stomach. *Is Martin here with news about my release?* I hoped. Bounding my way to the yard's doorway, I grasped the letter that Mundy handed me. "Looks like a bill collector has found you, Señor Gorman," he chortled.

On my way back to the bench where I'd been sitting, I flipped it over. By the handwriting, I knew it came from my mother. My gut tightened with apprehension and emotion. My hands shook as I tore open the envelope and read my mother's words:

Dear Paul,

We received your letter. Your dad and I want you to know we are doing everything we can to get you out of jail. The State Department has been in contact with us, and they have been very helpful. They have taken a keen interest in your case and are working on it diligently, so please don't do anything that would undermine their efforts and jeopardize your release.

My eyes watered, and I wiped them with my tanned bare forearms. I continued reading.

Your father wanted to fly there to help get you out, but the State Department said there was no need for him to come, and it would be better to let them handle it.

My mother's letter said how horribly cold March was. She told me how my fourteen-year-old brother and a friend had hot-wired my old VW Bug and snuck it out after school, while she and my father were still at work. Racing around the neighborhood, they rolled it going around a corner, sideswiping a neighbor's car and then plowed through his yard.

The neighbor called the police, and they said that since they are both under sixteen, they couldn't issue them tickets.

Your father is furious and put your brother on restriction for a month.

I just thought I'd let you know so when you get home, you're not mad because the car is sitting alongside the house and is totaled.

Anyway, we're just glad neither one of them got hurt. The officer said they were lucky to walk away from it with no injuries.

My mother concluded her letter with a piece of advice.

Paul, we all make mistakes in life, and it's how we deal with them that makes the difference in what kind of person we become. It's all part of being human and growing up. You are young and have many years ahead. I hope you will forgive yourself and use this experience as something you can learn and grow from.

Love,
  Mom

During siesta that afternoon, I reread my mother's letter two or three times. In between, I looked at two family photographs I had brought with me, taken several summers earlier in our front yard. Everyone looked so healthy and happy, except my mother, whose eyes had no sparkle. The image of her haunted me, especially combined with reading her letter.

The sound of breaking glass, screams, and shouting echoing up the stairwell abruptly interrupted siesta. Putting the letter and photographs away, I sat on my bed as my right leg bounced up and down involuntarily. Scanning the room, I noticed apprehensive looks on the faces of many cellmates. Ten minutes later, Gomer, Lurch, and Mundy arrived at our dormitory cell door. Mundy called Dominic's name and then mine. "Come with me," Mundy said, when we got to the door.

Clattering our way down the stone bell-tower-like stairway, Mundy told us a communist inmate named Enrique had just received a death sentence for sedition against Franco, and had broken a window slashing his wrists.

"Oh my God, is he okay?" I asked.

"He's lost a lot of blood and is in the infirmary," Mundy said. "Time will tell."

Mundy and the guards escorted Dominic and me down

the hallway to the officer's restroom close to Comandante Herrera's office.

"You've been brought here to clean up a mess," Mundy said, opening the bathroom door to reveal a broken window, glass shards scattered on the floor, and blood everywhere. Blood splattered on the walls ran down the American-style sit toilet, forming large pools on the tile floor.

"There're rags and a bucket in that corner over there," Mundy said, pointing to his right, "and the sink is over there," he nodded. "Don't put the glass in the toilet; put it in the waste can next to the sink. When you're finished, Gomez will return you to your cell upstairs. Any questions?"

Sickened, I glanced at Dominic, who had paled. We knew that prison officials had given us this task as a message to other communists in the prison, to not mess with Franco and his federalists. We bowed our heads in fear.

Fighting the urge to vomit, for the next hour Dominic and I mopped the metallic-smelling, coagulating blood. Neither one of us said a word. On hands and knees, we swirled our rags until they were bright red and then wrung them out in the bucket. Rinse and repeat, rinse and repeat.

The blood reminded me of when I was in second grade. As I stood on a chair drying dishes, the chair slid out from under me. When I fell, a fork stabbed me in the chest. My white tee-shirt turned scarlet with blood streaming onto the floor. I landed on my back and looked at the fork protruding from my chest in horror. Too frozen with fright to do anything about it, I shrieked in pain and terror. I panicked and scrambled to my feet.

My mother reached for me, and I started racing around the kitchen hysterically with the fork sticking out of me. She screamed for me to stop, but I kept running and wailing as blood kept spewing out of my chest, leaving crimson puddles on the floor. I could smell it and feel its slipperiness with my bare feet on the linoleum floor. All of the commotion caused my father to rush to the kitchen. With one quick motion, he grabbed me and pulled the fork from my chest. More blood gushed out. I screeched in terror and agony.

My father grabbed a dish towel, wetted it, and used it as a cold compress to stop the bleeding. Within minutes, my parents rushed me to the doctor for stitches. When I got home, I ate ice cream while I watched my mother mop up the dried blood with a wet rag, just as Dominic and I were doing now.

We scrubbed as fast as we could, trying to outrace coagulation setting in, which would be harder to remove. When the water in the bucket was so bloody that our rags remained red, we emptied it into the toilet and filled it with fresh water from the sink. Gradually we made progress. When we finished, the bathroom sparkled like new and smelled like fresh pine trees from the bottle of disinfectant we used afterward.

Soaked with sweat and blood, I was mentally and physically exhausted from cleaning up the mess, as Gomer and Lurch led us back to our cell. After changing my bloodstained clothes and rinsing them out, I settled onto my bed. Traumatized, I stared blankly at the cracks in the avocado-green ceiling. Sadistic inmates gathered around my bunk, and I shooed them away.

Following siesta, the exercise yard was abuzz with hushed conversations. The communists huddled together, whispering and eyeing me out of the corner of their eyes. They'd gotten the message that their fate could be exactly like Enrique's and had better watch what they said and did lest they receive the same treatment as him.

Gradually, the yard settled down, and by suppertime, things had returned to normal. It was Friday, so maybe that had something to do with it, which meant it was fish day. Generally, it was fish, Veracruz style over Arborio rice, or fish soup with French bread. It was my favorite dinner of the week, followed by Sunday's, when we usually ate beef or lamb stew with potatoes. Other times, it was meatloaf. Starved for protein, I savored those dinners more than the usual meal of garbanzo beans and potato soup.

Another day dragged by and I worried that Martin, Consul Brooks, and Ambassador Wagner had misled me. Much of my hope had dwindled. *What is taking so long? It's been nineteen days since my arrival here at Prisión de Barranco Seco, and five days since my meeting with the ambassador. They made it sound like my release was imminent. I can't believe they can't find the money. Then again, maybe the reason I'm still here is that the judge turned down my release.*

The waiting and uncertainty drove me crazy. I needed somebody to talk with other than Dominic, who I still avoided as much as possible. The only other person who spoke English was Abdul. While I liked him, there was definitely a cultural divide between us. He had grown up underprivileged and poor, and got no support from the Senegalese government.

Abdul could not relate to my situation. His eyes would go blank when I talked about money supposedly wired for me, consuls, petitioning the judge for my release, and my meeting with the ambassador. Even though we spoke the same tongue, he did not understand the language. I felt sorry for him and his Senegalese friends in the prison. Perhaps the court had turned down my petition, but he and his cadres never received representation to begin with.

To my astonishment, the following day a judge released Abdul and the rest of the Senegalese under the provision that they leave the Canaries and Spain within two weeks or face ten years in jail. I envied them and wished them good luck when they were released. Their departure left Nazi war criminal Kurt Mueller, Dominic, some of the communist university students, and me as the only English-speaking inmates—excluding Mundy, who was in an unapproachable league of his own. Extradited almost a week earlier, the Canadian jewel thieves Moe and Curly would face trial in England. I definitely didn't want to talk to Mueller, the communist students, nor be linked to Dominic any more than I already was.

Although I was a lonely, frightened, and despondent teenager, I didn't dare let the other prisoners see me cry. That would be a sign of weakness. I could end up being like the young inmate Muller smacked around. So I held in my emotions, kept to myself, and waited.

Since it was Sunday, it was movie night after supper. Ironically, they were showing the World War II prisoner of war escape story, *The Bridge on the River Kwai*. During high school, I saw the movie in a history class and was familiar with it. But from the perspective of being an inmate, it gave me an entirely new appreciation of the film. Granted, my conditions and treatment were nowhere near as bad as the soldiers in the movie, and for that, I was thankful. Notwithstanding, losing freedom is universal and something impossible to feel until it is lost.

The movie got me contemplating escape again. There was no point staying here. All my "friends," except Dominic, were gone and nothing seemed to be happening with my case. Thinking about it was better than dwelling on the prospects of spending four to six years in prison, which I increasingly believed would be the case.

30

Brits

May 26–28, 1969 — Las Palmas de Gran Canaria, Spain

The day after Abdul and his fellow countrymen left, several new prisoners arrived in the exercise yard. I overheard them speaking English with Mundy as he showed them around, explaining the rules. Mundy left, and it wasn't long before I made my way over to introduce myself. To my astonishment, one inmate was Tony, the disc jockey at El Cofre.

At first, I didn't recognize him with his shaved head. He resembled a featherless baby bird. Devoid of his thick sculpted blond hair, gone were his jet-set playboy looks. Coupled with his chic clothing and trim build, he always had beautiful Scandinavian girls hanging on him. I envied his style.

Today Tony wore black velvet stovepipe legged pants, a teal-colored, form-fitting shirt, a short-waisted black cashmere cardigan sweater, and black loafers. His eyes were full of fear, darting around as a group of men eyed him. *Man, I sure am glad I'm not dressed like that in here,* I thought. With his back to the bench and shoulders hunkered, he sat on the floor next to his friend. For once, I did not envy his hip clothing.

At El Cofre he would give me a tepid hello, but now that we were on the same playground, he finally talked to me. "Uh, hi Tony, remember me, man?" I said, standing above him.

Tony looked up and squinted. "El Cofre right?"

"Yeah, man, that's right."

"I was wondering what happened to you," Tony said, cracking a slender smile. "So how long have you been in this joint?"

"Three weeks now, not including the three days I spent in the city jail."

Tony scooted on the tiled floor out of the sunlight. "Wow, what're you in for?" he asked, furrowing his forehead in disbelief.

I told Tony about my crime, then asked him what he'd done. "I overextended my visa and will be here until I'm deported back to England ... Same with my mate Mark here." He pointed with a thumb toward his friend, then pulled out a pack of cigarettes and held it open.

"Oh, how long will that take?" I asked, lighting Tony's cigarette then taking one for myself.

"The British Consulate Service is working on it," Tony said, with his cigarette dangling from his lips. "Our consul says Mark and I should be free to leave in a day or two—soon as he gets us temporary visas."

"Well, I hope so, man," I said, before filling them in on all the broken promises and delays I'd gone through and how frustrating it'd been.

"Well, keep the faith man," Tony said with a scowl, as he

surveyed the busy yard. "This place looks like a real shit hole. I'm sure the U.S. is doing everything they can to get you out of here—the same with my government. Spain is trying to open up to the West. They want tourism and increased trade in Europe. The last thing they want is bad publicity."

I thanked Tony for his reassurance and wished him well just as we were summoned for roll call, followed by dinner.

Tony and fellow Englishman Mark were gone the next day, having received their temporary visas from their consulate.

If only I were British, I'd probably be out of here by now, I thought.

The optimism Tony gave me the previous day disappeared overnight. After more than three weeks, I was still rotting in Prisión de Barranco Seco, feeling more alone than ever as another acquaintance left. Meanwhile, I waited and hoped for my release. The silence was killing me. Increasingly, I became depressed and forlorn. Other than Martin, Brooks, and the ambassador, I hadn't had any other visitors. Terry and Judy knew about my incarceration, and probably John did, too. It bothered me they hadn't come to visit. Hurt and feeling forsaken, I tried getting my mind off of it by reading.

Four or five days earlier, Dominic gave me a book he'd picked out from the prison library, entitled, *The 38th Floor.* Written by Clifford Irving, it was a fictitious story about a black American diplomat who, because of an assassination, becomes Secretary General of the United Nations while the world teeters on the brink of nuclear war between the U.S. and China. Reading the book, I could see why Dominic recommended it. Vicariously, he probably saw himself as the protagonist. As for me, I found the story convoluted.

The book provided a pleasant distraction, though, temporarily enabling me to forget about my imprisonment. Intriguing as the book was, it was also interesting to learn that author expat Clifford Irving lived on Ibiza, a Balearic island in the Mediterranean. Because the Balearic Islands were part of Spain, his living there made the book personal for me.

31

Depression

May 28–30, 1969 — Las Palmas de Gran Canaria, Spain

Days and hours evaporated into a mist. I was in a fog—the fog of time. Time had no beginning, no end, no meaning. *Time cannot be measured, because it doesn't exist,* I reasoned. *I now understand eternity. I understand God, but don't know if I will go to heaven because of the bad things I've done, or if there even is a heaven and hell,* I asked God to forgive me. Clawing my way out of a slippery metaphysical and muddy pit filled with water, I regained my grasp of reality.

I spent my time in the exercise yard alone, watching the Nazi pummel the Spaniard, communists in the shadows whispering conspiracy theories, creepy men stalking the latrine, while I chain-smoked cigarettes and paced back and forth like the albino ape in the Barcelona Zoo. *How long could I hold out before I committed suicide? Could I last a year? Two years? Three years? Four years?* Thinking about it made me even more depressed.

To counter my declining mental state, I focused my thoughts on escape, my family, sex, and food. I imagined eating turkey dinner with all the trimmings and pumpkin pie with whipped cream for dessert. A grilled hamburger, along with French fries and a milkshake, was another one of my fantasies. Eventually, my daydreams ended, dropping me back into reality. It was frustrating, but at least it was better than thinking about killing myself.

During this period, I wrote another letter to my mother, telling her about my meeting with the ambassador and the bank having no record of receiving the money. I asked whether they'd really sent it. Once again, I coded my letter to avoid the censors.

Again, I spent hours studying the two family photographs, wishing I could go back in time and be there with them. Taken in the summer outdoors in our front yard, the grass was so green, and the rhododendrons were blooming. Jerry, our collie, smiled too, and my twelve-year-old sister had a dream-like gaze and tilt to her head.

My escape plans hadn't progressed past the planning or pipe-dream stage. The biggest problem was there weren't enough English-speaking prisoners for me to collaborate with, and even if there were, I didn't trust anybody.

Occasionally, I ran into Mundy in the exercise yard buying a chocolate bar or tea at the commissary and he would ask how I was doing, why I didn't bathe and shave, and how my case was going. I found him friendly enough, but I didn't fully trust him. Who is imprisoned for not paying alimony to an ex-wife? Perhaps he didn't pay because he murdered her. About the only people I trusted were the Senegalese prisoners.

Gradually, as weeks go by, you develop a routine as a means

of psychological and physical survival. You quickly learn who the terrible actors are and try your best to avoid conflict with them. Since the prison was crowded, it was difficult, but other than tattoo man, I'd had no altercations or threats. Sometimes inmates would want to borrow my comb and I'd let them. Afterward, I'd examine it for lice, even though I almost never used it. Other times they wanted to use some of my Old Spice After Shave and I'd loan it, not quite understanding for whom they were trying to smell good. Whatever the case, it was harmless and better than causing an argument or fight.

Being the only American in the prison made me somewhat of a curiosity. As one of the youngest, if not the youngest, I sensed some inmates would stick up for me—although I didn't want to test my theory. Becoming a rape victim worried me. Because of this, I never fully slept. Sometimes I could tell if a night-watch inmate stopped at my bed. Several instances when this happened, I lay perfectly still, listening, ready to fight back. Eventually, the person would continue walking.

Nights when I had the responsibility of being on night-watch duty petrified me. As I walked between the beds, I perceived some inmates were awake and observing me. I avoided making eye contact and wondered what I'd do if a disturbance occurred. Would I be brave enough to yell for the guards? If I did, surely I'd face retribution. Fortunately, I never had to make that decision.

There were two restrooms in the prison available to me, the one in my cell, and the one opposite the commissary in the exercise yard. The one in the exercise yard was filthy, infested with flies, and rarely sanitized.

Inmates were assigned once a day the wretched task of swabbing out the latrine in my dormitory cell with disinfectant.

In the weeks I'd been in the prison, I only had to do it once so far, and it was a dirty and disgusting job.

On that unlucky day, Mundy appeared at my cell room, called my name and handed me a mop. Holding my breath, I catstepped my way into a filthy stall. Tiptoeing across the porcelain slab to the hole in the floor, I stepped up onto the two raised foot pedestals. Then I used the mop to wipe excrement and soiled scraps of newspaper toward the hole in the floor. Finally, I pulled down on the handle of a chain dangling from a tank mounted on the wall six or seven feet above me. Water gushed down an open-ended pipe, flooding the area, as I swabbed furiously with bleach to sanitize it and rinse everything down. One stall done, two more to go.

The best time to use the dormitory's latrine was in the morning when it was clean. Of course, this was not always an option, and you just had to hold your breath and tiptoe between the feces to relieve yourself as quickly as possible. You also didn't want to linger because sometimes inmates would follow you in and spy on you while they masturbated.

There was one occasion when I went into the latrine to clean up and interrupted an inmate bathing in the urinal. He'd used his underwear to plug it up with water from the sinks that emptied into it. Disgusted by how unsanitary his bath was, I left and came back later to do my business.

Mornings, I'd wake up early and tug my pants on under the blanket. Then I'd trit-trot barefoot on the cold stone floor to the toilet. My routine was the same: pee, brush my teeth, wash my face, rinse off my feet. Sometimes there would be a bar of soap on the sink. Most mornings there wasn't.

Having completed my bathroom business, I'd return to bed and doze fully clothed until roll call.

By now, I'd given up hope of a release. I felt betrayed, lied to. But why? As hard as I racked my brain around this question, I couldn't solve it. It was a riddle that couldn't be unraveled. With this in mind, I resigned myself to a sentence of six years—two years awaiting my trial, and then a four-year sentence. I knew I'd never last that long. I'd either escape, kill myself, or be murdered. Like an approaching plague, a sense of impending doom overcame me. The darkening gloom pressed in on me. It was omnipresent. As hard as I tried shaking it, I couldn't. The best I could do was distract myself, but it was always there in the background, in the shadows, lurking, ready to torment me, ready to flare up at any moment.

32

Freedom

May 30, 1969 — Las Palmas de Gran Canaria, Spain

May 30, 1969, began like any other day. Latrine, roll call, breakfast, exercise yard, followed by lunch, and then we were returned to our cells for siesta. Not long after settling on my bunk, Gomer and Lurch were at our cell door calling my name: "Señor Gorman, el Señor Gorman, *venga aquí.*"

At this stage, I knew enough Spanish to understand their summons and got up from my bunk, ending my catnapping. I wasn't expecting visitors. *What have I done now?* I worried. *Am I in trouble for my coded letter to Mom? Did somebody see the key drawing? Am I being punished for talking to Dominic?*

As I arrived at the cell door, Gomer informed me to get my belongings within fifteen minutes for my release. I staggered back to my bunk, delirious with joy and confusion. Cellmates came up to me, patting me on the back, shaking my hand. Some sneered with jealousy, and others were apathetic. But most were happy about my release, calling out to me to do favors for them on the outside, which I couldn't possibly do even if I remembered. In a matter of minutes, I finished packing my French rucksack and went to say goodbye to Dominic. He handed me his letter. "Please mail this to my wife," he said, in a hushed voice.

I really didn't want to take it, but he forced it on me. Not wanting to create a commotion the guards might see, I stuffed the letter under my shirt. No sooner had I finished than Gomer called my name again. "Señor Gorman, Señor Gorman, *debe venir ahora.*"

I said goodbye with a brother's handshake to Dominic, then wandered in a daze to the cell door that Gomer and Lurch held open for me. They led me downstairs to Comandante Herrera's office. The young communists jeered me along the way. Mundy greeted me. "Ah, Señor Gorman, it is your lucky day," he said, gesturing for me to take a seat. "You are being released to the custody of Junior Consul Martin Alvarez. But first we need to do an inventory of your possessions held here and have you sign this release acknowledging you received them."

Gomer opened a locker and pulled out a basket with my name on it. He emptied the contents onto a table. Mundy then checked the items, including my passport, off a list and asked me to sign it.

"Stand at attention," Mundy ordered, translating for Gomer, who patted down my legs, arms, and finally torso. I sucked in my already emaciated belly, creating even more of a cavity. I held my breath as his hands skimmed over the letter. My heart pounded so hard I thought I would die, or he would hear or feel it. Luckily, he did not, and I relaxed. Relieved, I began breathing again. No telling what could have happened to me, although there's a good chance it would have jeopardized my release and possibly added to my sentence.

Finally, I was led to Herrera's desk, where he signed my release and then, snapping his watch wristband, said, "Señor Gorman, *todos los cargos en su contra han sido desestimados por la presente están siendo liberados de prisión.*" Translating it back to me, Mundy said, "Señor Gorman, all charges against you are dismissed. You are hereby released from prison."

Handed over to Martin's custody with the stipulation he would see that I paid back Mr. Bhatt the hundred dollars I owed him, I walked out of the prison with him.

Before Martin dropped me off at Parque Santa Catalina, he took me to lunch. Having not eaten vegetables for almost a month, I craved a salad and ordered one. While eating, Martin pulled out several black-and-white photographs. One was of me sitting in the cell, head hanging low, looking forlorn, and the ambassador standing alongside with his hand on my shoulder. "We never had to use these," was all Martin said, tucking them back into his leather satchel.

Still trying to make sense of the ambassador's visit and the U.S. government's involvement in my case, I could only muster a nod. As much as I liked Martin, my trust in him had diminished.

On our drive from the restaurant to Parque Santa Catalina, he handed me a letter from my mother and the two hundred dollars my parents had wired.

"Thank you, Martin, for everything you've done for me," I said.

"I'm sorry it took so long, but the money was sitting there in the bank all this time, under my name."

"No kidding?"

"Yes, we all assumed it would be under your name. Nobody ever thought to check if it was under my name. You could've been released weeks ago if we had known."

Pulling to a stop at Parque Santa Catalina, Martin cleared his throat and impatiently tapped his fingers on the steering wheel.

"Well, it doesn't matter now," I said, not fully believing him. "I'm free, and for that I will always be grateful."

Martin gave me a half grin. It was the same uneasy smile Danny gave me when he said goodbye before boarding the ferry to Morocco.

Martin extended his hand, and I shook it. He wished me well before driving away.

33

Goodbye

May 30–June 1, 1969 — Las Palmas de Gran Canaria, Spain

L

ate in the afternoon of my release, I deposited Dominic's letter at the post office and then went to Mr. Bhatt's shop.

"Thank you, Mr. Bhatt, for dropping the charges," I said, handing him a hundred dollars in the backroom of his shop. "Here's the money I owe you."

Mr. Bhatt shook my hand and smiled. "You are most welcome. I could tell you were a good boy who made a mistake, and not someone who there is no chance for learning from their errors. I hope this will be a good lesson for you in the future."

"It will, Mr. Bhatt. I will never forget it and your kindness." Mr. Bhatt bowed to me. Saying goodbye to him, I waved at his smiling kids playing outside as I exited his shop through a side door.

My next stop was to pay Mama Gallenda the money I owed her. When she saw me, she stopped washing dishes, dried her hands, and smiled, giving me a huge hug.

"Pablo, I have been worried about you. The police were here weeks ago asking questions about you. They said you were in prison. Is that true?"

"*Sí*, Mama Gallenda, I did something wrong and am sorry for that. I am free now and am here to pay the money I owe you ... I'd also like to see if I can rent a room for a few days...I'll pay you in advance."

"Your old bed is rented, but I have a single room available. It costs more, fifty pesetas a night. Do you want to see it?"

"*Sí*, I'd like to see it."

I ended up renting the room. With no support in the middle, the bed was uncomfortable, but the room had its own bathroom and shower—a definite plus. That evening I took a long hot shower, washing away almost two months of dirt, grime, and body oils, and, to my satisfaction, little hair. It felt good to be clean again.

The next day, I washed my clothes at a laundromat, bought a ferry ticket to Algeciras, Spain, and then stopped by to see Terry. Packing to return to London, he'd purchased a sailboat, and along with Judy, intended to sail it there. Back in London teaching until the school year ended, she planned to fly to the Canaries the day after tomorrow to assist him. I asked Terry about Danny, and he said, "Danny's in London now, staying at my flat. He bought five kilos of hash in Morocco and shipped it there. I'll be taking his bag along with us and will meet him there."

"How about his nose surgery? Did he have it yet?"

"No," said Terry, tossing toiletries into a cosmetic bag.

"He's on the waiting list. They're saying it'll be about nine months. In the meantime, he will stay with Judy and me. You're welcome to come visit us if you'd like. I told Danny about your arrest and he's concerned about you. I know he'd like to see you."

"Uh, I want to go home, you know, but say hi to Danny for me, will you?"

"I will," Terry replied, as he went back to his packing.

I left Terry's feeling he cared little about my prison experience. It also still bothered me that he and Judy hadn't come to visit me at the prison.

On the way back to my pension, I ran into by black Cuban friend, Miguel, who greeted me with a twinkled-toed pirouette, followed by a royal bow. He'd heard from John about my imprisonment. Miguel told me that John had left for Barcelona. It made me wonder if John had thought I might nark on him for introducing Kenneth the drug dealer to me.

Telling Miguel I'd be leaving the day after tomorrow, he hugged me. "Goodbye, my sweet darling boy," he said, batting his eyelids. "El Cofre will be a mortuary without you." Then he performed a little Greek tragedy dance in my honor, shedding crocodile tears and writhing in anguish before fluttering off down a nearly empty street, flapping his arms like a butterfly. I chuckled and thought, *I'm gonna miss this place, not for what it is, but for what it was.* It just wasn't the same without Danny and John, and now Terry and Judy were leaving, too. Overcome with emotion, I buried my head in my hands, fighting to keep my emotions in check.

Seeing me from a nearby bench, Abdul came up. "Why are you sad? You are a free man now?"

"Abdul, how are you?" I said, collecting myself. "It's good

to see you, man."

"It's good to see you too, man." Abdul smiled broadly, exposing ivory-white teeth while giving me a brotherly handshake. "When did you get out?"

Returning Abdul's smile, I replied, "Yesterday. I'm leaving on the ship to Algeciras tomorrow."

"So am I, man," he said, "and so are my Senegalese mates."

"Wow, what a nice coincidence, man. Well, I'll see you then," I grinned. "Where are you staying?"

Abdul pointed eastward. "We're sleeping on the beach, man, near the port. I was just going to buy some food for our last meal here. Do you want to join us, man?"

Late that afternoon, after helping Abdul buy fresh vegetables, potatoes, rice, tomatoes, spices, and fresh tuna, he cooked up an enormous pot, combining all the ingredients. The group of us sat around the campfire, eating the mixture with our bare hands. It was delicious and filling, and an excellent bonding experience.

The morning I left, I said goodbye to Mama Gallenda and thanked her. She gave me a big hug and kiss on my cheek. "Go home to your mama now."

"I will, Mama Gallenda," I assured her. "Thank you again."

I waved at her and her children, then closed the door behind me. Half an hour later, I was in the port boarding the ship to Algeciras. Rather than a five-night cruise like the one from Barcelona, this was a two-night cruise. From there, my plan was to hitchhike to Barcelona, spend the night, then take a train the following day across the border into France.

34

Reflections

June 1–3, 1969 — Atlantic Ocean to Mediterranean Sea

On my way to mainland Spain aboard the ship, I stayed mostly to myself. Now and then, I'd chat with Abdul and his friends. On the morning of the third day, we docked in Cádiz for six hours to unload cargo. I spent the port call wandering around town and listening to songs in a record shop. It'd been about a month since I'd heard music and it soothed my soul. At two p.m., we set sail for Algeciras.

It was seven p.m. when we arrived and went ashore. Across the bay, we could see Gibraltar basking in the golden rays of the setting sun. Since it was June 3, the sun would not set until eight thirty, which meant there was still daylight to hitchhike toward Barcelona. The main problem was that Abdul and his six fellow countrymen had the same thought. I couldn't imagine anybody stopping for a collection of seven black men and one white guy. It's not that I found Spaniards to be racist, other than the police; there just wasn't room for so many passengers in their small cars.

Two hours later, we called it quits and returned to the port, where we could sleep on the beach. Still full from the lunch we had eaten on the ship and food we stuffed into our pockets, we didn't need to cook anything. We just huddled around our campfire, trying to stay warm. Eventually, I crawled into my sleeping bag and fell asleep.

Upon awakening, the sun had risen, and the campsite was empty. Apparently, Abdul and his friends had already left to try hitchhiking. I resolved before falling asleep the night before to catch a bus to Almería. That way, I'd be able to leapfrog the logjam of Abdul's group.

As the bus raced its way along the rocky coastline, I held my breath and grasped a handle on the back of the seat in front of me. Looking several hundred feet down at the ocean ripped apart on jagged rocks, I prayed. The bus drove excessively fast for my comfort. Occasionally, at wide spots, I'd see clusters and sometimes stragglers of Abdul's band hitchhiking or walking along the road. I pitied them. But there was no point in joining their party, and nothing I could do to help. I barely had enough money to get myself to Amsterdam, where I hoped to buy a charter flight back to the States.

In various cities, I'd seen tickets for sale advertised on bulletin boards in youth hostels. Many of the tickets were charter flights going to and from Amsterdam. The Dutchman named Dirk, who had sold me his charter flight ticket to Amsterdam owed me a favor for being unable to use his ticket. I still had the name and address of his father and decided to see if he could help me.

With this in mind, once I got to mainland Spain, I planned

to hitchhike to Amsterdam. With a little luck, I'd be home within a week. But I wouldn't relax until I got out of Spain. The government could change their mind at any moment.

As the bus raced on toward Almería, I continued to reflect on my meeting with the ambassador. *Was my release a bargaining chip between the U.S. government and Spain over a military contract?* I began to believe it was. *Why else would the ambassador to Spain do a photo op with me? Things at that level happen for a reason.*

The more delays that occurred, the more Martin's story sounded fishy. His lies rumbled through my head: "The money's been wired by your folks. You should be released within several days."

"We're still waiting for the money."

"The State Department checked with your parents and according to them the money was wired."

"As soon as it's here, you will be released."

"We checked with the bank and they have no record of receiving it."

"The U.S. ambassador to Spain is very interested in your case and wants to meet you."

"It's very important when you meet the ambassador to shake his hand when he greets you, and don't smile."

I concluded that I had been a political pawn foisted by the State Department as propaganda against the Franco regime in order to get the arms deal they wanted. I could see the headline: "American teenager faces up to six years in prison in Franco's Spain for cashing a hundred dollars' worth of stolen traveler's checks."

Within that context, the fact it took almost four weeks for me to be released made perfect sense. All they had to do was make up a story about being unable to find the money until they got what they wanted. Of course, this was speculation on my part. However, for the bank not to be able to find the money for almost a month stretches credibility. All they needed to do was to trace the money order. Likewise, the State Department could have called my parents and asked them to whom they sent it. But they never did.

35

Paranoid

June 4–6, 1969 — Almeria, Spain to Perpignan, France

The bus pulled into Almeria, dropping me off in the quiet, quaint town center. It was dusk. For ten or fifteen minutes, I walked around town, stretching my legs, looking for a pension to spend the night. Because they usually advertised their rates outside, it wasn't hard to find one within my budget—which was only fifty pesetas.

At that time in Spain, you had to fill out a registration card stating your name, address, nationality, and passport number. This card went directly to the local police, where they would check it against lists of people wanted by the police or Interpol. This was the case in Las Palmas where I'd rented the car for Rolf. When he didn't return it, the next day, police barged into my room. *It could happen here too*, I fretted.

Remembering that experience, I lay in my bed, staring at the dark box beam ceiling, counting the bolt heads. At any moment,

I expected police, having gone through hotel registration cards, to barge into my room and arrest me. Paranoia is what nearly four weeks in a Spanish prison will do to you. Desperate to get out of Spain, it took me several hours to fall asleep. And then I awakened whenever a car pulled up outside, or a siren approached, not falling back to sleep again until the sounds subsided.

I caught a morning bus to Barcelona. Apprehensive that somebody at the youth hostel might report me to the police for the meal I'd skipped out on in February, I rented a pension just to be safe.

First thing in the morning, I purchased a train ticket to Perpignan, France, leaving in two hours. I went to the central market off La Rambla and bought fruit, cheese, salami, and a baguette for my breakfast. Shopping done, I went to Plaça Reial to eat, hang out, and wait for my train. Sitting on the stone bench encircling the fountain, I ate breakfast, feeding crumbs from the baguette to a flock of head-bobbing pigeons.

It was then I noticed a stout, bald-headed man with a brown beard. Wearing a tattered army coat, he entered the courtyard from La Rambla. As he got closer, I recognized him. It was John. He heard my voice as I called out to him and strutted over to me, guitar slung over his back.

"So, I see they let you out," he said. "We heard they were going to give you four years and a day."

"Who'd you hear that from?" I asked.

"Tony, the DJ at El Cofre."

"Tony, oh yeah that's right he was in there for a day or two."

"So, how'd you get out?" John asked, lighting a cigarette and offering me one.

I explained what had gone down as John lit my smoke.

"Then it must have been some sort of a deal," John said. "Franco's been getting a lot of bad press lately for his fascist policies. The last thing he needs is for word to get out about some American teenager getting four years for forging stolen traveler's checks."

"Yeah, man, that wouldn't look good," I agreed, checking my watch. "Anyway, Miguel told me you were here."

"Yeah, I broke up with Kate and didn't know if you said anything to the police about me ..."

"I didn't say a thing, man. You've got nothing to worry about in the Canaries."

"Well, now that Kate and I are history, there's not much point in going back to Las Palmas," John said, taking a final drag from his cigarette. "Besides, tourist season is finished there. I can make more money playing here." For a moment, he looked wistful, as if he was trying to convince himself.

We talked for several minutes, and then John said he needed to play a gig at the market. Before he left, I asked him to play "Tambourine Man" one more time for me, and he did. As John poured his guts out, my eyes panned around the wonderful placa, at the scattering of palm trees, the exquisite feminine fountain and countless mysterious archways that beckoned.

My mind entered them one at a time. Each one contained a memory—real life synapses, not fake eight millimeter family films, but a fragment, a sliver in time, an etching, like graffiti carved into the Las Palmas city jail, a testimony of *I was here*. In my mind, the archways held a time record of human souls, human interactions, human dreams. They were a spiritual archive for anyone having passed through this magical placa.

After John finished singing, we exchanged brotherly hand-shakes and hugs. Less than an hour later, I boarded my train for Perpignan. As the train neared the French border, it slowed to a stop. My stomach knotted, and my tongue thickened like the cow's tongue Grandma Gronzy served me. Spanish border police boarded the train, making the rounds to inspect passports. I sweated. Afraid my release from prison had been a nasty trick, I believed they were going to re-arrest me.

Packing machine guns, a clean-shaven officer and one with a mustache stopped at my seat. "*Pasaporte*," the mustached one ordered.

I handed him my passport and took several deep breaths, hoping they wouldn't notice the moisture on my forehead.

"Ah, Americano," the mustached officer said, looking at my passport and then at me. *Does he know who I am?* I fretted. The same guard studied me, inspected my passport, then me again.

"*Destino?*"

"Uh, uh, Amsterdam," I said, immediately regretting it because it was common knowledge Amsterdam was the drug capital of Europe.

The mustached guard glanced at the clean-shaven officer, who grabbed my passport and flipped through it. I prayed he wouldn't notice I had over extended my visa. My stomach growled. The mustached officer heard it and glanced at me. I patted my belly. "Salami," I said.

After what seemed like an hour, the clean-shaven officer turned to me. "*Propósito de viaje?*"

"Huh?" I responded, not understanding the question. The same officer simplified his question.

"*Propósito?*"

"*No comprendo*," I said, as my mind swirled with confusion. He then asked, "*Turista?*"

"*Sí, sí, turista*," I replied, bobbing my head like the pigeons in Plaça Reial.

The clean-shaven guard flashed me a wry grin, then handed me my passport before moving on to another passenger. Within minutes, they left the train. As we started moving again, the knot in my stomach loosened, and the tightness in my chest eased. Although I was relieved, I was going to miss Spain; I loved the culture, the people I'd met, the architecture, and the weather in the Canaries. If I hadn't been arrested, I would have enjoyed staying longer.

In less than five minutes, French border guards entered, asking to see our passports. I wasn't nervous. The train had just entered France. I was safe.

36

Hitchhiking

June 6–8, 1969 — Perpignan, France, to Amsterdam

L ess than half an hour after getting off the train in Perpignan, France, I caught a ride from a Frenchman in his early thirties who was on his way home to Cannes. He proudly told me about the city's film festival. Never having heard of it, I was intrigued.

Outside of Hollywood, I had little knowledge of foreign films other than David Lean's films, *Bridge on the River Kwai, Doctor Zhivago,* and *Lawrence of Arabia,* along with Hitchcock, James Bond, and Peter Sellers' movies. Of course, they were all British films, financed by American Studios. Having never seen a French film, I only knew of Brigitte Bardot. The Frenchman's arms waved and his face turned into a rubbery eddy of expressions as told me all about French cinema.

As he let me off in Avignon, my head churned with French film titles and actors' names I could hardly pronounce, let alone remember. His passion and knowledge of cinema made an impression on me I've never forgotten. It wouldn't be until my early twenties that I would see my first French film, and then many other foreign films. Years after my ride with the Frenchman, I screened a trailer at the Cannes Film Festival's Marché du Film for a feature film I co-wrote and produced called *The Last Mirage.* The market is for film producers and buyers.

Before I left Barcelona, I vowed to avoid hitchhiking as much as possible in France, because it had been so difficult getting rides from Paris to Barcelona in February. Plotting my course on a Michelin map, I chose a route up through Switzerland and Germany, then to the Netherlands.

The Frenchman dropped me off several kilometers from the road I needed to take, requiring me to walk there. It wasn't a big deal, because it was early June and a beautiful day in Provence. Besides, it felt good to stretch my legs after the train and car ride.

Lavender and flower blossoms filled the air with a bouquet of fragrance, stimulating my libido. Apparently, it had the same effect on a brunette French housewife who stood in the upstairs window of her stone-and-stucco farm chalet, exposing her breasts. She whistled and motioned for me to come join her. Horny as I was, sex terrified me—not to mention what her husband might do if he caught me. As she waved, I kept walking, listening to her pleas fade away.

Shortly after reaching the correct road, I thumbed a ride from two Swiss guys in their mid-twenties heading home to Geneva after vacationing in St. Tropez. As we wound through the French countryside in their Porsche Cabriolet, the balmy sweet air refreshed my soul like sheets hanging out to dry.

Sitting in the cramped back seat, I could barely hear them over the roar of the engine, so we didn't talk much.

Up through the villages of Orange, Montélimar, and Valence, we sped through the Rhône River Valley. I was awestruck by the beauty of the countryside as sunlight filtered through fresh deciduous trees and vineyards stitched their way from the mountains to the banks of the river. Meanwhile, the Porsche's performance impressed me. The Swiss driver sped like a Grand Prix racer, but I never felt unsafe as I had in Rolf's VW Beetle joyride.

Passing the turnoff for Grenoble, we began climbing. The road became windy, and the temperature dropped. It was early evening. I pulled on my favorite sweater, that I wore for special occasions ... and today was one of those, as was Danny's farewell party. Riding in a Porsche convertible, skirting the Alps on a sunny day, didn't get any better than this. I savored every minute. *Ah, freedom; there's nothing like it,* I thought, as it coursed through every cell in my body.

An hour passed, and we stopped at the Swiss border to go through customs. French and Swiss flags flapped lazily near a guard station, with a red-and-white gate barricading the road. We waited behind a small line of cars for our turn. At the guard station, an officer asked for our passports. My hand quaked slightly as I handed him mine. To my relief, he stamped it, asking no questions. On our way again, we were soon in downtown Geneva and I said goodbye to the two Swiss guys.

I wandered around town, admiring the grandfather clocks in shop windows, telling myself I'd make a point of exploring them the following day. By then, the sun was melting away, and I was hungry. First, I needed to buy food. I hadn't eaten since morning and was ravenous. Most of the shops had closed for the day. I settled for Lindt and Toblerone candy bars at a souvenir shop selling miniature cuckoo clocks, tiny Swiss flags, Hansel and Greta toys, Heidi dolls, and postcards. Strolling through a park afterward, I purchased a wiener and sauerkraut at a stand.

As we had entered the city, I noticed pastures with trees about half a mile outside town in an area known as *la forêt.* My bivouac for the night. Retracing the way we'd entered town, I found a vacant pasture. Checking to make sure nobody was watching, I stepped over a waist-high stone wall. Night had closed in, few cars were on the street, and there were enough trees to hide behind if one passed by. Fortunately, a nearly full moon made it easy to see where I headed in the mid-calf-high grass. Spotting a large, distinctive beech tree, I camped beneath it.

Early in the morning, I rose and spent the hours before noon exploring the Jardin Anglais flower garden, along with the grandfather clock shops. To my surprise, cuckoo and grand-father clocks fascinated me. I admired the exquisitely hand-carved wood, the steady ticking of the gears, the rhythmic swaying back and forth of the pendulums, the different tones of the chimes, not to mention the cuckoo birds all popping out and then going off in unison in a cheerful cacophony.

As afternoon sunshine chased away the morning chill, I strolled on the boardwalk along beautiful Lake Lucerne, watch-ing swans embrace. It reminded me of Lake Washington in Seattle, with the Alps in the background taking the place of the Cascade Range and Mount Rainier. Stopping for a lunch of salami, cheese, and the baguette I'd bought earlier in the day, I wrote a postcard to my parents, encouraging them to come see Geneva someday.

Late in the afternoon, I bought a train ticket, leaving in the morning, for Basel, Switzerland, where I planned to hitchhike up the German autobahn to Dusseldorf and then spend a night there at the youth hostel. The day after that, I would then hitchhike to Amsterdam—which I hoped would be the last destination of my European odyssey. I couldn't wait to get home, despite the draft and having to face my father.

After dark, I returned to the pasture to sleep. It was easy finding my tree since it was the largest of the grove. My backpack and other items were still there, not that I was concerned. But during my travels, I had collected postcards, knick-knacks, and gifts for my siblings. My most prized possession was a bottle of peach brandy I'd purchased for my parents in Las Palmas shortly before I left. Las Palmas was a free port, and the purchase was duty-free.

Not wanting to oversleep and miss my train, I only spent a few hours spread out beneath the tree, catnapping before packing my gear and leaving for the train station. My train departed at five a.m., so I spent two or three chilly hours waiting across the street at Basilica Notre-Dame, sitting on a bench. To pass the hours, I sang Simon and Garfunkel's song "Homeward Bound" to myself.

As the train pulled out of the station, I fell asleep, exhausted. The next thing I knew, the train was in Zurich and a conductor roused me, telling me to get off the train. Explaining that I'd overslept, I pleaded with him to let me ride back to Basel on the return trip. Apparently, sympathetic to my plight, he let me take the train back to Basel where I got off. From there, it was only a short walk to the German border and the A-5 Autobahn.

Going through customs was easy. The farther I got away from Spain, the less it concerned me going through checkpoints. Of course, there was always Interpol. They could arrest me at any moment and extradite me back to Spain if they suddenly reconsidered—but it was a long shot. My offense was petty compared to some inmates in Prisión de Barranco Seco.

Standing at the on-ramp of the autobahn, I watched a BMW 2002 pull over. A couple in their late thirties picked me up. It was my lucky day because they were going to Dusseldorf. The little BMW was surprisingly quick. Porsches, Ferraris, Maseratis, and Lamborghinis were much faster, however, and came from out of nowhere. They flashed their lights, warning us to get out of the passing lane or they were going to run us over. We spent most of the drive in the slow lane. Occasionally, the driver darted into the passing lane and drove like a maniac until an exotic car came roaring up behind us. The driver zipped back into the slow lane and slammed on the brakes. Scary as it was, we made good time, and I was in Dusseldorf by five p.m.

I didn't connect much with the married couple. They were professors at Freiburg University heading to Dusseldorf, where they lived. I'd hoped they would invite me to stay at their place, or at least offer me a meal, but they didn't. It was a little uncomfortable when I ran into them later at a supermarket. They merely waved from a distance, and that was it. Oh well, I would stay at the same youth hostel where the two Canadians had gotten me drunk, which seemed like a lifetime ago.

The next day I caught a ride all the way to Amsterdam in a Ford Escort MK1 Twin Cam, the German driver boasted. The day before, we were frequently on the receiving end of fast cars racing up behind us. Now, we were mostly on the giving end as the thirty-something German tore up behind a slower moving car in the passing lane, slammed on his brakes, flashed his lights, and cursed until the car moved over. It was the weekend, and Hans, a mechanical engineer from Cologne, was heading to Amsterdam to party and partake in the girls of the red-light district. No wonder he was in such a big hurry.

37

Favor

Pulling into Amsterdam, I marveled at the canals and row houses where Hans dropped me off at the youth hostel. It would be my home for a week. The hostel bustled with privileged, hyper-energetic, boisterous, American college students on summer break. Despite being younger than most, I felt older than they acted. My experiences over the past five months had matured me. Psychologically, I had aged a hundred years. I had lost my innocence. I could no longer be carefree.

After registering and settling in, I checked the bulletin board for return charter flights to the States and found one for sale. Somebody named Steve had a ticket to L.A., leaving in a week, for ninety dollars. I called him and put a hold on it, explaining it would take me a few days to come up with the cash. I only had forty-four dollars and it would have to last me until I got home. I had my plan, though. I would contact Dirk Vander Holm's father to see if he could loan me money for the ticket, with the stipulation that I would pay him back when I got home and cashed my 1968 tax return—which amounted to $330. I would then have money to reimburse him, and still have enough left to enroll in college fall semester.

The next day, I located Mr. Vander Holm's address on a map and found his house. I knocked on the door. Luckily, almost all Dutch people spoke English. A sandy-haired man in his late forties, wearing a white tee-shirt and brown slippers, answered the door. I stammered when I introduced myself, explaining my predicament.

"Dirk is not here. He is still in Seattle," Dirk's father said. "He won't be here until September. You will have to take it up with him when he returns."

"It can't wait until then. I need to buy the ticket now, and will repay you when I get home," I pleaded. "I want to go home."

Rubbing his neck, Mr. Vander Holm contemplated briefly. "I'll tell you what. I will call Dirk and ask him. Come back tomorrow and I will let you know then."

"Thank you, Mr. Vander Holm," I said, shaking his hand. "I'll see you tomorrow afternoon."

As directed, I showed up at Mr. Vander Holm's residence the following day. I knocked on his door and waited. I knocked again and there was no answer. Sighing, I turned to leave when Mr. Vander Holm opened the door. "Come in. I spoke with my son and he vouched for your story. He felt sorry you could not use his ticket. Make yourself comfortable while I get the money."

I sat in the living room, where an episode of *Bonanza* played on a black-and-white TV in English without subtitles. It seemed a little surreal to be here in Amsterdam, watching an American TV show. When Mr. Vander Holm entered the living room, he noticed me watching *Bonanza*.

"We Dutch people love American TV shows," he said. "We all speak English. Some say it's our first language and Dutch our second." He smiled, thrusting his chest out proudly.

Dirk's father handed me ninety dollars and shook my hand. "I'm glad to help you get home," he beamed. "When you bought my son's ticket, you did him a favor. Now I do one for you since you were unable to use his ticket."

"And I will repay you as soon as I get home and cash my tax return," I promised. I don't know if he believed me, or cared, before I said goodbye and left.

The next five days I spent sightseeing, going to Anne Frank's House, the Rembrandt House Museum, and the Rijksmuseum, spending hours studying Rembrandt's *Night Watch* and other masterpieces. One day, I toured the Heineken Brewery after hearing they served free beer and appetizers. Mostly, though, I just meandered around the city admiring the architecture, canals, light-green linden trees, flea market, beautiful Dutch girls on bicycles, and trams in this most charming city. I'd been in a lot of European cities and towns on my journey. Wonderful as they all were, this was my favorite. What a great place to end my European trek.

When I wasn't exploring the city, I spent my afternoons people-watching in Dam and Leidseplein Squares, where somebody told me about an area known as a "free zone," meaning you could buy and use drugs there legally—and where they played live music. Not interested in the drugs, I just wanted to hear music.

On my way there one evening, I walked through the red-light district. I had cut through that area many times during daytime hours, never realizing I was in the red-light district. What a difference a few hours made. Seducing me to come inside, gorgeous, scantily clad women sat in windows illuminated by red lights. As enticing as they were, I barely had enough money left to live on until I got home. Even if I did, I didn't want to lose my virginity this way. I did a little window-shopping, then continued through the area toward the free zone, past strolling elderly folks waving at their neighbors in the windows. *What a different way to look at prostitution*, I thought.

In the free zone, I listened to live music by a Dutch band named Golden Earring. They were new to me, but were popular in the Netherlands, Holland in particular, and were great. Afterward, I browsed around, looking at arts and crafts, hash pipes, bongs, hookahs, roach clips, and drugs. It bothered me. Having drugs blatantly on display and promoted openly felt wrong.

As I prepared to leave, to my surprise, I ran into Andy. The last time I'd seen him was in Las Palmas, shortly before my incarceration. Back then, he spent most of his days in Arguineguín. Sitting at a table in the free zone, he was selling hashish, hash pipes, and chillums.

Andy and I talked about what each other had been doing. He'd heard about my arrest and I filled him in on the details. I asked about him, and he told me he'd met an elderly woman who owned a VW van. They had traveled to Morocco together, bought ten kilos of hashish, hid it in the van, and then smuggled it to Amsterdam to sell. The woman was old enough to be his grandmother, so nobody really questioned her, nor bothered to search the van when they crossed borders.

"This place is great," Andy said, taking a hit from a hash pipe. "I can sell our stuff here and toke hash all day long."

"That's great," I responded, checking my watch.

"Yeah, man, if you want to earn some bucks you can help me sell this shit here."

Glad I had an excuse, I replied, "Thanks, but I'm leaving tomorrow for Los Angeles."

"I'm from L.A.," he reminded me. "Tell you what, man," he said, opening his backpack and pulling out two kilos of hash. "You take these with you to Los Angeles, deliver one to a friend of mine, and keep the other one for yourself. How does that sound?"

I mulled it over for a second. Thoughts of my arrest, arraignment, Consul Brooks telling me it would be a miracle if he could get me out of my predicament, and Prisión de Barranco Seco flashed in my mind. There was only one answer, and that was *no*.

I said goodbye to Andy and wished him good luck. Mostly, though, I was concerned about him, knowing what lay in store for him if busted. The smuggling he had done, and wanted me to help with, was similar to Danny's plot. Unlike Danny, though, Andy's persona screamed *drug dealer*. I didn't worry much about Danny, but I did about Andy.

I left the youth hostel the following evening, having checked out earlier in the day, and caught a bus from Leidseplein Square to Amsterdam Airport Schiphol, where I met Steve at the gate for my midnight flight. We had met five days earlier at the youth hostel where I paid him for the ticket. The plan was that Steve would check in with the ticket, hand it to me, and then leave. We waited until they called his name. When they did, Steve checked in, then milled around several minutes before slyly handing me the ticket. A moment later, he slipped away. *So far, so good*, I thought.

They called my flight, and I boarded the plane, hoping they wouldn't check IDs against ticket names. To my relief, they didn't.

I grabbed a window seat on the Boeing 707 sitting next to an elderly woman returning home after visiting her Dutch relatives. Shortly after the flight took off, she fell asleep. Not long afterward, so did I. About five hours later, stewardesses awakened me as they handed out immigration cards and notified us we would land soon in Bangor, Maine, where we would go through customs.

One question on the card asked if we had any liquor to declare. I had the bottle of brandy I'd bought for my parents. Not wanting to lie, I answered *yes*. Since I was under twenty-one, I bit my nails, worrying they would bust me for it and deny my entry. Standing in line, I also grew concerned they were checking names on passports against the passenger list. It made me wonder if they would notice my name was not on it and deport me back to Europe. My mind spun from lack of sleep. Finally, it was my turn. The immigration officer glanced at my passport, looked at the card I filled out, then stamped my passport.

"Welcome home," he said with a smile.

Back on the plane, I thought, *Man, they never checked my backpack. I could've easily smuggled those two kilos for Andy, and sold one for five grand.* I quickly put the thought out of my mind, realizing how stupid it was. Perhaps they went through my rucksack when they unloaded it, or my behavior would have tipped them off. More than likely, it would have resulted in my arrest and imprisonment. If this happened, I wouldn't be so lucky. I would have to serve years.

From Bangor to L.A. I didn't sleep. The old woman awoke about the moment we passed over the neon lights of the Las Vegas Strip, shining in the darkness like a hundred Orion's belts. She wanted to hear about my trip and I told her about it, except for the bad things I did.

"My, what a lot of experiences for somebody who's only nineteen," the old woman said.

She was right. I'd done a lot, seen a lot, and changed a lot in the five months since my brother dropped me off in the snow at an Interstate 90 freeway on-ramp. I felt like a different person than when I'd left home.

38

Home

June 15–17, 1969 — Los Angeles, California, to Bellevue, Washington

Never having been to California, I arrived unprepared for the America I encountered. The streets were wide, the buildings new, the cars big, the skies smoggy, orange Union 76 balls vibrated on car antennas, and American flag decals reflected off car windows.

I already missed the quaintness and charm of Europe. Getting out of Los Angeles International Airport to a freeway entrance required several miles of walking. It was a good thing it was morning because I dripped with sweat by the time I got my first ride. Suffering from jet lag, lack of sleep, and culture shock, the next few rides were a blur. It wasn't until I got a ride on Highway 101, just south of San Francisco, from a middle-aged black woman, with a Diana Ross hairstyle, faux leopard-skin jumpsuit, and wearing pink sunglasses, that a ride stuck in my memory.

She asked me what I'd been doing and was unprepared for the extensive travel experiences pouring out of me. I assumed she'd never left the country, so I felt a little self-conscious rattling off the names of cities, towns, churches and museums halfway around the world. I didn't want her to think I bragged, so I toned down my tale, emphasizing how I'd slept on beaches, in cars, pastures, youth hostels, and fifty-cent-a-night pensions. She appreciated my humbleness.

"Honey, you don't need to sugarcoat ol' Belinda here," she said, with a mock sassy voice. "I know you think I ain't been nowhere, but I spent twenty years in the military, so I've been all over the world. I've been shot at by every gun and man thing there is … That's why I carry my rod. I can blast any male that tries to mess with me into the stratosphere," she chortled. "But I never had to sleep in no car or on no beach."

She laughed, and so did I.

"Now sugar, my advice is if you ever want to travel again, join the Army," she laughed again, teasing me.

"Oh no, I'm not joining the Army."

"I was just teasing you, sugar," she grinned. "You're too sweet for the service. Don't you ever join them, you hear me?"

I chuckled. "Don't you worry. I have no intention of ever joining."

"Good, now that this is settled, this is where I turn off," she pointed. "You're welcome to come home with me, sugar. I can be your worst enemy, and sometimes your best piece of ass at the same time, but there wouldn't be much of your skinny white ass left after I'm done with you, or you can get out here, sweetie."

"Uh, I guess, I'll get out here," I replied, grasping the door handle.

"Okay," she said, as I got out of the car. "Stay sweet, honey."

Belinda blew me a kiss and then chuckled as she pulled away in her Pontiac Bonneville. Sobered by her, I was completely awake and ready for anything.

Three hours later, I was in Williams, California, and it was dark. I really didn't want to hitchhike at night, and the adrenaline rush from Belinda had worn off several hours ago. A veil of tiredness clouded my vision, and my empty gut rumbled like a semi-truck. There was a Denny's on the other side of the freeway. I ordered a piece of blackberry pie and a cup of coffee, then I called home from a pay phone in the lobby.

"Hi Mom, I'm in Williams, California, and am going to spend the night here. I'll be home tomorrow or the next day," I said, doing my best to keep my emotions in check.

"Where are you staying?" she asked.

"I don't know," I said, fiddling with the metal jacketed phone cord. "I'll probably just sleep outside."

"Oh no, don't do that," she implored. Trying to support my tired body, I held onto the wooden phone cubby bolted to the wall.

"Mom, I can take care of myself. I've been on my own for the past five months."

"That's what I worry about."

"Well, don't worry. I'll see you in a day or two."

I said goodbye and hung up the phone. *Some things never change.*

That night, I slept in a field of tall dry grass about two hundred yards off I-5. In the middle of the night, a shaking awakened me. *Is it an earthquake?* Terrified, I sat up as a single bright light shone straight into my pupils. Blinded, I shielded by eyes with a hand. *What is it?* Like a cyclops, whatever it was headed straight for me. The light grew bigger and brighter. As the thundering sound grew louder, the earth shook. And then I heard the startling blare of a train's whistle. *Oh my God, it's a train!* The noise was deafening. I couldn't tell which way the tracks were. Were they to the left or right of me? Frozen with fear, I sat motionless as an Amtrak train passed just three or four feet to the left of me. Good thing I hadn't rolled in that direction.

It took a while to settle down enough to doze. The rest of the night, I tossed and turned, never really sleeping. As the sun came up, I went back to Denny's and ordered another piece of pie and a cup of coffee. Awake enough now, I got back to hitchhiking and caught a ride to Yreka. Several minutes after being dropped off there, a beer bottle whizzed past my ear as the occupants of a passing pickup truck flipped me off and hurled hippie insults. *Welcome home. This place is crazy!* I lamented.

In Yreka, a teenager about my age, Curtis, offered me a ride in his mid-fifties Chevy pickup truck. It was late afternoon, around four or five, and hot—probably in the high nineties. Just outside town, I-5 starts climbing precipitously until reaching 4,000-foot Siskiyou Pass, where you enter Oregon.

The more we climbed the pass, the hotter his engine became, and the more times we stopped to add water to the radiator from a gallon jug he had. We didn't discuss it. We just popped the hood, used a rag to unscrew the radiator cap, and jumped back from steam so hot it could blister your skin off in a split second. But wisely, the California Department of Transportation had set up water stations periodically along the steeper sections, and we used all of them—from what I could tell.

When we crested Siskiyou Summit, Curtis put his pickup in neutral as we coasted the entire seven miles to Ashland. The farther downhill we went, the more his truck's temperature dropped. The steam that once billowed from under the truck's hood disappeared.

His family's farm was located a short distance off I-5. Chickens, goats, pigs, and ducks greeted us when we pulled into a circular dirt driveway in front of a large, weathered white farmhouse shaded by gigantic oak trees. Almost immediately, excited dogs and children burst out of every opening imaginable to greet us.

I spent the night there, sleeping on a davenport in the living room. We all ate a huge country breakfast in the morning comprising eggs, bacon, and pancakes. I stuffed myself. It was the best breakfast I'd had since leaving home. Satisfied, I said goodbye to his family, and within minutes, he dropped me off at an I-5 northbound on-ramp. I thanked him before he pulled away in his pickup, billowing white smoke in its wake. By the looks of it, the head gasket had blown, which would explain the overheating, and white exhaust—too bad, because he came from a poor family.

Focused on what my reception would be when I got home, I didn't remember the rides between Ashland and the street my folks lived on. I was in a fog. From there, it was a half-mile walk to their place. Within ten minutes, I arrived at the top of their gravel driveway and stopped to take it in. When I had left, snow covered the lawn. Now the grass was bright green. Flowers and rhododendrons bloomed, just like in the two photos in my backpack. When looking at those photographs in prison, I would frequently hear in my head Tom Jones' song, "Green,

Green Grass of Home."

Entering the kitchen moments later, my mother welcomed me with hugs, kisses, and tears. Several hours later, my father arrived home from work and my mother, like an excited contest winner, rushed to tell him the news. I could hear her say, "Richard, Richard, come here! It's Paul. He's in the family room!" My mother led my father to where I was telling some of my siblings about my experiences. Upon entering, he stopped and glared at me, his eyes burning with anger.

"Get rid of that beard," he growled with disgust, and then left the room.

The end.

Epilogue

In the process of writing this book, I did some research and discovered that approximately three weeks after my release from prison, the U.S. government and Spanish government signed an extension to the Pact of Madrid of 1953 (a military agreement). This information validated what I had already come to believe, that the U.S. Government used me as a pawn in their negotiations with Spain. I was elated. All indications seemed to point in that direction, but I now had the smoking gun. Nevertheless, I am lucky for my early release, and grateful to the U.S. Department of State, Martin, Brooks and Ambassador Robert Wagner for their efforts. Without their political string pulling, and possible arm twisting, there's little doubt in my mind that I would have served up to six years in prison.

According to pp. 38 and 40 of the U.S. Air Force's report "Military Relationships Between Spain and the United States Since 1953," written by Capt. James T. Roberts and Capt. Edwin R. Ruhmann IV and published in June 1979: "The renegotiation of the Pact of Madrid of 1953 was again requested by Spain at the end of the first extension in 1968. ... After much debate and bargaining between the two countries, it was mutually agreed on June 20, 1969, that the Pact of Madrid of 1953 would be extended to September 26, 1970, retroactive to 1968 (65:17230;

69:15).""

After returning home, I never spent much time there adjusting to family life again. I'd been independent for too long. Within a week, I moved to Eugene, Oregon, with two high school friends for the summer. The father of one of my pals owned a truck rental business in Seattle. He had just opened a satellite office in Eugene. Before long, I was shuttling trucks up and down the West Coast for the company.

Prior to leaving for Eugene, I inspected the remnants of my old VW Bug. Before coming home, my youngest brother and some neighbors had removed the dented body. They called it the "flying frame." As they drove it around the neighborhood, the neighbors would gawk or yell for them to slow down. Eventually, my father sold it, and somebody who planned to turn it into a dune buggy carted it off.

In the fall, I moved back home and enrolled at Bellevue Community College and was given a 2S deferment, keeping me out of the draft.

A year later, I moved out of my parents' house over disagreements with my father concerning the length of my hair. I moved in with neighbors. Early one evening, I got a call from my mother saying somebody named Danny, who knew me in Las Palmas, had called, asking about me.

"When did he call?" I asked, as my eyes danced around the room my friend's mother used for spinning yarn and sewing.

My mother's voice squawked in the phone's black handset. "Oh, I'm not sure. It must have been five or six hours ago."

"Did he say where he is?"

Informing me that Danny had called from Seattle International Airport during a layover, my mother said he had a connecting flight at six p.m. I glanced at my Timex watch;

it was now five fifteen. There was no way I could get to the airport in forty-five minutes. Irritated with my mother for not telling me earlier, I asked what Danny had wanted.

"He just thought he'd see how you were doing."

"And what did you tell him?"

"I said that you were going to school and were living some-place else."

"Did he say where he was going?"

"No, that's all he said."

I cupped a hand around the mouthpiece so nobody would hear as I raised my voice. "Why didn't you give him my phone number here?"

"I didn't think of it."

"And why didn't you tell me earlier?" I said, my voice growing louder.

"I was going to, but I didn't know who he was and if you wanted to hear from him. For all I knew, he could've been somebody from that prison."

"Come on, Mom, give me more credit than that," I grumbled. "Geez, I can't believe you didn't tell me earlier!" I slammed the phone down and emptied my lungs with a loud *whoosh*.

I never heard from Danny again, and wondered why he had passed through Seattle and where he was going. Over the years, I've also pondered what he did with his life. I guess I'll never know, but would bet he's had a successful one. I hope, after hearing about my incarceration from Terry, it convinced him to abandon his India smuggling plan.

A few more months passed, and I stopped by my folks' place to say hello. Seeing me, my mother stopped her cooking and opened a drawer. "I've got a piece of mail for you from London," she said, handing me a manila envelope.

My mind raced, wondering whether it was from Danny. Upon opening it, I pulled out a black-and-white photograph of me burning my old high school draft card taken at the youth hostel in Barcelona.

"What is it?" my mother asked.

"Oh, just a picture of me in Barcelona," I replied, dismissing her with a hand wave.

"Here, let me see," she said, reaching for the photograph. I handed it to her.

"My goodness, you look so much better now without the beard. What is that you're burning?"

"I don't remember," I said, suddenly feeling ashamed.

"Well, whatever you do, don't let you father see this," my mother said, handing back the photo. She frequently said something like that when she caught me doing something wrong. Just to emphasize her point, she would tell stories about her childhood and say, "You're lucky I'm not your grandmother."

As for my father, he rarely talked about his childhood. It wasn't until years later that I would learn about his past. That knowledge helped explain his lack of warmth and volatile temper. Raised in Chicago by a mean alcoholic uncle during the Depression, he attended seminary school in Mount Carmel, Canada, just across the river from Niagara Falls to get away from him. Heavily leveraged during the 1929 stock market crash, my grandfather lost his construction business, forcing the family to move into a two-bedroom apartment Uncle Lou owned. With four kids in the family, there just wasn't room for all of them. As the eldest, my father had to live with Uncle Lou.

The abandonment my father experienced, along with the harshness Lou and the seminary inflicted on him, hardened him. Occasionally, he would see his siblings when he passed through Chicago on business trips, but would never stay with them. Learning all of this gave me a better appreciation of why my father was incapable of showing his affection toward us and the angry outbursts he sometimes had where he would hit us.

Years later, having learned about my father's past, I reconciled with him. I apologized for everything I'd put him and Mom through and thanked him for bailing me out. For the first time in my life, shortly before he passed away, he told me he loved me.

"I love you too, Dad," I said, holding back tears, sorry that he was dying so young, sorry he never could retire, and sorry that he would never get to know his grandkids.

Despite my father's shortcomings, he had more influence on my life than anyone. As a good provider, he taught me to set long-term and short-term goals. He showed me how to hunt and fish. Being a perfectionist, he taught me how to do a job right and the meaning of hard work as I helped him build our new home, repair cars, and work on the apartment building my folks owned. Those skills have served me well over the years.

Other than my father, Danny Zorro probably had more impact on my life than anybody else. He instilled the understanding that you have to have a plan and believe in it in order for it to work. If you want to be successful, act and think rich, and that means improving yourself every way you can, even if it means bathing, shaving, and cutting your hair.

Danny's outlook taught me that anything is possible, if you believe it is, and nothing was possible if you believe otherwise. What Danny was saying is, if you think you'll never be successful, you'll never be successful. From that moment forward, I have always been an optimist, thought big, and believed I can accomplish anything if I set my mind to it.

When I left home, I was a messed-up nineteen-year-old looking for the love I hadn't gotten from my father, running from the draft, and seeking independence and adventure.

When I returned, I'd flushed wanderlust out of my system, gained my independence, and still faced the draft. Although still screwed up, I had grown up somewhat. I was in a much better position to become a responsible and productive person. A few years later, I would finally get there. However, my experiences in Europe laid the foundation and gave me confidence. If I could spend five months traveling halfway around the world, nothing was impossible. More than anything, my stint in prison taught me a valuable lesson in honesty, reinforcing the morals instilled in me, making me the law-abiding person I am today.

I am glad I saw Europe when I did. It was before Schengen, and before there were hordes of tourists, Starbucks, and McDonald's. Each country had a border, its own language, customs, currency, and culture. Crossing a border was an adventure and meant another stamp mark in my passport. Immediately my senses were jolted awake and I was on high alert. The Europe of yesteryear challenged my ability to adapt, leaving me awestruck, as I experienced artworks, architecture, languages, foods, customs, and cultures thousands of years in the making. Sadly, I believe it is an era gone forever. Having been there five or six times since, I vastly prefer the Europe of 1969. Sure, the buildings and art are still there, but to what purpose ... and for how much longer if the culture is lost? That is what concerned Danny and motivated him to save the art.

And so my story has come to an end, but it's only one chapter of my life. It's funny how one's perspective changes after fifty years. Here I am today writing about it, trying to relive and reconcile my past with the person I am today. What I learned is that I had already reconciled it a long time ago. I'm not the same person I was then. Today I'm wiser, more honest, better educated and happier. I can now relieve those experiences and marvel at all of the crazy things I did, the amazing sights I saw, the unique and outrageous people I met, and the wild adventure I had.

If you enjoyed this book, I would greatly appreciate you leaving a review at Amazon or your favorite online bookstore!

Thank you!

About the Author

Paul Gorman is a filmmaker, writer and producer of numerous short films, stage plays, and feature films. His works have appeared in film festivals in North America and Europe, and on stage in Seattle. His film "Ride The Sky" can be found streaming on Roku channel DocsNow Plus. In addition, he spent years working in the high tech industry designing circuit boards, parts, and assemblies for fortune five hundred companies, including Boeing.

Paul lives in Tacoma, WA with his wife and two dogs.

You can connect with me on:
- http://www.raincitycinema.com
- http://twitter.com/RainCityCinema

Also by Paul Gorman

Running Down A Dream: The Making of a Film

Haunted for thirty years by a dream of a female friend's death eight years before she died in a skydiving accident, Filmmaker Paul Gorman hopes to unlock the mystery of his dream by making a film about her. Gorman's book tells the remarkable story about the making of his 2014 award winning documentary film, "Ride The Sky". During his quest, he discovers the meaning of his dream locked away in a painful secret from her past. In the end, her past reconnects with the present in a most surprising and emotional way.

Lightning Source UK Ltd.
Milton Keynes UK
UKHW011546291221
396337UK00003B/693

9 780578 948478